PROLEGOMENA
on Biblical Hermeneutics
and Method

2nd Edition

christopher cone

Prolegomena On Biblical Hermeneutics and Method
2nd Edition

(1st Edition published as *Prolegomena: Introductory Notes on Bible Study and Theological Method)*
© 2012 Christopher Cone
Published by Tyndale Seminary Press
Hurst, TX

ISBN-10: 1938484037
ISBN-13: 978-1-938484-03-2

All Scripture quotations, except those noted otherwise are from the New American Standard Bible,
©1960,1962,1963,1968,1971,1972,1973,1975, and 1977 by the Lockman Foundation.

As well might a medical doctor discard his books on anatomy and therapeutics as for the preacher to discard his books on Systematic Theology; and since doctrine is the bone structure of the revealed body of truth, the neglect of it must result in a message characterized by uncertainties, inaccuracies, and immaturity.

-- Lewis Sperry Chafer
Systematic Theology, Vol. I, Preface

To my precious Lord,
Thank you for your mercy. Please confirm the work of my hands, and may I be honoring and glorifying to you. Thank you for your love.
I love you.

To my lovely bride, Catherine,
I love you. Thank you so much for your amazing love and unwavering support. Many have done nobly, but you excel them all.

To my dear daughters, Christiana and Cara Grace,
Thank you so much for your patience with me throughout this project. I love you both and pray that you will both continue to grow in the love of our Lord.

CONTENTS

INTRODUCTION

Inasmuch as Scripture is the product of one Mind, it seems that a proper approach to understanding the message of Scripture will result necessarily in a cohesive and consistent system of theology that represents God accurately insofar as He has chosen to reveal Himself. This work seeks to demonstrate the foundations for such an approach - namely definition, aim, prerequisites (pillars), and method - and to offer an introductory overview of the conclusions of that approach.

As an introduction to theological method this work will be built upon the framework of four pillars, which are (1) the existence of the Biblical God, (2) His authoritative revelation of Scripture, (3) natural man's incapacity to comprehend (or spiritually appraise) revelation, and (4) the necessity (in approaching that revelation) of a consistent hermeneutical approach which does not violate any of the first three pillars. The literal grammatical-historical method will be argued as the only interpretive method which can function within this framework, and will thus lead naturally to an inductive exegetical process which will inform the synthetic and systematic processes, effectively providing a scaffold for derivation of a Biblical theology.

This theological methodology seems best characterized as beginning with the presuppositional epistemology, and resulting necessarily in normative dispensational conclusions. Therefore, it is here suggested that *Presuppositional Dispensationalism* be the most appropriate description of this system, emphasizing its particularly definitive elements.

DEFINITIONS IN BIBLICAL THEOLOGY

Theology is a compound of *theos* (God) and *logos* (word, reason, or idea), and represents a discourse concerning God[1] generally including (but not limited to) the following branches: *Biblical theology* generically refers to the development of theological themes directly and exclusively from the Biblical record itself, typically examining the Bible "bit by bit and writer by writer."[2] *Systematic theology* topically systematizes information exclusively from the Biblical record.[3]   *Historical theology* discusses the historical development of

---

1   Charles Hodge, *Systematic Theology*, (Peabody, MA: Hendrickson, 2001), 1:19.

2   W.G.T. Shedd, *Dogmatic Theology*, (Nashville, TN: Thomas Nelson, 1980), 1:11.

3   Some would suggest that systematic theology also deals with information from other sources outside the Biblical record (e.g., The Moody Handbook of Theology), however, this writer does not follow such definitions here, as this text will treat systematic theology as being a direct outworking of Biblical theology, and therefore finding its derivation strictly in the Biblical record.

theological doctrines. *Dogmatic theology,* like traditional definitions of Biblical theology, derives its doctrinal body from the Scriptures alone, but differs from such definitions in that it deals with the whole of Scripture rather than isolated parts. W.G.T. Shedd used the term to distinguish his theology from liberal theological thinking, as well as from a partial view of Scripture.[4] *Natural theology* is the necessarily limited observance of information about God as revealed in nature (Rom. 1:20). *Practical theology* discusses the practical application of theological doctrines.

This text is concerned primarily with the overarching aspects of theological method and theology as derived exclusively from Scripture without external considerations impacting the formulation of either the method or the results. Based on this premise the general study of theology will be referred to here as *Biblical theology* – not to be defined in the traditional sense as partial and isolated, nor in reference to any liberal movement, but rather referencing *a discourse concerning God which is based entirely and exclusively on the Biblical record.* Millard Erickson offers an excellent definition for this kind of *Biblical theology,* which complements the meaning implied by this text when the term *Biblical theology* is here referenced:

A final meaning of the expression "biblical theology" is simply theology that is biblical, that is, based on

---

4   W.G.T. Shedd, *Dogmatic Theology,* (Nashville, TN: Thomas Nelson, 1980), 1:11.

and faithful to the teachings of the Bible. In this sense, systematic theology of the right kind will be biblical theology. It is not simply based on biblical theology; it is biblical theology. Our goal is systematic biblical theology.[5]

THE AIM OF BIBLICAL THEOLOGY

God possesses incomparable glory. He created as an expression of His glory (Rev. 4:11). He reveals Himself to His creation that it might be filled with His glory (Num. 14:21) and that all will ascribe to Him the glory due His name (1 Chr. 16:28-29; Ps. 29:1-2; 96:7-8). The existence of all things serves the purpose of Divine Self-expression, i.e., Self-glorification (Rom. 11:36), in perhaps the same manner as the symphony reflects the skill of the composer, the masterpiece reflects the brilliance of the painter, and the piercing words reflect the heart of the poet. God's overarching revealed purpose in all things is to bring glory to Himself. Psalm 86:9-10 says the nations shall glorify Him because of His great deeds." Revelation 15:3-4 notes that His deeds reveal His holiness and glory. All God's works function in concert to achieve this, His *doxological purpose* – that is, His Self-glorification.[6] God's doxological purpose then is, as Ryrie explains, "A

---

5 Millard Erickson, *Christian Theology* (Grand Rapids, MI: Baker Books, 2001), 26.

6 From the Greek *doxa* (honor, glory) and *logos* (word or discourse), speaking of or attesting to glory.

basic and working conception of the purpose of God as His own glory..."[7]

The major works of God revealed in Scripture *all* serve the doxological purpose (Ps. 86:9-10; Rev. 15:4); as a matter of fact, Scripture identifies no greater purpose for each of the following: God's predestining and calling works (Eph. 1:5-12; 2 Pet. 1:3); the ministry of Christ (Jn. 13:31-2; 17:1-5; 21:19; 2 Cor. 1:20; Heb. 13:21); creation (Ps. 19; Is. 40; Rev. 4:11); the Keeping of His word (Rom. 3:1-7);   salvation (Ps. 79:9; Rom. 15:7;16:25-27;   Eph. 1:14; 1 Tim. 1:15-17; 2 Tim. 4:18; Jude 24-25); the church (1 Cor. 10:31; 2 Cor. 4:15; Eph. 1:12; Php. 1:11; 2 Thes. 1:11-12; 1 Pet. 4:11,16); fruitfulness of believers (Jn. 15:8; 1 Cor. 10:31); the kingdom (Php. 2:11; 1 Thes. 2:12; Rev. 1:6); sickness, death, and resurrection (1 Sam. 6:5; Lk. 17:11-18; Jn. 9:1-3; 11:4); judgment (Rom. 3:7; Rev. 14:7); deliverance of Israel (Is. 60:21; 61:3); and the fulfilling of covenants and summing up of all things (Is. 25:1-3; 43:20; Lk. 2:14; Rom. 4:20; 15:8-9; 2 Cor. 1:20; 2 Pet. 1:3-4; Rev. 19:7).

This doxological purpose is at the center of God's revelation to man, and there is therefore no higher purpose for man but to glorify God – this is indeed man's chief end.[8] But at this point we must exercise caution, for this doxological purpose is not only man's highest calling, but it is the intended design of all that

---

7 Charles Ryrie, *Dispensationalism Today* (Chicago, IL: Moody Press, 1965), 48.

8 *Westminster Shorter Catechism*, Q. 1.

is. To emphasize man's role in accomplishing this task to the exclusion of other aspects of creation can be anthropocentric – drawing the attention from God and placing it wrongly upon man. It is therefore this doxological purpose which provides the continuity between the Old and New Testaments, the various covenants, the dispensations, and all other revealed outworking of God's program.

The aim therefore of Biblical theology is to communicate the truth about God, to the extent to which God has revealed Himself in Scripture, and for His own doxological purpose. Rightly understanding then the primacy of the doxological design is a necessity without which no consistent and coherent theology can result. With this significance in view, Ryrie includes doxological purpose as the third element of dispensational theology's *sine qua non,*[9] identifying it as a basic and outworking conception of the purpose of God as His own glory rather than as the single purpose of salvation. [10]

Understanding the dependence of the first two elements of Ryrie's *sine qua non* (the distinction between Israel and the church and a consistently literal principle of interpretation) upon this third element, this writer suggests that the doxological purpose consistently understood and applied is *the central tenet* upon which a truly Biblical theology must

9 Latin: without which not, meaning indispensable aspects.

10 Charles C. Ryrie, *Dispensationalism Today* (Chicago, IL: Moody Press, 1965), 48.

be built, for it provides the obvious foundation for acknowledgment of God-centered and God-defined reality. The right understanding of the revelation of God will be accompanied by the sentiment of Jn. 3:30 – He must increase, but I must decrease. This is antithetical to the self-exalting methodology of the evil one (Gen. 3:1-5; Is. 14:13-16), and begs the question: Who is at the center of theology - is it man or is it God? The Biblically correct answer is readily identifiable (Ps. 16:5-11; 144:15; 86:9, 12; Is. 12:2; Ezek. 39:13;   Lk. 2:10; Jn. 17:3-4; Rom. 11:36; 12:1-2; 1 Cor. 6:20; 10:31; Eph. 2:8-10; Php. 4:4; 1 Tim. 1:5;   1 Pet. 4:11; Is. 6:3 and Rev. 4:11; 21:3-4, etc.).

Despite this clarity, however, based on a variant interpretation of, for example, Jn. 5:39 some see the Christological redemptive element as the center of Biblical revelation. This is a significant developing factor in the formation of alternative theological frameworks (particularly covenant theology). Shedd says of this approach,

> While this method is interesting because it makes sin and salvation the principal theme and brings Christ the Redeemer into the foreground, yet it is neither a natural nor a logical method. God incarnate is only a single person of the Godhead; redemption is only one of the works of God; and sin is an anomaly in the universe, not

an original and necessary fact. The
Christological method, therefore, is fractional.[11]

The Biblical evidence suggests (from Jn. 17:4 and 1 Pet.
4:11, for example) the Christological purpose is
primarily doxological by way of redemptive
methodology. The redemptive achieves the doxological.
The redemptive is a means to an end – the doxological
end. Such precise distinctions are important and will
arise further down the theological road.

Regarding Biblical theology's aim to present the
truth about God, it is evident that even three
prevailing theories of truth demonstrate the need for
certain prerequisites or presuppositions: The
correspondence theory of truth identifies as truth that
which corresponds with fact, being objective and
absolute. But as certain elements of reality are not
empirically demonstrable, this is an inadequate theory
of truth unless based on the presupposition that fact
begins with God (the presuppositional approach), in
which case the correspondence theory becomes fully
adequate in identifying truth. The *coherence theory*
posits that the more consistent the system, the more
truthful. Biblical theism is demonstrable by a
presuppositional epistemology to be the only fully
coherent system, and therefore, by definition of the
coherence theory, using presuppositional methodology,
Biblical theism would be understood in this approach to

---

11 W.G.T Shedd, *Dogmatic Theology,*   (Nashville, TN: Thomas
Nelson, 1980), 1:5.

be truth. The *pragmatic theory* suggests that which works is that which is true. Just as in the other two theories, a presuppositional approach will demonstrate Biblical theism to be truth, as all things are shown to work together for the glory of God.

All truth is God's truth, and the fear of the Lord is the beginning of knowledge and wisdom (Pr. 1:7; 9:10). Proper attention to a *Biblical theology* should be requisite to *all* pursuits of truth, whether philosophical, scientific, or otherwise. Any approach to learning or knowledge which does not first account for the truths of *Biblical theology* will result in a misguided conclusion about the nature of reality, and will therefore be much less productive (if not entirely destructive) than if it had begun with the right foundation – the fear of the Lord. As Van Til observes, there is nothing in this universe on which human beings can have full and true information unless they take the Bible into account.[12]

This premise invites the unbeliever (he who worships the creature, i.e., himself) to approach Scripture as foundational and authoritative in order to see for a moment what his world is really like when the veil of falsehood and atheistic pretense is lifted. The premise likewise demands that the believer (he who worships the Creator in spirit and in truth) maintain grounding in *Biblical* theism, no longer submitting his intellect to the fallacies of non-Biblical foundations.

---

12 Cornelius Van Til, *Christian Apologetics* (Philipsburg, NJ: Presbyterian and Reformed Publishing, 2003), 20.

Biblical theology stands as the foundation which undergirds and underwrites such studies as philosophy, science, worldview, epistemology, and ethics.

> Scripture gives definite information of a most fundamental character about all the facts and principles with which philosophy and science deal. For philosophy or science to reject or even to ignore this information is to falsify the picture it gives of the field with which it deals.[13]

BIBLICAL THEOLOGY AS A FOUNDATION FOR PHILOSOPHY

Biblical Theology functions neatly as a philosophical system, or I should say, as *the* philosophical system. By very definition philosophy is love of wisdom, and as the Proverbist tells us, "The fear of the Lord is the beginning of wisdom" (Pr. 9:10). Thus philosophical pursuit must begin properly with the fear of the Lord. Plantinga advises Christian thinkers to remember this key, saying,

> The Christian philosopher quite properly starts from the existence of God, and presupposes it in philosophical work, whether or not he or she can

---

13 Ibid., 61.

show it to be probable or plausible with respect
to premises accepted by...philosophers.[14]

Plantinga's agreement here with Solomonic wisdom
unveils a contrast between really only two systems of
thought, directly opposing one another: one which
begins with God, and one which begins without God.
Theology has been influenced through the centuries by
philosophical contributions from both systems of
thought. Presently it seems that theology bears too
significant a brand from the latter of the two
approaches, when in fact proper theology should be the
guiding light for philosophical pursuit, and not vice
versa. It is notable that the various fields of philosophy
in many cases work together systematically to provide
theological answers. For example, the presuppositions
one brings into perspectives of metaphysics will direct
systems of epistemology (and vice versa) and will in
turn lay perhaps the most defining groundwork in
principles of ethics.

Philosophy's unfortunate imprint upon
theological understanding is easy to identify. Despite
this influence it is profoundly evident that a Biblically
sound theology forms the base of correct philosophical
method (again, in accordance with Solomonic premises
of Prov. 1:7; 9:10, etc.). Philosophy, *rightly defined* as
affection (and pursuit) of wisdom, must operate under
the confines of the Biblical definition of process of

---

14 Michael Beaty, ed., *Christian Theism and the Problems of
Philosophy* (Notre Dame: IN: Notre Dame Press, 1990), 24.

arriving at wisdom. Ultimately then, correctly applied, philosophy should be considered an aspect of theology itself, seeking the ultimate end of greater knowledge of God.

BIBLICAL THEOLOGY AS A FOUNDATION FOR SCIENCE

Science, from the Latin *scientia*, meaning *knowledge*, implies knowledge gained from study. Scientia is not independent of presuppositional ties. It is evident that the framework of worldview adopted by the scientist profoundly impacts conclusions derived from study (worldview precedes observational interpretation). A cursory examination of the widely held threefold division of scientific eras (pre-modern, modern, and postmodern) provides illustration of the impact of presupposition.

The premodern world was one of traditional authorities – feudal lords and ecclesiastical hierarchies – which shaped society in every respect. From economics to education (in most cases, lack thereof), the individual was not a unit of impact, but rather a means to an end. The problem then, was not one of authority, but rather one of terribly abused and falsely assumed authorities.

But by the fifteenth and sixteenth centuries, the power base of these authorities began to buckle, in no small part due to the Reformation, begun in 1517, and of course pre-Reformation developments, including Gutenburg's printing press (1445) and William

Tyndale's (illegal) use of it, as he translated the New Testament into the common vernacular in 1526. English citizens were able for the first time to read the Bible in their own tongue, and what resulted was a sweeping recognition that the religious system which dominated their society bore no resemblance to what was described on the actual pages of the holy book. Also of immeasurable import was Columbus' 1492 voyage, which, even as it shrunk the world, made the horizon that much broader. The previously unthinkable became plausible. The world was indeed much bigger than it had earlier seemed.

By the late eighteenth century, and inspired in no small part by the Reformation and the scientific progress of Galileo (1564-1642) and Newton (1643-1727), the Enlightenment brought with it a new momentum leading to, "a distinct epoch of historical development marking the inauguration of the economic and socio-cultural disruptions which founded industrial capitalism and the nation-state."[15] The modern world was born, with a view toward the progress of man in understanding, and to at least some degree, the conquering of the world around him.

The collective trust had shifted from the traditional authorities of premodernity to the power of individual reason in the modern age. Descartes' *cogito ergo sum*[16] created an inviting epistemology wherein

---

15   Robin Usher and Richard Edwards, *Postmodernism and Education* (New York: Rutledge, 1994), 8.

16 "I think therefore I am."

reason bridged cultural and religious gaps. The great hope was now fixed upon the idea of collective progress and agreement – primarily through the vehicle of reason. But even as technological progress increased by virtue of reason and the scientific method, world war, holocaust, and numerous other sociopolitical, socioeconomic and religious failures proved the two ideas of progress and agreement to be unachievable by the modern mindset.

Fueled by Kierkegard's subjectivity and Nietzche's rejection of absolutes, post World War II into the 1960's brought a rapid development of postmodernist ideas and methodology, acknowledging the failures of the modern era. Derrida (deconstruction), Foucault (society and power), Lyotard (literary theory and critique of the metanarrative), and Baudrillard (social theory) are just a few key developers of postmodernism, and these gave rise to a new postmodern era.

Postmodernism is a way of doing science, of interpreting the world in an age of postmodernity. It is decidedly not modern and seeks to correct errors of modernity. As Vanhoozer puts it, postmodern[ism] is largely a reaction to the subject-object distinction and to its concomitant assumption that truth can be discovered by induction and deduction.[17]

---

17 Kevin J. Vanhoozer, "One Rule to Rule Them All," Craig Ott and Harold A. Netland, eds., *Globalizing Theology* (Grand Rapids, MI: Baker Books, 2006), 89.

Rozzi, et al, provide a secular scientific perspective on the delineations between the three eras, particularly in the context of scientific observation:

> Pre-Modern represents the emphasis on observation of the natural world started by scholars toward the end of the Middle-Ages. Modern, includes the scientist, who no longer perceives natural beings of processes in themselves but rather as phenomena represented in his/her mind, that may or may not correspond with the "external" material world. Post-Modern, emphasizes the influences of the social and cultural context upon scientific observations and explanations. (Rozzi, et al, 1998)

Due to its consideration of previously de-emphasized factors (namely social and cultural context), postmodernism is perceived by its adherents as a much better way – willing, of course to utilize implements of modernity, but unwilling to submit to the modern ideas of inevitable progress through rationality and science,[18] and certainly refusing to submit to any singularity of truth beside the relative realities of cultural impact.

It is at this point that postmodernity and postmodernism are most easily distinguishable, with postmodernity referencing a specific era of scientific

---

18 Usher and Edwards, 9.

perspective and postmodernism encompassing *a broad and somewhat unsystematic mode of interpretation.* Objective scientific observation is and must be colored by presuppositions and shaped by methodology. Biblical theology asserts to be fundamental truth, it must be seen as ultimately governing science, and thus provides the proper framework of worldview with which to begin scientific study.

BIBLICAL THEOLOGY AS A WORLDVIEW

Sire defines a worldview as,

A set of presuppositions (assumptions which may be true, partially true or entirely false) which we hold (consciously or subconsciously, consistently or inconsistently) about the make-up of our world.[19]

Using Sire's definition, at least four critical elements can be identified as requisite for the framework and content of a worldview: presupposition (the basis of the worldview), method (how the presuppositions and conclusions are derived), motivation (why is the method used and the presuppositions held), and authority (upon what basis the presuppositions, method, and motivation are used).

---

19 James W. Sire, *The Universe Next Door* (Downers Grove, IL: InterVarsity Press, 1988), 17.

At the start of any worldview reside certain assumptions of reality, self-justifying bases for the validity of the worldview. A reduction of presupposition to point of origin will show the necessity to move beyond the observable and empirical into the historical, and to some degree, even metaphysical. This is the realm of faith. As an example, Freud's secular approach is discussed. In his 1933 lecture "The Question of Weltanshauung," Freud described a Weltanshauung[20] as

> An intellectual construction which solves all the problems of our existence uniformly on the basis of one overriding hypothesis, which, accordingly leaves no question unanswered and in which everything that interests us finds its fixed place.[21]

It is that *one overriding hypothesis* that a worldview seems to require, and must be rooted in presupposition. Freud's worldview included such conclusions as the pleasure principle and its extensions,[22] and was based on the premise that an understanding of meaning in

---

20 Trans., View of the universe.

21 Sigmund Freud, "The Question of Weltanschauung," in *New Introductory Lectures on Psycho-Analysis* (New York: Norton, 1965), Lecture XXXIV.

22 Freud initially held that the desire to fulfill sexual drives enveloped all human aspirations, while later expanding his view of such foundational drives to include death instinct, etc.

life was unattainable outside of the observable forces of nature. But his premise had a deeper presupposition. He said in a 1939 letter, "Neither in my private life nor in my writings have I ever made a secret of being an out-and-out unbeliever," and further confirmed his atheistic presupposition by calling religion a *universal obsessional neurosis*, portraying religion in similar fashion to Marx's *Opium des Volkes*.[23] Freud further says,

> While the different religions wrangle with one another as to which of them is in possession of the truth, in our view the truth of religion may be altogether disregarded. Religion is an attempt to get control over the sensory world, in which we are placed, by means of the wish-world, which we have developed inside us as a result of biological and psychological necessities. But it cannot achieve its end. Its doctrines carry with them the stamp of the times in which they originated, the ignorant childhood days of the human race. Its consolations deserve no trust. *Experience teaches us that the world is not a nursery.* [emphasis mine] The ethical commands, to which religion seeks to lend its weight, require some other foundation instead, for human society cannot do without them, and it is dangerous to link up obedience to them with religious belief. If one attempts to assign to

---

23 Trans., opium of the people.

religion its place in man's evolution, it seems not so much to be a lasting acquisition as a parallel to the neurosis which the civilised individual must pass through on his way from childhood to maturity.[24]

Freud begins, then, with the belief that God is not. This is his foundational presupposition. It is his *one overriding hypothesis*, and it is based on (according to his assertion) the teaching of experience, yet human experience is necessarily limited. To therefore trust in this ultra-limited experience as the basis of the hypothesis is an exercise in faith. Freud's observations of human nature are heavily influenced by his atheistic view, and he defends his atheism with these same observations.

This is an example of circular reasoning, and illustrates the real challenge in deriving a presupposition: a (foundational) presupposition begins with some degree of circular reasoning. Every overriding hypothesis has at its foundation, faith. Freud's asserted basis of *authority* is experience; his *method* is empiricism; his *motivation* seems an ordering of the universe in a fleshly and sensual way, perhaps justifying certain of his own experiences; and his presupposition, at the heart of his worldview, is an atheistic one.

---

24 Sigmund Freud, "A Philosophy of Life," in *New Introductory Lectures on Psycho-Analysis* (New York: Norton, 1965), Lecture XXXV.

A worldview is a matter of presupposition and thus faith. The question becomes not one of whether or not faith is fitting or even necessary (it is), the question rather becomes, "what kind of faith is the *right* kind?" Beginning, then, at the right point becomes the defining focus of a worldview.

> Only on the basis of a correct starting point is it possible to provide a transcendental foundation for the possibility of experience. Starting from a false point leads thought inexorably to turn into its opposite and to destroy itself.[25]

Example: There is no absolute truth (a self defeating statement, as the assertion requires that it, in itself, is a statement of absolute truth).

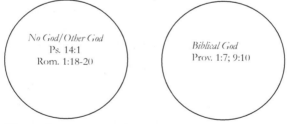

No God/Other God
Ps. 14:1
Rom. 1:18-20

Biblical God
Prov. 1:7; 9:10

Two beginning circles (and *only* two) become apparent when examining various worldviews in this

---

25 Robert Knudsen, "Progressive and Regressive Tendencies in Christian Apologetics," in E.R. Geehan, ed., *Jerusalem and Athens: Critical Discussions on the Theology and Apologetics of Cornelius Van Til* (Philipsburg, NJ: Presbyterian and Reformed Publishing, 1980), 281.

light: (1) the one beginning without the Biblical God, and (2) the one beginning with the Biblical God.

Circle #1: Beginning without the Biblical God: Atheism in particular
Five particular presuppositions in this circle are impactful here.

(1) Incompatibility between Science and Religion: Steven Jay Gould references this concept as *NOMA* (Non-overlapping Magesteria)[26] – also recognized as the distinction between *mythos* (the mystical) vs. *logos* (the rational), or between reason and revelation. This dichotomy creates a disconnect between these two elements, usually enthroning reason over revelation.

(2) There is no supernatural; the elevation of the material: The late evolutionist Carl Sagan opens his *Cosmos* with the assertion of faith that "the Cosmos is all that is or ever was or ever will be."[27] His assumption underscores the human proclivity to deny the supernatural, and to attribute to the creation the divine characteristics of the Creator. Harvard Research Professor of Zoology Richard Lewontin makes a very bold admission regarding anti-supernaturalism (materialism) as a necessary foundational assumption:

26 Steven Jay Gould, *Rocks of Ages* (NY: Ballantine, 1999), 5, 49-67.

27 Carl Sagan, *The Cosmos* (NY: Ballantine, 1980), 1.

Our willingness to accept scientific claims that are against common sense is the key to an understanding of the real struggle between science and the supernatural. We take the side of science *in spite* of the patent absurdity of some of its constructs, *in spite* of its failure to fulfill many of its extravagant promises of health and life, *in spite* of the tolerance of the scientific community for unsubstantiated just-so stories, *because we have a prior commitment, a commitment to materialism.* [emphasis mine] It is not that the methods and institutions of science somehow compel us to accept a material explanation of the phenomenal world, but, on the contrary, that we are forced by our *a priori* adherence to material causes to create an apparatus of investigation and a set of concepts that produce material explanations, no matter how counter-intuitive, no matter how mystifying to the uninitiated. Moreover, that materialism is absolute, for we cannot allow a Divine Foot in the door.[28]

(3) Death came before sin,[29] therefore death is unrelated to sin. Here death is completely distinct from the realities of sin and divine judgment.

(4) Social Darwinism and the ascent of man is the new Babel (Gen. 11), man's means of creating a stairway to

---

28 Richard Lewontin, "Billions and Billions of Demons," *New York Review of Books*, January 9, 1997.

29 Note the counter claim of Gen. 2:15-17.

heaven. Here, man is not descending, but is rather on a steady (albeit sometimes interrupted) path to godlikeness.

Four defining elements of this fourth point are evident. First, creatures are evolving from crude and violent to refined and peaceful (a kind of secular postmillennialism). Interestingly, Charles Darwin's own beliefs regarding the evolution of man were guided significantly by his observation of uncivilized inhabitants (he calls them savages) of Tierra del Fuego and westward. Of these inhabitants he says,

> Those poor wretches were stunted in their growth, their hideous faces bedaubed with white paint, their skins filthy and greasy, their hair entangled, their voices discordant, and their gestures violent. Viewing such men, one can hardly make one's self believe that they are fellow-creatures, and inhabitants of the same world...Whilst beholding these savages, one asks, whence have they come? What could have tempted, or what change compelled a tribe of men, to leave the fine regions of the north...? I believe, in this extreme part of South America, man exists in a lower state of improvement than in any other part of the world.[30]

---

30 Charles Darwin, *The Voyage of the Beagle*, edited by Charles Eliot (New York: PF Collier and Sons, 1909), 228-246.

As Darwin observes men living "as animals," he ultimately assumes their derivation from animals, thus creating almost a hermeneutic circle, albeit one unrelated to scientific observation or reality. Yet his observations raise an interesting question about observation and perception of origin: as one might observe men living as described in the progression of Romans 1:28-32, from whence would they appear to have come? Would they appear to have been derived from a Holy Creator? Or would they appear to have come from some lesser source? In short, Darwin seems to assess origins based on the observation of present condition, while the Biblical record asserts a dramatic distinction between the two because of sin. Perhaps if Darwin had considered sin in his equation he might have come to a sounder conclusion regarding the origins and development of man. But since he did not, he attributes even the progress of nations to natural selection rather than to Divine blessing and grace. On this Darwin says,

> The remarkable success of the English as colonists over other European nations...has been ascribed to their 'daring and persistent energy'; but who can say how the English gained their energy. There is apparently much truth in the belief that the wonderful progress of the United

States, as well as the character of the people, are the results of natural selection.[31]

Sadly, Darwin does not even consider the possibility of the supernatural here.

Second, is the Utopian idea that progress is imminent. Erasmus Darwin borrows from Hume, suggesting the ascent not only of man, but of all things:

> The late Mr. David Hume...concludes that the world itself might have been generated rather than created; that is, it might have been gradually produced from very small beginnings, increasing by the activity of its inherent principles, rather than by a sudden evolution by Almighty fiat...Thus it would appear, that all nature exists in a state of perpetual improvement by laws impressed on the atoms of matter by the great cause of causes; and that the world may still be in its infancy and continue to improve forever and ever.[32]

Third, man is presently a highly evolved animal and he is therefore justified in living as an animal; and fourth, life is composed of matter and energy, therefore the supernatural and the personal are denied.

---

31   Charles Darwin, *The Descent of Man* (1871 reprint, New Jersey: Princeton University Press, 1981), 179.

32 Erasmus Darwin, *Zoonimia*, (New York: AMS Press, 1974), 2:245-246.

(5) Practical Denial of the Biblical God: atheism - The practical result of the other presuppositions is atheism, as all elements of the divine are denied. With respect to method, four tactics are in use here.

The first tactic is re-definition of key terms (a technique used by Satan, e.g., Gen. 3:4-6): Smith considers atheism not to be a positive assertion, but rather the absence of a positive assertion of the existence of God. He makes his case, saying,

> Atheism, therefore, is the absence of theistic belief. One who does not believe in the existence of a god or supernatural being is properly designated an atheist...Atheism, in its basic form, is not a belief: it is the absence of belief. An atheist is not primarily a person who believes that a god does not exist; rather, he does not believe in the existence of a god.[33]

and,

> If one presents a positive belief...one has the obligation to present evidence in its favor. The burden of proof lies with the person who asserts the truth of a proposition. If the evidence is not forthcoming, if there are not sufficient grounds for accepting the proposition, it should not be

---

33 George Smith, *Atheism: The Case Against God* (New York: Promotheus Books, 1989), 7.

believed...Atheism refers only to the element of nonbelief in a god, and since there is no content here, no positive beliefs, the demand for proof cannot apply.[34]

Conveniently, Smith asserts his belief system not to be a positive assertion and thus has no obligation to offer evidence.   Note the absurdity: Could not believers positively assert that they are a-atheists: having a *non*-belief in the *non*-existence of God? Whose would be the obligation then?

Fundamentalism is another term that is redefined. Particularly notable is Karen Armstrong's definition, offering a stark distinction from more traditional usages of the term. Here is Armstrong's characterization:

> Fundamentalists have no time for democracy, pluralism, religious tolerance, peacekeeping, free speech and separation of church and state. Christian fundamentalists reject the discoveries of biology and physics about the origins of life and insist that the Book of Genesis is scientifically sound in every detail.[35]

(Note the implied characterization of Biblical Christianity as a threat.)

---

34 Smith, 15 and16.

35 Karen Armstrong, *The Battle for God* (New York: Ballantine, 2000), xi.

Here is a historical definition:

> Historically, fundamentalism has been used to identify one holding to the five fundamentals of the faith adopted by the General Assembly of the Presbyterian Church of the USA in 1910. The five fundamentals were the miracles of Christ, the virgin birth of Christ, the substitutionary atonement of Christ, the bodily resurrection of Christ, and the inspiration of Scripture.[36]

A second tactic employed in the practical denial of God is the suppression of truth, and is illustrated in Genesis 3:4-5 and Romans 1:18-20. In both passages, that which is known about God is suppressed, not in ignorance but in deliberate rebellion.

A third tactic is speculation (Gen. 3:1; Rom. 1:21). Note Darwin's closing comments in his *Origin of Species*:

> There is grandeur in this view of life, with its several powers, having been originally breathed by the Creator into a few forms or into one; and that, whilst this planet has gone cycling on according to the fixed law of gravity, from so simple a beginning endless forms most beautiful

---

36 Paul Enns, *Moody Handbook of Theology*, (Chicago, IL: Moody Press, 1989), 613.

and most wonderful have been, and are being evolved.[37]

While Darwin's biological conclusions were not an outright denial of God, they served as a practical one, by means of speculation (tool used by Satan, Gen. 3:1). (4) Eliminate absolutes (Gen. 3:4). Smith explains well the natural consequence of the elimination of such foundational elements, saying,

> Once the theist removes himself from the framework of natural causality and the general principles or 'laws' by which man comprehends the universe, he forfeits his epistemological right to the concept of explanation and precludes the possibility of explaining anything.[38]

If here he is correct, then in seeking to demonstrate the needlessness of the existence of God, he has just logically disproved his own thesis by stating that (a) there is no need for first cause, (b) there is therefore no first cause, and (c) since there is no first cause the theistic explanation of reality is irrelevant and thus untrue. Essentially, in order to destroy the theistic position, the atheist here destroys even his own basis of explaining reality. Before examining evidence he has already made his conclusion, tautology not

---

37 Charles Darwin, *The Origin of Species* (1859 reprint, New York: Modern Library, 1993), 374.

38 George Smith, 234.

withstanding. The absolute denial of first cause is the beginning of the defining circle here.

The motivation seems to stems from a desire to supplant God, or to be like God in a self-prescribed manner (Gen. 3:1-6); steeped in falsehood, saying in one's heart what one knows with the mind not to be true (Ps. 14:1); and seeking to suppress the truth in unrighteousness (Rom. 1:18-20).

The basis of authority is anthropocentric and revolves around the worship of creation rather than the Creator, as illustrated by Sagan's conclusion to *The Cosmos*:

> ...we are the local embodiment of a Cosmos grown to self awareness. We have begun to contemplate our origins: starstuff pondering the stars; organized assemblages of ten billion billion billion atoms considering the evolution of atoms; tracing the long journey by which, here at least, consciousness arose. Our loyalties are to the species and the planet. We speak for Earth. Our obligation to survive is owed not just to ourselves but also to that Cosmos, ancient and vast, from which we spring.[39]

Circle #2: Beginning with the Biblical God
The primary presuppositions here are that God is (Gen. 1:1); and God has revealed Himself authoritatively (2 Tim. 3:16). Therefore, it is not

---

39 Sagan, 286.

enough to say that God is, but if we would be accurate in the matter, we must in fact assert that the *Biblical* God is.

As for method, any pursuit of knowledge must begin with the proper respect for Him (Prov. 1:7; 9:10). Consistent with this is a requisite submission to the authority of His word, interpreting it literally, and thus allowing Him to speak rather than enthroning the interpreter (2 Tim. 2:15).

Further, the proper methodology seems best facilitated by a motivation grounded upon the proper perspective of humility on the part of the inquirer (Jn. 3:30), and on a desire to know God as He is (Jn. 17:3).

In respect to authority, due to the self-authenticating nature of the Biblical record, the Scriptures alone provide the authoritative base for this worldview (2 Tim. 3:16; Heb. 1:1 [Jn. 5:39]; 2 Pet. 1:20-21). To begin with any other authority base would result in gross contradiction and irreparable incompatibility.

BIBLICAL THEOLOGY AS AN EPISTEMOLOGY

From the Greek *episteme*, (knowledge) and *logos*, (word), epistemology deals with the question "*How do we know?*" Scripture defines knowledge as finding its base in the fear[40] of the Lord (Prov. 1:7, 9:10). Only a right perspective (rightly applied) of God can provide the impetus for proper perspective of all other aspects of reality.

This theology will follow a presuppositional approach to epistemology, being based upon the objective, self-authenticating truth claims of Scripture.[41] While some have criticized this approach as *fideism* (truth based upon faith rather than reason), it must be said that there can be absolutely no reason and no truth unless the self-authenticating truths of Scripture be true (Prov. 1:7; 9:10). While the term *fideism* is not particularly desirable here, truth *is* based on the claims of Scripture, as taken by faith, and not upon the reasoning faculty of man, and therefore

Biblical theism is asserted to be the only rational interpretation of reality. Natural man has no ability to rightly assess reality, and Biblical theism here will not be submitted to mere probabilities of proof for its

---

40 From the Hebrew *yirah*, definitions of which include fear and terror. Note Calvin's statement on the fear of the Lord: "Hence that dread and wonder with which Scripture commonly represents the saints as stricken and overcome whenever they felt the presence of God. Thus it comes about that we see men who in his absence normally remained firm and constant, but who, when he manifests his glory, are so shaken and struck dumb as to be laid low by the dread of death — are in fact overwhelmed by it and almost annihilated." (John Calvin, *Institutes* (Philadelphia: Westminster, 1940), 38-39).

41 James Emery White, *What Is Truth?* (Nashville: Broadman and Holman, 1994), 44.

reality. It must also be stated that any epistemology must also be based in faith, as certain key elements cannot be observed but rather must be believed. In truth, any epistemology could, with some degree of fairness, be referenced as *fideism*.

Foundationalism
Philips defines foundationalism as

> The view that a belief is a rational belief only if it is related in appropriate ways to a set of presuppositions which constitute the foundations of what we believe. It assumes, from the outset, that belief in God is not among these foundational propositions.[42]

Essentially, foundationalism requires that in order to believe anything, there must first be adequate evidence to substantiate the belief. Regarding the existence of God, A.B. Davidson recognized that the Biblical writers were certainly not foundationalist in their approach, observing that it never occurred to any prophet or writer of the Old Testament to prove the existence of God.[43]

   Foundationalism either defeats the premise of Biblical revelation (which presupposes the existence of

---

42 D.Z. Phillips, *Faith After Foundationalism* (London: Routledge, 1988), 3.

43 A.B. Davidson, *Theology of the Old Testament* (Edinburgh, 1904), 30.

God), or the Biblical revelation demonstrates the fallacy of the foundationalist approach. I suggest the latter. Yet, this flawed epistemology is paramount in the thought of many theologians, resulting in flawed conclusions such as theistic evolution, antisupernaturalism, replacement theology, and an evidentialist approach to truth.

Presuppositions of Biblical Theology

All worldviews must necessarily begin with circular reasoning, and thus with faith of some kind. The secularist can purportedly trace his origin back to the big bang, yet when challenged with the task of identifying the origin of the initial colliding substances he is left without any plausible explanation of first cause (whether a first cause is necessary in this worldview or not is irrelevant) and therefore he must accept by volitional faith that these things came into existence.

The late evolutionist Carl Sagan opens his popular book with the assertion of faith that the Cosmos is all that is or ever was or ever will be.[44] Sagan never attempts to justify this statement; rather it is the defining circle with which he begins. As a result of his presupposition, naturally the Cosmos becomes the object of worship, and his system categorizes itself as one of the many systems which worship the creature rather than the Creator, as illustrated by Sagan's closing comments in *Cosmos.*

---

44 Carl Sagan, *The Cosmos*, 1.

The irony here is that, Sagan seeks to worship, but does not seek to acknowledge God. Therefore his defining circle leads him to transmogrify the created into the creator.

The atheist George Smith denies the need for first cause, and then asserts that there is no evidence for the existence of God, and lacking such evidence concludes against Him.[45] But why the presuppositional denial of the need for first cause? Smith answered the question, providing a means whereby "the concept of explanation" is done away.[46]

If Smith is correct, then in seeking to demonstrate the needlessness of the existence of God, he has just logically disproved his own thesis by stating that there is no need for first cause, there is therefore no first cause, and since there is no first cause the theistic explanation of reality is irrelevant and thus untrue. Essentially, in order to destroy the theistic position, the atheist here destroys even his own basis of explaining reality. Before examining evidence he has already made his conclusion, tautology notwithstanding. The absolute denial of first cause is the beginning of the defining circle here.

We should not be critical of the atheistic use of first principles, or defining (presuppositional) circles here, for the Biblical theist begins with one too. The simple identification of God as Creator necessitates

45 George Smith, *Atheism: The Case Against God* (New York: Promotheus, 1989), 223-225.

46 Ibid., 234.

presuppositions regarding the reality of God Himself, creation, and His sovereign control over that creation. This is the beginning of the defining circle for Biblical Christianity.

All systems of thought – epistemologies, philosophies, and religions systems - begin with defining circles. There is nothing inherently illogical in beginning with a circle, for there is no other place to begin. The flaws of any system, however, are evidenced when the defining circle of presuppositions is demonstrated to be incoherent, inconsistent, or otherwise impossible. Knudsen illustrates the significance of the matter:

> Only on the basis of a correct starting point is it possible to provide a transcendental foundation for the possibility of experience. Starting from a false point leads thought inexorably to turn into its opposite and to destroy itself.[47]

In seeking to start at the *correct* starting point, theological method should begin with a very simple defining circle of presuppositions. The prerequisites that make up this circle, in this writer's estimation, provide the foundations of the Biblically theistic system. It should at this point be noted that by

---

47 Robert Knudsen, "Progressive and Regressive Tendencies in Christian Apologetics," in E.R. Geehan, ed., *Jerusalem and Athens: Critical Discussions on the Theology and Apologetics of Cornelius Van Til* (Philipsburg, NJ: Presbyterian and Reformed Publishing, 1980), 281.

identifying prerequisites or presuppositions necessary to understanding Biblical theology, I do not at all mean to say that man in his depraved, natural state can arrive at saving faith (belief *in* Jesus Christ) by simply postulating these presuppositions, for it is clear that the unregenerate mind, while intellectually capable of understanding, cannot attain to the necessary spiritual understanding.

Still, by presupposing these prerequisites, even the unregenerate mind can intellectually comprehend Scripture as a unified message that proclaims powerfully the glory of God. "It is God's plan, God's comprehensive interpretation of the facts that makes the facts what they are."[48] Therefore, if the unregenerate mind would seek a truthful basic perspective of reality he must begin at the beginning.

Whether or not God allows this basic perspective to be unified with saving faith in the heart and mind of the unbeliever (thus making him a believer) is entirely God's business (Jn. 6:44), and is only to be achieved by His own volition (Rom. 9:14-18; Eph. 2:8-9), convicting (Jn. 16:8-9), power (Rom. 1:16-17), and regeneration (Tit. 3:5), as Calvin said,

> ...it is one thing to feel that God as our Maker supports us by His power, governs us with providence, nourishes us by His goodness, and attends us with all sorts of blessings — and

---

48 Van Til, *Christian Apologetics*, 27.

another to embrace the grace of reconciliation offered to us in Christ.[49]

Recognizing such truths as intelligent design, providence, and sustenance requires a keen awareness of Biblically theistic truths, even if the recognition of these truths are simply originated from the pages of natural theology (God's general revelation in creation). It is not by the recognition of truth that one is given spiritual life, but rather by belief *in* the Truth Himself.

Further, by presupposing these prerequisites, the believer can avoid being conformed in thought to the pattern of this world – being unstained by the myth of neutrality and the myth of objectivity outside of the necessary conclusion of God and His laws. By avoiding these myths, the believer, by illumination of the Holy Spirit through Scripture can see the full counsel of God in context as a divine and purposed revelation of Himself, and can thus avoid allowing the errant fundamentals of human thought to invade his epistemology, his mindset (Col. 3:1-4) and ultimately his practice and his walk.

Just as Van Til perceived two basic presuppositional foundations for a Christian apologetic (that men must presuppose God in all their thinking and that natural man will resist this necessity entirely), there seems likewise to be no less than *four*

---

49 John T. McNeill, ed., Ford Lewis Battles, trans., John Calvin, *Institutes of the Christian Religion*, (Philadelphia, PA: Westminster Press, 1940), 1:38-39.

prerequisite pillars vital to a truly Biblical theology: (1) the existence of the Biblical God, (2) God's authoritative revelation of Himself to man, (3) natural man's incapacity to comprehend God's revelation, and (4) a consistent hermeneutic for interpreting that revelation.

Without these pillars the Biblical worldview as a basis for a Biblical theology is compromised, leaving the unbeliever with an unwarranted confidence in his own reason and his ability to arrive at that which he must understand through his own faculties and administration, and likewise leaving the believer with the illusion of a practical substitute (human objectivity) for the inherited mind of Christ, therefore hindering the believer's obedience to the imperative of Colossians 3:1-4:

> *If then you have been raised up with Christ, keep seeking the things above, where Christ is, seated at the right hand of God. Set your mind on the things above, not on the things that are on earth. For you have died and your life is hidden with Christ in God. When Christ, who is our life, is revealed, then you also will be revealed with Him in glory.*

PILLAR #1

THE EXISTENCE OF
THE BIBLICAL GOD[50]

A brief examination of Scripture will unveil, in particular, the central assumption of the existence of God (Gen. 1:1, Ps. 14:1, etc.). Never does Scripture seek to prove His existence; rather it presents His reality as the foundational starting point of Biblical theology. In light of this, it must also be understood that Scripture makes no case for a deity in general, but rather for a specific Deity, self-disclosed and explained to His desired extent in Scripture.

Therefore theism in the general sense is not an acceptable definition for the reality presented by Biblical theology, for it does not go far enough – as far as Scripture goes – in defining God Himself. Rather, it is *Biblical* theism, or the existence of the *Biblical* God that is the foundational reality upon which Biblical theology is built; and therefore an efficacious investigation (meaning one that will portray an accurate reflection of its Subject) of the revelation of

---

50 The Four Pillars concept discussed here is adapted from Christopher Cone, "Presuppositional Dispensationalism" in *The Conservative Theological Journal*, 10/29 (May/June 2006).

God in Scripture requires, first and foremost, a certain belief in the God of the Scriptures.

Kuyper recognizes the centrality of this truth, saying "Faith in the existence of the object to be investigated is the *conditio sine qua non* of all scientific investigation."[51]   Augustine suggested that man recognizes the imprint of the Divine upon man:

> We ourselves can recognize in ourselves an image of God, in the sense of an image of the Trinity. Of course, it is merely an image and in fact, a very remote one. There is no question of identity nor of co-eternity nor, in one word, of consubstantiality with Him. Nevertheless, it is an image which by nature is nearer to God than anything else in all creation, and one that by transforming grace can be perfected into a still closer resemblance.[52]

Calvin likewise asserted that man has an innate awareness of Deity, saying,

> There is within the human mind, and indeed by natural instinct, an awareness of divinity. This we take to be beyond controversy. To prevent anyone from taking refuge in the pretense of

---

51   Abraham Kuyper, Principles of Sacred Theology (Grand Rapids: Baker Book, 1980), 48.

52 Augustine, City of God, 11:26, translated by Marcus Dods, in *Nicene and Post-Nicene Fathers of the Christian Church*, edited by Philip Schaff (1886 reprint, Grand Rapids: Eerdmans,1988), 2:220.

ignorance, God has implanted in all men a certain understanding of His divine majesty.[53]

He has set eternity in our heart (Eccl. 3:11), and all are aware, and thus without excuse because He has revealed Himself to all men (Rom. 1:18-32).

Without the existence of God as Absolute, as the first and final reference point for reality, man could make no appeal to the laws of logic (which are generally understood to include (1) the law of identity – everything is what it is, and this can be affirmed; (2) the law of non-contradiction – everything is not what it is not, and this can be affirmed; (3) the law of exclusion – of two contradictory propositions one must be false and the other true, thus if one is affirmed the other must be denied; and (4) the law of reason and consequent – logical reason is followed by logical consequent, thus dealing with cause and effect. These four fundamental principles require absolute truth, which the atheist denies either in theory, practice, or both.

Appeals to intellect and morality, likewise ultimately require God to be the first and final reference point, as these elements also require origin in their absolute form from God. The atheist assumes these elements (logic, intellect, and morality), but yet interprets them in light of his own will. Thus he recognizes certain necessary Biblical premises, while rejecting their Designer. As Van Til noted,

---

53 John Calvin, *Institutes of the Christian* Religion, 1:43.

> ...if God is not self-sufficient and self-explained then He is no longer the final reference point in human predication. Then God and man become partners in an effort to explain a common environment. Facts are not what they are, in the last analysis by virtue of the plan of God; they are partly that, but they partly exist by their own power.[54]

Ultimately, even the very premise of seeking to prove the existence of God smacks of humanism, as the creature seeks to ascertain the Creator by submitting the Creator to an empirical standard greater than Himself. Here the creature has the illusion of authority by neutrality of reason, when in fact there is no such neutrality.

The natural outworking of the Biblically theistic presupposition also assumes the veracity of Scripture as the revelation of God, since it is the Biblical God that we seek to understand. For the mere existence of a god in the abstract sense is not sufficient to answer the questions that are presented,[55] nor does the idea of god in the abstract fit at all the character ascribed to the Biblical God of Scripture. It is therefore a prerequisite

---

54   Cornelius Van Til, *A Christian Theory of Knowledge* (Philipsburg, NJ: Presbyterian and Reformed, 1969), 12.

55   Essentially this is Hume's accusation (Hume's Stopper) that any argument based solely on natural theology does not prove the Biblical God.

of Biblical theology to understand that God is, and that He is the source of all knowledge, not only regarding Himself specifically, but also regarding all truth. All truth, after all, will be seen to be God's truth.

Regarding the existence of God, Greg Bahnsen said

> We can prove the existence of God from the impossibility of the contrary. The transcendental proof for God's existence is that without Him it is impossible to prove anything.[56]

Bahnsen's statement underscores the importance of the foundations of epistemology in approaching the existence of God, and ultimately concludes that Biblical theism is the only beginning point for a consistent epistemology. The basic premise here is that the reality of God is inescapable and quite necessary as the starting point for any truly rational thought. Ultimately, the atheistic position, taken to its logical conclusion completely destroys all reason and science.

It is at this point helpful to view epistemological conclusions in order to (1) demonstrate the immeasurable chasm between the musings of the Almighty God and the fallen ramblings of the human mind (Is. 55:8-11) and (2) recognize that man will consistently rebel against the knowledge of the truth (Jn. 3:19, and even if he were to seek after God, he does

---

56 "The Great Debate: Does God Exist?" Dr. Greg Bahnsen versus Dr. Gordon Stein At the University of California, Irvine, 1985.

not possess, in his fallen state, the ability to rightly appraise spiritual things (1 Cor. 2:14), therefore, only God can sufficiently draw man into the experiential knowledge of Himself (Jn. 6:44).

Thus there is no consistent epistemology other than that which presupposes the existence of the Biblical God. In fact, there is no truth, logic, or fact without the existence of the Biblical God. As Van Til suggests, "unless you believe in God you can logically believe in nothing else."[57]   Any argument for the existence of God that does not begin with His existence is wrongheaded.

Historically, various arguments concluding positively in favor of the existence of God have been made, however, most of these arguments share the same flaw in their beginning assumptions.

The *Ontological Argument* suggests that since man possesses being and the idea of God, He must exist. Anselm of Canterbury (1033-1109), in his *Proslogion,* postulated that God was that "than which no greater can be conceived." John Frame characterizes this argument as follows:

Premise 1: God has all perfections.
Premise 2: Existence is a perfection.
Conclusion: Therefore, God exists.[58]

---

57   Cornelius Van Til, *Why I Believe in God* (Philadelphia: Presbyterian and Reformed, n.d.), 20.

58 John Frame, *Apologetics to the Glory of God* (Philipsburg, NJ: Presbyterian and Reformed, 1994), 114.

In this argument, the very idea of existence attests to the existence of God.

The *Cosmological Argument* asserts that a first cause is necessary for the existence of every finite thing, and the logical First Cause is God. Thomas Aquinas offered, in his *Summa Theologica*, five "proofs" for the existence of God, the first three of which are cosmological.

The *Pantheistic Argument* perceives God as all and in all. That there is anything at all necessitates His existence. This is a type of ontological argument used in particular by Parmenides, Spinoza, and Hegel.

The *Teleological Argument* is the metaphysical argument from design. The order of the universe provides evidence that there was a Designer. In particular, that non-thinking entities can function in harmony of purpose seems a strong evidence for the reality of a Designer.

The *Moral Argument*, the argument from the existence of morality, points to the existence of absolute morals and is indicative therefore of a Primary Moralist.

These arguments lack a sound epistemological grounding. While at best they serve to demonstrate probabilistically the existence of God, at worst, due to the failure to acknowledge Solomon's definition of sound epistemology, they give rise and credibility to atheistic arguments which deftly identify the logical flaws in the theistic arguments. In essence, by seeking to prove the existence of God, the failure here is in assuming an empirical standard to which He must submit. Logically, if such a standard exists to which God must be submitted, then it is that standard itself which must be greater than God. Seemingly here would be presented greater argument for the non-existence of God than for His existence. One argument does not possess such intrinsic flaws:

The *Transcendental Argument* seeks to demonstrate the reality and necessity of the existence of God by arguing, in particular, the impossibility of the contrary. It is the only basic argument which argues *from* God's existence rather than *to* His existence. While the other arguments suggest the probability of God, only this one demands the necessity of God. Knudsen aptly summarizes Van Til's use of the transcendental argument and his presuppositional approach:

> Van Til's apologetics pointed in two directions at once. It tried to show that it is only on the foundation of Christian presuppositions that meaningful discourse is possible. It also tried to show that the failure on the part of non-Christian thinking to attain the true starting point of thought means that it is impaled on the horns of a dilemma. Its attempt to interpret everything according to a criterion acceptable to the autonomous man means that it is driven inexorably to the opposite, namely, to an irrationalism in which meaningful discourse has become impossible. No matter what the difficulties may be, considered in detail, there is

the possibility of a meaningful approach to thought and to life only when one is entrenched solidly behind the walls of a full-orbed expression of the Christian theistic position. The method is, then, not to reason to the full theistic position from a standpoint outside of it, but to stand within the Christian theistic position itself.[59]

A presuppositional approach to the existence of God will uncover dualisms in the universe in several senses: first, the personal versus the impersonal; second, singularity versus plurality; third, the rational versus rationalism; and fourth, the absolute versus the relative. These dualisms pit principles of Biblical theism on one side, and all other philosophical and religious conclusions on the other. These dualisms do not provide proof for the existence of God. These are not arguments for his existence. Rather they illustrate in a practical way the lucidity of the transcendental argument. In a sense, these dualisms provide a picture of where the two opposing philosophies (the one beginning with God, and the other beginning without Him) lead.

---

59 Robert Knudsen, "Progressive and Regressive Tendencies in Christian Apologetics," in E.R. Geehan, ed., *Jerusalem and Athens* (Philipsburg, NJ: Presbyterian and Reformed, 1980), 340.

PERSONAL VS. IMPERSONAL

Schaeffer's explanation of the personal vs. the impersonal shines valuable light on the epistemology of the beginning:

> What is involved is the reality of the personal God in all eternity in contrast to the philosophic other or impersonal everything which is frequently the twentieth-century theologian's concept of God. What is involved is the reality of the personal God in contrast to a theoretical unmoved mover, or man's purely subjective thought protection....
>
> An impersonal beginning, however, raises two overwhelming problems which neither the East nor modern man has come anywhere near solving. First, there is no real explanation for the fact that the external world not only exists, but has a specific form....
>
> Second, and more important, if we begin with an impersonal universe, there is no explanation of personality. In a very real sense the question of questions for all generations – but overwhelmingly so for modern man – is, "Who am I?"....
>
> In short, an impersonal beginning explains neither the form of the universe nor the personality of man. Hence it gives no basis for understanding human relationships, building

just societies, or engaging in any kind of cultural effort.[60]

Schaeffer's approach underscores the importance of understanding the personal God as the initiator of all, for without the presupposition of His existence all that is left are unanswered questions and illogical lines of thought. That there is a universe fashioned in an orderly manner with a personal purpose is a fact witnessed by David's exclamation that "the heavens are telling of the glory of God; and their expanse is declaring the work of His hands." (Ps. 19:1). An impersonal presupposition gives no explanation for reality, rather it simply asserts negatively that God is not at the heart of the matter. The basis of an impersonal presupposition is relativism and the result is humanism – the elevation of man to the highest position as individual deities autonomously in charge of their own lives, and thus eliminating in the minds of those adherents any need for God. Schaeffer sees the impersonal approach as being, in its denial of the personal God, far-reaching and tremendously effectual in its result:

> Those who hold the material-energy, chance concept of reality...not only do not know the truth of the final reality, God, they do not know

60 Francis Schaeffer, *The Complete Works of Francis Schaeffer, Vol 2: Genesis in Time and Space* (Wheaton, IL. Crossway Books, 1982), 9 and 11.

who Man is. Their concept of Man is what Man is not, just as their concept of the final reality is what the final reality is not.[61]

As a result, in Schaeffer's approach, there is no basis for a sound epistemology – or sound reasoning at all. The impersonal approach results in "no sufficient base for either society or law,"[62] while the personal approach provides a sound epistemology, that which is based upon the personal God, and by virtue of this, the only logical explanation for the questions of the external world and personality.

SINGULARITY VS. PLURALITY
(The One and Many Problem)

Plotinus understood the One as

the first principle, the origin of being, the cause of all good...All proceeds from the One without diminishing or changing it, for the One does not give of its substance.[63]

---

61 Francis Schaeffer, *The Complete Works of Francis Schaeffer, Vol 5: A Christian Manifesto* (Wheaton, IL. Crossway Books, 1982), 428.

62 Ibid.

63 P. Zachary Hayes, *The General Doctrine of Creation in the Thirteenth Century* (Germany: Verlag Ferdinand Schoningh, 1964), 63.

Diogenes of Apollonia (c. 460 BC) previously suggested that all existing things are created by the alteration of the same thing, and ultimately *are* actually the same thing.[64] This is the problem of finding unity in the midst of the plurality of things.[65] Or more specifically, non-Christian worldviews' failure to adequately relate the unity of the universe to the diversity and plurality that is found within it. The difficulty of the problem has been well stated by Rushdoony:

> ...to pursue the problem of the one logically in terms of ultimacy of the one leads to monism, a course taken by much Eastern philosophy. The end result has been disillusion; the one has been affirmed, but the triumph of the one has been the triumph of meaninglessness. As a result, Buddhism and other philosophies proclaimed the ultimacy of nothingness. But if the many be affirmed, the end result of such a philosophy is to proceed from dualism to total atomism and anarchy...[66]

---

64 Rousas John Rushdoony, "The One and Many Problem – the Contribution of Van Til," in E.R. Geehan, ed., *Jerusalem and Athens* (Philipsburg, NJ: Presbyterian and Reformed, 1980), 340.

65 Cornelius Van Til, *The Defense of the Christian Faith* (Phillipsburg, NJ, Presbyterian and Reformed Publishing, 1967), 24.

66 Rousas John Rushdoony, "The One and Many Problem – the Contribution of Van Til," 341.

Van Til suggests that the Biblical presupposition of a triune God offers the only suitable explanation in both the realms of the eternal and the temporal. In terms of the eternal, God was and is and will be. He is both Plurality (note the constant use of the Hebrew plural *elohim* in identifying God, as well as the ever-present doctrine of the Trinity, see Is. 48:12,16), and Unity (note the *shema* of Deut. 6:4 – "...the Lord is *one!*"). It is based upon this principle that Van Til says,

> It is only in the Christian doctrine of the triune God, as we are bound to believe that we really have a *concrete universal.*"[67]

In terms of the temporal, the one and the many are therefore (as demonstrated by the eternal one and many) created by God, and thus find both unity and plurality under God.

> Thus the created one and many may in this respect be said to be equal to one another; they are equally derived and equally dependent upon God who sustains them both. The particulars or facts of the universe do and must act in accord with universals of laws. Thus there is order in the created universe...Thus there is a basic equality between the created one and the created many, or between the various aspects of created

---

67 Cornelius Van Til, *The Defense of the Christian Faith*, 26.

reality. On the other hand, there is a relation of subordination between them as ordained by God...It is this subordination of one fact and law to other facts and laws that is spoken of in Scripture as man's government over nature.[68]

This, in Van Til's estimation, explains the order in the universe (between the one and many), and thereby gives the Biblical worldview yet another means of superiority over the non-Biblical worldview in explaining reality.

Occam's razor[69] pertains here. In this context, the simplest explanation is usually the best, and the Biblical God is the simplest solution for the one and many problem.

RATIONAL VS. RATIONALISM

Rationalism's Platonic pronouncement that "knowledge through reason is the end of all things" stands in dramatic contrast to the Biblical worldview that the noetic effects of sin have left such a stain on mankind that man's reason is utterly unreliable. The wisdom of man is foolishness to God (1 Cor. 1:20). Revelation of God was given to man and it was understood and clearly seen (Rom. 1:19-20), yet man in his finite wisdom represses the truth of that which he

---

68 Ibid., 27.

69 Pluralities ought not be supposed without necessity.

knows (Rom. 1:18). Why? Because of his presupposition – he loved the darkness rather than the light (Jn. 3:19). Man's reason leads him to ignore the truth in this context by virtue of a deceptive hermeneutic of revelation. The heart of man is deceitful (Jer. 17:9). Every intent of his thoughts are evil continually (Gen. 6:5). The mind set on the flesh therefore accomplishes the opposite of what it intends (Rom. 8:6), just as obedience to Satan's deceptions provided an effect opposite that which Eve expected – death rather than godlikeness (Gen. 3:4-5).

It is with this severe handicap that rationalism seeks the truth, and it is because of this severe handicap that a rationalistic – or any other man centered approach to truth falls far short of discovering it. Ramm identifies the crux of rationalism as the fundamental assertion that whatever is not in harmony with *educated* mentality is to be rejected.[70] Rationalism fails to consider the noetic affects of sin, and thus its definition of education is inadequate.

In contrast, the Biblical approach is quite simple. There is none who seeks after God (Ps. 14:1-3; Rom. 3:11); even those who appear to seek after Him accomplish worthless works which are not pleasing to God (Is. 64:6). Man cannot of his own volition approach God; God must draw him to Himself (Jn. 6:44). The powerlessness of human reason leaves man helpless before his Creator, but by virtue of His love (Jn. 3:16)

---

70   Bernard Ramm, *Protestant Biblical Interpretation* (Grand Rapids: Baker Book House, 1995), 63.

God has provided the gift of salvation (Eph 2:8-10) – even providing the very vehicle for receiving it, faith (I Pet. 1:5). Therefore, the Biblical response is the polar opposite of the humanistic rationalistic mindset:

> The Christian is not rationalistic; he does not try to begin from himself autonomously and work out a system from there on. But he is rational... However, he does not end with only rationality, for in his response to what God has said his whole personality is involved.[71]

Rationalism seeks to place man at the center, autonomous from the Creator. Biblical theology is contrastingly rational in that it correctly identifies man's plight and offers a solution outside of the efforts of man, yet involving the whole of the human person in the plan of redemption. These two approaches are inconsistent with one another; therefore only one can be chosen. But one of them must be chosen, for these two options encompass epistemology. Either true knowledge comes from man (a totally illogical conclusion), or true knowledge comes from something or someone other than man (a conclusion which is best explained by the revelation of Biblical theism). There are no other options. Biblical theism is the only truly rational interpretation of the universe.

---

71 Francis Schaeffer, *The Complete Works of Francis Schaeffer* (Wheaton, IL: Crossway Books, 1982), 1:124.

ABSOLUTE VS. RELATIVISM

Protagorus, because of his statement that "Of all things the measure is man, of the things that are, how they are, and of things that are not, how they are not,"[72] is commonly recognized as the father of relativism. His principle taught that man is the standard of truth, and that truth can vary from man to man. In short, because of his anthropocentric epistemology, he illogically concluded that there is no absolute save for the absolute that all things are relative to man. Plato quoted him as saying, "The way things appear to me, in that way they exist for me; and the way things appears to you, in that way they exist for you,"[73] illustrating the contradictory nature of the belief – truth is relative to each man, in this view; and therefore to the one who believes relativism to be false, it is therefore false, and becomes a self defeating argument. Biblical theism, on the other hand, offers the only explanation of the absolute. Christ claims to be "the way the truth and the life" (Jn. 14:6). As a result,

> Jesus' absolute claim that He is the way, the truth, and the life means categorically that

---

72 Kathleen Freeman, *Ancilla to the Pre-Socratic Philosophers* (1952 reprint, Cambridge: Harvard Univ Pr., 1983), 125.

73 *Theaetetus* 152a.

anything that contradicts what He says is by definition false.[74]

Again, a choice must be made. Man will either suppress the truth of the absolute Christ, or God in His mercy will allow the individual to come to the saving knowledge of Him.

Is it presumptuous to offer the conclusion that only Biblical theism is the plausible explanation of absolute truth when other religions make similar claims? The Qur'an, for example, states with conviction "The only true faith in God's sight is Islam."[75] A survey of Biblical theology will show that the God whom is revealed in the Old Testament (predating the Qur'an by as many as 2200-1200 years) is the same God revealed in the New Testament in Christ, who makes exclusive claim to deity, and by so doing contradicts the claims of the Qur'an, therefore resulting in two opposing and not complimentary systems. An examination of Biblical theism against any other system claiming absolute truth will have the same result as this one, because the Biblical revelation of God is mutually exclusive (Jn. 14:6; Acts 4:12, etc.). Warfield aptly expresses this:

> The religion of the Bible thus announces itself, not as the product of men's search after God, if

---

74 Ravi Zacharias, *Can Man Live Without God*, (Word Publishing, 1994), 101.

75 *Qur'an*, Sura 3:19.

> haply they may feel after Him and find Him, but as the creation in men of the gracious God, forming a people for Himself, that they may show forth His praise. In other words, the religion of the Bible presents itself as distinctively a revealed religion. Or rather, to speak more exactly, it announces itself as the revealed religion, as the only revealed religion; and sets itself as such over against all other religions, which are represented as all products, in a sense in which it is not, of the art and device of man.[76]

Because of this exclusivity, there are once again only two options – to suppress the truth and embrace relativism (and the humanistic side of the universal dualisms), or to be drawn by the Father into a right and personal understanding and knowledge of the Absolute Christ – the Way the Truth and the Life.

The attribute of God that is most emphatically ascribed to Him in both the Hebrew and Greek testaments is holiness (Is. 6:3; Rev. 4:8), which at its heart refers to God as being *totally other and above* that which He created (Hos.11:9b). It is fitting then, that Biblical theism would be in direct conflict with all forms of human philosophy, religion, and thought, and that any agreements of these humanisms with Biblical

---

76   B.B. Warfield, *The Works of Benjamin Warfield Vol. 1, Revelation and Inspiration* (Grand Rapids, Baker Book House, 2003), 4.

theism are due to the fact that in that particular instance they are borrowing from the Biblical worldview. All truth is God's truth, and man, in his depravity and suppression of the truth, will try to hold on to whatever truth he may, yet so as to suppress the truth which he knows about his Creator.

These humanistic suppressions of truth (the impersonalist, pluralist, rationalist, and relativist epistemologies) illustrate man's love of the darkness and desire to avoid submission to God's truth. They demonstrate the lengths to which man will go in order to maintain the philosophical equivalent of the boy thinking he can hide from oncoming danger by simply covering his eyes. Man left to his own devices is at best an atheist. Psalm 14:1 identifies the atheist as a fool. Not just a fool in the sense of one who is unwise, but in the sense of one who is sinister and vicious in his attitudes toward God.

> The fool, a term in Scripture signifying a wicked man, used also by the heathen philosophers to signify a vicious person, *gabal* as coming from *nabal* signifies the extinction of life in men, animals, and plants; so the word *nabal* is taken, a plant that hath lost all that juice that made it lovely and useful. So a fool is one that hath lost his wisdom, and right notion of God and divine things which were communicated to man by creation; one dead in sin, yet one not so much void of rational faculties as of grace in those

> faculties, not one that wants reason, but abuses his reason.[77]

This kind of fool rejects not the notion of an abstract supreme being, but rather he rejects the notion of God as revealed in Scripture.

> There is no God...It is not Jehovah, which name signifies the essence of God, as the prime and Supreme Being; but Eloahia, which name signifies the providence of God, God as a rector and judge. Not that he denies the existence of a supreme being that created the world, but his regarding the creatures, his government of the world, and consequently his reward of the righteous or punishments of the wicked.[78]

The counter to this type of foolishness is not simply theism, instead it is Biblical theism. A Biblical theology must therefore be built not upon the simple presumption of the existence of *a* god, but rather must stand firmly upon the demanded presupposition of the existence of *the* God as He reveals Himself in Scripture.

It should be understood that Scripture never attempts to prove God's existence but rather assumes it. Consequently the apologetic imperatives of Scripture

---

77   Stephen Charnock, *Discourses Upon The Existence and Attributes of God.* (Grand Rapids, MI: Baker Book House, 1993), 23.

78 Ibid., 24.

center around the gospel itself – that we be ready to defend the gospel (Php. 1:7, 16; 1 Pet. 3:15).

PILLAR #2

GOD'S AUTHORITATIVE
SELF REVELATION TO MAN

God has made Himself known to man by way of divine self-disclosure. Solomon acknowledges as much in Ecclesiastes 3:11: "He has made everything appropriate in its time. He has also set eternity in their heart, yet so that man will not find out the work which God has done from beginning even to end." God has revealed Himself with

> divine self disclosure, the purpose of which is, by intervention in history and communication in language, the calling of men into fellowship with God.[79]

This is not to say that His divine purpose in all things is man centered – we understand His divine purpose to be doxological – to bring glory to Himself, i.e., to manifest His character, but rather it is to simply say that in His *revelatory* purpose He calls men to a relationship with Himself.

---

79 Clark Pinnock, *Biblical Revelation* (Chicago, Moody Press, 1971), 29.

God has revealed Himself in *general (natural) revelation* (Acts 14:14-17) divinely by (1) the creative work itself (Is. 40), (2) other marvelous divine activities using creation (Ex. 15:1-21), and (3) within the creation itself (Ps. 19:1-6; Rom. 1:20). However, general revelation only provides enough information of God to present every man without excuse (Rom. 1), and does so sufficiently. General revelation does not present the content necessary for response resulting in regeneration. Therefore, more revelation is necessary.

He has also revealed Himself, in many portions and in many ways (Heb. 1:1), through men moved by the Holy Spirit of God (2 Pet. 1:21), in *special (supernatural) revelation* by the progressive revelation of God-breathed (2 Tim. 3:16) Scripture. This Scripture is inerrant (it is the word of truth, 2 Tim. 2:15) in its original text and authoritative for all aspects of life, as it functions as the final authority (being God's written revelation) for life in Him. It is therefore sufficient in presenting him as He wishes to be presented, and it is clear and precise in that presentation.

This special revelation ultimately points to His *personal revelation* (Jn. 5:39) in His Son, Jesus Christ (Jn. 1:18; Heb. 1:1). Christ, as the personal Revelation of God is both representative (Col. 1:13-18; Heb. 1:3) and hortatory (Jn. 1:18).

> As self-explanatory, God naturally speaks with absolute authority. It is Christ as God who speaks in the Bible. Therefore the Bible does not appeal to human reason as ultimate in order to

justify what it says. It comes to the human being with absolute authority.[80]

All elements of His revelation require human response, and man is held accountable for his response. Chafer identifies the assumption of the inspiration and authority of Scripture as the first of his essential requirements for theological study.[81]

INSPIRATION

"God in the past used various methods to communicate His word to man, as...He spoke long ago to the fathers in many portions and in many ways" (Heb. 1:1b). Although the methods varied, the Giver of revelation is always the same. The claim of inspiration (2 Tim. 3:16) is regarding the (1) origin of Scripture - proceeding from the mouth of God (there are over 150 references in Scripture to "the Lord spoke" or "God spoke" and over 400 to "Thus says the Lord," also see Col. 3:16; Heb. 1:1-2, etc.); and regarding the (2) purpose of Scripture – for training unto being fully equipped for ministry. The Scriptures are the revelation of God, given via inspiration of God. The revelation is what God said; the inspiration is the instrument of revelation.

---

80 Cornelius Van Til, *A Christian Theory of Knowledge*, 15.

81 Lewis Sperry Chafer, *Systematic Theology* (Grand Rapids, MI: Kregel, 1993), 1:7.

Old Testament revelation was delivered to prophets, although not exclusively so, as Kuyper observes,

> The divine speaking is not limited to prophecy. God spoke also to others than prophets, e.g., to Eve, Cain, Hagar, etc. To receive a revelation or a vision does not make one a prophet, unless it be accompanied by the command to communicate the revelation to others. The word "nabi," the Scriptural term for prophet, does not indicate a person who receives something of God, but one who brings something to the people. Hence it is a mistake to confine the divine revelation to the prophetic office.[82]

All that is revealed in Scripture is divine revelation, and is inspired, or God-breathed *(theopneustos)* by the Holy Spirit. There are two distinct categories of revelation identified in the Old Testament: speaking and dreams/visions/trances.

With respect to speaking as a revelatory tool, a comparison of Is. 6:1-10 and Acts 28:25 shows that the Holy Spirit is equated with God and is the One speaking. It is vital to understand that the literal interpretation of this method would require audible communication in linguistic terminology understandable by the recipient – in other words, the

---

82 Abraham Kuyper, *The Work of the Holy Spirit* (Grand Rapids: Eerdmans, 1975), 70.

use of human language and words (note Ex. 19:9 and 1 Sam. 3:1-14).

Dreams, visions, and trances were valid, although secondary, methods for the receiving of revelation (Gen. 20:3-7, 31:10-13, 24, 37:5-20, 40:5-16, 41:11-13, 15-32, 42:9, etc.). God specifically identified dreams as a valid method of revelation (Num. 12:6). In contrast to dreams, visions comprised revelation given normally while the recipient was awake (1 Kin. 22:19; Is. 1:1, 6:1; Ezek. 1:3, etc.). Trances usually were simply a condition created by God to facilitate the delivering of revelation via dream or vision.

In the New Testament, there are some specific purposes and limitations identified in God's revelatory program: (1) the person of Christ is the apex of God's revelation (Heb. 1:1-2), and all of the Holy Spirit's working in revelation points to Him (Jn. 5:39, 15:26). (2) Revelation through Scripture – at the completion of the New Testament text (1 Cor. 13:10; Eph. 2:20-21; 4:12-13; Heb. 2:2-3; Rev. 22:18-19), the revealing work of the Holy Spirit in this dispensation - in terms of *new* revelation – is complete.

While *revelation is the content of the message, inspiration is the means of the recording of the message.* In regard to Scripture, inspiration refers to the quality of being *God-breathed* – from the very mouth of God. There must be, at this point, a reminder that indeed it is the Scriptures themselves that are inspired (2 Tim. 3:16), while the men who wrote the words were moved by the Holy Spirit, and thus spoke the words of God (Is. 59:21; Jer. 1:9; 2 Pet. 1:20-21). Christ affirmed the Holy

Spirit's role in both revelation and inspiration (Mt. 22:42-43; Mk. 12:36), as did the apostles (Acts 1:16, 4:25, 28:25; Heb. 3:7, 9:6-8, 10:15). Apostles, therefore, make authoritative claims for their writings (i.e., note Paul's claims in 1 Cor. 2:13; 14:37; Gal. 1:7-8; 1 Thes. 4:2,15; 2 Thes. 3:6, 12, 14).

Without the Holy Spirit's work of inspiration, we could not know the revelation of God, and any examination of the identity, character, and works of God would be purely speculative. As it is, we have an authoritative revelation from God, via the Holy Spirit's work of inspiration of Scripture. *Verbal Plenary Inspiration* seems the most accurate description of this instrument.

Inspiration is *verbal* in the sense that the Holy Spirit strongly influenced the selection of the very words used by the human writers, utilizing their personalities and vocabulary, while avoiding the intrusion of error.[83] Inspiration is *plenary* (from the Latin *plenus*, meaning full) in the sense that inspiration extends to every aspect (not just in regard to the 'doctrinal' elements) and even the very words of Scripture.

---

83 Chafer, 71.

Excursus: Outline of Prophecy as Instrument of Inspiration by the Holy Spirit

God Has Spoken
(1) The content is special revelation (Ps. 19:7-11; Heb. 1:1), which is the revelation by God through the Holy Spirit, of His Son (Jn. 5:39) who glorifies the Father.

(2) The method is inspiration (2 Tim. 3:16).

(3) The final form is Scripture (2 Tim. 2:15; 3:16).

(4) The Revealer is the Holy Spirit.
　　(A) The interactions involved the Holy Spirit's moving of men (2 Pet. 1:20-21).

　　(B) The recipients were the apostles and prophets (Jn. 14:26; Eph. 3:5).

　　(C) The content was the truth and remembrance, of Christ, to the glory of the Father (Jn. 14:26; 15:26-27; 16:13).

　　(D) The characterizations included the sword of the Spirit (Eph. 6:17; Heb. 4:12), and the witness and words of the Holy Spirit (Is. 59:21; Zech. 4:6; Acts. 21:11; 1 Tim. 4:1; Heb. 3:7; 9:8; 10:15; Rev. 2:7, 11, 17, 29; 3:6, 13, 22).

Prophetic Eras in the Old Testament
(1) The Pre-Abrahamic era involved direct revelation rather than messages to be delivered to an audience (e.g., Adam and Eve, Cain, Enoch, Noah, etc.).

(2) The Abrahamic era included direct revelation of personal and covenant blessing.

(3) The Mosaic era was characterized by direct revelation with a particular message to be delivered to specific audiences.

(4) The time of Judges included occasional direct revelation (1 Sam. 3:1); The names of the prophets are generally not recorded (except Deborah, Jdg. 4:4).

(5) During the Monarchy, Exilic, and Post-Exilic eras, revelation is extensive, and primarily in the context of messages to be delivered: messages of judgment, restoration, and Messianic hope.

The Ministry of Christ
(1) Christ claimed to be a prophet (Mt. 13:57; Mk. 6:4; Lk. 4:24; 13:33).

(2) He was recognized as a prophet (Mt. 21:46; 21:11; Mk. 6:15; Lk. 7:16; 24:19; Jn. 4:19; 6:14; 7:40; 9:17).

(3) He is both the Revealing Prophet and the Revelation (Jn. 5:39; Col. 1:15; Heb. 1:1-3; 2:2-3).

(4) He is the coming appointed Prophet (Deut. 18:15-19; Acts 3:19-26).

The Apostolic Age
(1) Apostles and prophets were sent ultimately to be persecuted, and killed (Lk. 11:49-51, *note the implication here that the normative prophetic office would conclude with that generation*). Regarding priority in the church, apostles were first, and prophets second (1 Cor. 12:28).

(2) Men were appointed by God within the church as prophets (1 Cor. 12:28).

(3) They were to speak in the name of the Lord (Jam. 5:10).

(4) They were to prophesy in an orderly manner (1 Cor. 14:29-32).

(5) Apostles and prophets were significantly related (Eph. 3:5; 2 Pet. 3:2; John, for example was both and apostle and prophet, see Rev. 22:9), and yet distinct (Eph. 4:11).

(6) Apostles and prophets, are *given* to the church as foundational (Eph. 2:20; 3:5; 4:11), building upon the Rock of Christ (Mt. 16:18; 1 Cor. 3:11).

(7) They were authenticated by signs, miracles, wonders, gifts of the Holy Spirit (2 Cor. 12:12; Heb. 2:3-4).

(8) The foundational ministry of prophecy, in context of revealed knowledge, would be done away at the coming of the perfect or the complete (1 Cor 13:10).

The word translated perfect, or complete in 1 Corinthians 13:10 is *teleion*, and is a neuter (note the *to* article instead of *ton*), an adjective that does not refer to Christ, but rather to an *it*. The preposition *ek* (v. 9) denotes 'from the partial' (lit. division or section) *ek merous* (from a division) and is contrasted with *to teleion* (not with *nepios*). Some suggest *to teleion* refers to the eternal state, the second coming of Christ, or the maturating of the church. But in context, the completion of special revelation is in view here. (Note the mirror concept of 1 Cor. 12:13, 2 Cor. 3:14-16, and Jam. 1:23). In contrast to *partial*, complete (rather than perfect) is the best rendering.

(9) Some are identified as apostles, including Paul, Christ (Heb. 3:1), Peter, the Twelve (Mt. 10:2), Matthias (Acts 1:26), Barnabas (Acts 14:14), James (Gal. 1:19), Silas (Silvanus) and Timothy (1 Thes. 1:1, 2:6, etc.).

(10) Some are identified as prophets, including, Agabus, others from Antioch (Acts. 11:27), Barnabus, Simeon (Acts 13:1), Judas, Silas (Acts 15:32), and Agabus (Acts 21:10).

False Apostles and Prophets
(1) False apostles and prophets have arisen (2 Cor. 12:11-15; 2 Pe. 2:1; 1 Jn. 4:1).

(2) False apostles and prophets will arise (Mk. 13:22), and false teaching will be desired (1 Tim. 4:1-2; 2 Tim. 3:1-8).

The Tribulation Age
(1) The two prophets are granted the required authority to prophesy (Rev. 11:3-10).

(2) The False Prophet assists the beast during the tribulation (Rev. 16:13), performing signs to deceive (19:20), and is seized and thrown alive into the lake of fire (19:20; 20:10).

Prophets, Apostles, and Inspiration
        Prophets and apostles were revelatory tools of the Holy Spirit. Definitions in this regard dramatically impact the doctrines of inspiration, inerrancy, infallibility, and therefore the authority of Scripture. If these gifted roles are misrepresented, ultimately the authority of Scripture is undermined, leaving the reader with either a humanized text or a fluid canon to be influenced either by ecumenical bodies or by pseudo-authoritative gifted figures who on a whim offer new revelation. If these gifted roles are rightly understood, the reader may consequently grasp the necessity of learning to skillfully wield the divine sword, and will

perhaps abandon the fruitless task of trying to sharpen it.

Alternate Theories of Inspiration

Liberalism teaches that the Bible contains the word of God. Neo-Orthodoxy teaches that the Bible becomes the word of God (ala Karl Barth). The dictation theory suggests God dictated the words without any utilization of the author's personality. The partial inspiration or concept theory asserts that inspiration extends only so far as doctrine but denies inerrancy in other aspects. The talent inspiration theory holds that God inspired the writer rather than the words. Each of these is countered by a literal interpretation of 2 Tim. 3:16; 2 Pet. 1:21. As the Scriptures are God-breathed, they are both inerrant (free from error) and infallible (incapable of error), and are thus the final authority for all.

CANONICITY

Canonicity deals with the church's *recognition* of Divine authority of the books of the Bible. In this sense, canonicity does not itself provide the authority of Scripture (God does that), but rather gives testimony to it:

> the original meaning or the term canon can be traced to the ancient Greeks, who used it in a literal sense: a *kanon* was a rod, ruler, staff, or measuring rod. The Greek word *kanon* is

probably a derivative of the Hebrew *kaneh* (reed), an Old Testament term meaning measuring rod (Ezek. 40:3; 42:16)...Galatians 6:16 comes closest to the final theological significance of the word, as Paul says, "Those who will walk by this rule [*kanon*], peace and mercy be upon them."[84]

During the early generations of the church the idea of the canon referred primarily to the rule of truth or the rule of faith[85] as descending from Christ and the apostles. Soon thereafter and also more recently the term has come to refer to the list of books considered authoritative as Scripture.

The idea of a closed canon is emphasized in several contexts: Deuteronomy 4:2 and 12:2 highlight the completeness of the Law; Amos 8:11 reveals a stoppage in new revelation for an extended period of time; 1 Corinthians 13:9-12 outlines that there would be a final end to revelatory gifts; and Revelation 22:18-19 underscores the completeness of God's revelation to man. F.F. Bruce emphasizes the reality of a closed canon:

The words "to which nothing can be added...and from which nothing can be taken away"...seem

---

84 Geisler and Nix, *A General Introduction to the Bible* (Chicago: Moody, 1986), 203-204.

85 F.F. Bruce, *The Canon of Scripture* (Downers Grove: IL: Intervarsiy Pres, 1988), 18.

certainly to imply the principle of a closed canon... Such language about neither adding nor taking away is used in relation to individual components of the two Testaments.[86]

While there are many evidences for the validity of the canon, perhaps the most significant and most resounding is Christ's stamp of authority on both Testaments:

The Old Testament

The 24-book Hebrew Old Testament has come to be known as the TaNaKh (an acronym for the Torah, the Nevi'im, and the Ketuvim). The Torah (Law) is comprised of Genesis, Exodus, Leviticus, Numbers, and Deuteronomy (Deut. 31:24-26 indicates a completed law [five books of Moses], and is alluded to in Josh. 8:31; Neh. 8:1-9:38, etc.). The Nevi'im (Prophets) consists of two groups: (1) The Former: Joshua, Judges, Samuel, Kings; (2) The Latter: Isaiah, Jeremiah, Ezekiel, and the Twelve (Minor Prophets) which include Hosea, Joel, Amos, Obadiah, Jonah, Micah, Nahum, Habakkuk, Zepheniah, Haggai, Zechariah, and Malachi. (Prophets recognized the authority of other prophets: Zechariah references former prophets [1:4; 7:7] as those preceding the exile; also note Jer. 7:25; Ezek. 38:17. Dan. 9:2 indicates that by the early 6th

---

86 Ibid., 22.

century BC there was a collection of prophetic books.[87])
The Ketuvim (Writings) includes three groups: (1)
Psalms, Proverbs, and Job; (2) The Megillot (scrolls):
Song of Solomon, Ruth, Lamentations, Ecclesiastes,
and Esther; (3) Daniel, Ezra-Nehemiah, and Chronicles

Jesus' testimony in Luke 11:50-51 indicates that
this basic structure of the Hebrew Bible as Genesis-
Chronicles was recognized in Jesus' day. Although
Chronicles is not chronologically the last book of the
Old Testament (the events of Ezra-Nehemiah followed
those of the Chronicles), it apparently was the last to
be added to the canon. Note Jesus' observation: "The
blood of all the prophets since the foundation of the
world may be charged against this generation from the
blood of Abel to the blood of Zechariah who was killed
between the altar and the house of God" (Lk.
11:50b-51a). Abel was the first identified in Scripture
(Gen. 4:8) to have been killed for his faithfulness;
Zechariah, while not the last chronologically, is the last
listed in Chronicles (2 Chr. 24:20-22), which
traditionally has been the final book of the Hebrew Old
Testament. Jesus, therefore, by his statement
emphasizes the present (at the time of His statement)
generation's accountability for all the martyrs of the
Old Testament. Wenham's observations of Christ's
validation of the Old Testament are especially helpful:

Jesus consistently treats Old Testament historical
narrative as straightforward records of fact. He

---

87 Ibid., 39.

refers to Abel (Luke 11:51), Noah (Matt. 24:37-39; Luke 17:26,27), Abraham (John 8:56), the institution of circumcision (John 7:22; cf. Gen. 17:10-12; Lev. 12:3), Sodom and Gomorrah (Matt. 10:15; 11:23, 24; Luke 10:12), Lot, (Luke 17:28-32), Isaac and Jacob (Matt. 8:11; Luke 13:28), manna (John 6:31, 49, 58), the snake in the desert (John 3:14), David eating the consecrated bread (Matt. 12:3, 4; Mark 2:25, 26; Luke 6:3,4), David as a psalm writer (Matt. 22:43; Mark 12:36; Luke 20:42), Solomon (Matt. 6:29; 12:42; Luke 11:31; 12:27), Elijah (Luke 4:25, 26), Elisha (Luke 4:27), Jonah (Matt. 12:39-41; Luke 11:29, 30, 32), and Zechariah (Luke 11:51). The last passage brings out Jesus' sense of the unity of history and His grasp of its wide sweep. His eye surveys the whole course of history from 'the creation of the world' to 'this generation.' He repeatedly refers to Moses as the giver of the Law (Matt. 8:4; 19:8; Mark 1:44; 7:10; 10:5; 12:26; Luke 5:14; 20:37; John 5:46; 7:19). He frequently mentions the sufferings of the true prophets (Matt. 5:12; 13:57; 21:34-36; 23:29-37; Mark 6:4 [cf. Luke 4:24; John 4:44]; 12:2-5; Luke 6:23; 11:47-51; 13:34; 20:10-12) and comments on the popularity of the false prophets (Luke 6:26). He sets the stamp of His approval on such significant passages as Genesis 1 and 2 (Matt. 19:4, 5; Mark 10:6-8). These quotations are taken by our Lord more or less at random from different parts of the Old Testament, and some periods of its history are covered more fully than others. Yet it is evident that

He was familiar with...the Old Testament and that He treated all parts of it equally as history.[88]

(Also see: 2 Sam. 23:2; Ezek. 2:2; 8:3; 11:1,24; Mic. 3:8; Mt. 22:43; Acts 1:16; 4:25; 28:25; Heb. 3:7, 9:6-8, 10:15; Lk. 24:44, etc.) The validity of the Old Testament revolves around the authority and testimony of Jesus Christ.

The New Testament

Further, Christ, in promising the coming of the Holy Spirit, identified His role in revelation and inspiration of New Testament writings (Jn. 16:12-15), and commissioned the apostles to bear witness of the truth He would reveal (Mt. 10:14, 15; 28:19; Lk. 10:16; Jn. 13:20; 15:27; 16:13; 17:20; Acts 1:8; 9:15-17; compare Ex. 4:15 and 1 Cor. 14:37; Rev. 22:19). Apostles, therefore, make authoritative claims for their writings (i.e., note Paul's claims in 1 Cor. 2:13; 14:37; Gal. 1:7-8; 1 Thes. 4:2,15; 2 Thes. 3:6, 12, 14). Those specifically referenced as apostles account for the greatest volume of New Testament writings.

---

88 John Wenham, "Christ's View of Scripture," in *Inerrancy*, Norman Giesler, editor, (Grand Rapids, MI: Zondervan, 1980), 6-7.

Writer	N.T Book(s)	Identified as Apostle
Matthew	Gospel of Matthew	Mt. 9:9
John	Gospel of John, 1, 2, and 3 John, Revelation	Mk. 1:19
Paul	Romans, 1 and 2 Corinthians, Galatians, Ephesians, Philippians, Colossians, 1 and 2 Thessalonians, 1 and 2 Timothy, Titus, Philemon	Acts 9:4-6
James	Epistle of James	Gal. 1:19
Peter	1 and 2 Peter	Mt. 4:18

However, not all of the New Testament books were written by apostles. Those writers who did not have apostleship most certainly must have had the gift of revelatory prophecy (as identified in 1 Cor. 13:8-13), and each had significant ministries in direct association with the apostles.

Writer	N.T. Book(s)	Identified w/ Apostle(s)
John Mark	Gospel of Mark	2 Tim. 4:11; Paul
Luke	Gospel of Luke Book of Acts (Hebrews?)	2 Tim. 4:11; Paul
Apollos	Hebrews	1 Cor. 16:12; Paul
Barnabus?		Acts 4:36; the apostles Acts 11:24-26; Paul (Saul)
Luke?		*See above*
Jude	Jude	Jude 1; James

Because the books of the Bible have the stamp of divine authority, and they were recognized as authoritative from the beginning, over time by the church, the New Testament was finally recognized in its current form by the Third Council of Carthage (397 AD). Bahnsen recognizes the importance of this divine stamp:

> The Christian faith is based upon God's own self-revelation, not the conflicting opinions or untrustworthy speculations of men. As the Apostle Paul wrote: "your faith should not stand in the wisdom of men, but in the power of God" (I Cor. 2:5). The world in its own wisdom would never understand or seek God (Rom. 3:11) but always suppress or distort the truth in unrighteousness (Rom. 1:18, 21). So Paul concluded that "the world in its wisdom did not know God" (I Cor. 1:21), and he set in sharp contrast "the words which man's wisdom teaches" and those which "God revealed unto us through the Spirit" (I Cor. 2:10, 13). In light of that contrast, we need to see that the apostolic message did not originate in persuasive words of human wisdom or insight (I Cor. 2:4). The light of the knowledge of God's glory in the face of Jesus Christ was, as they said, "of God and not from ourselves" (II Cor. 4:6-7). Paul thanked God that the Thessalonians received his message "not as the word of men, but as it is in truth, the word of God" (I Thes. 2:13). As Peter wrote, "no

prophecy ever came by the will of man, but men spake from God, being moved by the Holy Spirit" (II Peter 1:21). Paul said of the sacred writings which make us wise unto salvation that every one of them is "God-breathed," inspired by God (II Tim. 3:15-17). It is for this reason that the Scriptures are profitable for our doctrine, correction, and instruction.[89]

BIBLICAL CRITICISM

Biblical/textual criticism examines internal and external evidence in order to arrive at such conclusions as the dates and authorship of books and the legitimacy of textual readings. While Biblical/textual criticism can be a valuable tool in understanding where the books of the Bible fit in context, some use it to undermine the authority of the Scriptures, possessing faulty motivations and using flawed methods resulting in a suppression of the authority of the Scriptures. This approach is commonly identified as *liberal criticism*, and does not possess the intent of simply understanding the books, but rather seeks to destroy the authority of the books altogether. There are generally two schools of Biblical criticism: higher criticism, addressing issues of authorship and setting, etc., and lower criticism, addressing the manuscripts themselves.

---

89 Greg Bahnsen, "The Concept and Importance of Canonicity" in *Antithesis* Vol. 1, No. 5.

Some Elements of Higher Criticism.[90]

(1) Regarding the Torah

Moses' authorship of the Torah (or Pentateuch - the first five books of the Bible) is affirmed throughout Scripture, thus the Biblical literalist will conclude that Moses was indeed the author. There are numerous claims within the Torah of Mosaic authorship,[91] as well as other Old Testament books containing statements of the same,[92] and Christ Himself identified Moses as the writer of the first five books on more than 15 recorded occasions.[93] Most significantly, in Luke 24:44, He refers to the entire Old Testament, divided - as the Jews of that day recognized – into three categories: "the Law of Moses and the Prophets, and the Psalms."

Only in recent years has the Mosaic authorship of these books been challenged, most notably by Julius Wellhausen (1844-1918). Wellhausen argued for the Documentary Theory, also known as the JEDP theory – a theory that suggested several men as being responsible for the authorship of the Torah:

---

90 section contains selections reprinted and adapted from Cone, *The Promises of God: A Bible Survey* (Arlington: Exegetica, 2005).

91 Ex. 17:14; 24:4; 34:27; Num. 33:1-2; Deut. 31:9.

92 Josh. 1:8; 8:31; 1 Kgs. 2:3; 2 Kgs. 21:8; Ezra 6:18; Neh. 13:1; Dan. 9:11-13; Mal. 4:4.

93 Mt. 8:4; 19:7-8; Mk. 1:44; 7:10; 10:3-5; 12:26; Lk. 5:14; 16:29-31; 24:44; Jn. 5:45-46; 7:19-22.

"J" is for "Jahwist," as this supposed author seemed to prefer to use the name Jehovah (in Hebrew, Yahweh) in describing God. This author wrote in approximately 850 BC. Exodus 34:10-26 is claimed to have been authored by "J," yet Exodus 34:27 makes clear claim to Mosaic authorship.

"E" is for "Elohist", as this author penned the Hebrew word Elohim when referring to God. His writing was done around 750 BC. Exodus 17:8-13 and 20:22-23:33 are supposed examples of this writer's work, yet again Exodus 17:14 and 24:4 claim Mosaic authorship.

"D" is for "Deuteronomist" – the unnamed redactor of 650 BC, who edited and combined documents "J" and "E" to arrive at the deuteronomic account. Deuteronomy 5-30 and 32:1-42 supposedly fall into this category, yet Deuteronomy 31:9 and 32 evidence Mosaic authorship.

"P" is for the priestly author - primarily of Leviticus – but of other priestly and institutional sections as well. Leviticus 18:5 is purportedly an example: yet again, Romans 10:5 demands Mosaic authorship. Also compare Numbers 33:3-49 and Numbers 33:2.

This form of criticism assumes that because there are variances in the writing 'style' and because there is found within these books a very broad range of subjects, time, and information covered, that it could not possibly be the work of just one author; and the theory dismisses completely the idea of God's inspiring and revealing work.

While Wellhausen was not the primary originator of this theory (Richard Simon, a Catholic priest, hypothesized in 1678 that there were two authors of the Pentateuch. Later Jean Astruc [1684-1766] and Johann Eichhorn [1752-1827] advanced the theory), he seemed to be it's loudest proponent. And the issue at stake is not simply the question of who wrote these books. The process by which Wellhausen and others arrive at their conclusions is a dangerous one, as Gleason Archer points out:

> The Documentary Theory has been characterized by a subtle species of circular reasoning; it tends to posit its conclusion (the Bible is no supernatural revelation) as its underlying premise (there can be no such thing as supernatural revelation)...Unfortunately...it rendered impossible any fair consideration of the evidences presented by the Scripture of supernatural revelation. Furthermore, it made it absolutely obligatory to find rationalistic, humanistic explanations of every miraculous or God-manifesting feature or episode in the text of Scripture.[94]

It is imperative that the Bible student recognize the conflict between Biblical claims and the claims of

---

94 Gleason Archer, *A Survey of Old Testament Introduction* (Chicago: Moody Press, 1995), 113.

liberal criticism. They are mutually exclusive; and as a result, we must make a choice to either acknowledge God's sovereign and supernatural work in revealing Himself, or to thoroughly discount it. But again, despite any lack of clarity in the arguments or intentions of the critics of Mosaic authorship, the Bible stands clear in its testimony that Moses was the mouthpiece chosen by God to pen the Torah.

(2) Regarding Isaiah

Because of the predictive nature of Isaiah's ministry, some modern (as early as the late eighteenth century) critics have promoted a documentary theory regarding the authorship of Isaiah. It is suggested that in addition to the historical Isaiah, who authored the first thirty-nine chapters, there was a redactor who lived in Babylon after the fall of Jerusalem who completed the latter part of the book (thereby justifying prophetic mentions of the coming fall of the city), and who is commonly referred to as Deutero-Isaiah. Some even refer to a third author, Trito-Isaiah. These critical methods are unjustifiable and simply seek to explain away the miraculous aspect of predictive prophecy with which God revealed His plan. However, Jewish traditions, as well as New Testament writers, acknowledge the genuineness of Isaiah's authorship:

Matthew attributes Isaiah 40:3 and 42:1 to Isaiah (Mt. 3:3, and 12:17-18). Luke recognizes Isaiah's authorship of 40:3-5 (Lk. 3:4) and 53:7-8 (Acts 8:28). Paul also acknowledges that Isaiah wrote the latter portion of the book, attributing Isaiah 53:1 and 65:1 to

Isaiah (Rom. 10:16, 20). The authority and legitimacy of Isaiah's authorship was further verified by Christ Himself, as He quoted both the earlier section of the book (Is. 29:13 in Mt. 15:8-9), and the latter part of the book (Is. 61:1 in Mt. 11:5), as authentic and prophetic of Himself.

(3) Regarding Daniel

Due to the amazing precision of Daniel's prophecies, critics have suggested a later date of 167 BC, citing the book's placement in the ketuvi'im rather than the nebi'im (this conclusion overlooks the fact that Daniel did not minister as a prophet as did those writers in the nebi'im, rather he was a head of state serving under the Chaldeans.). Keil says of the book of Daniel,

> Its place in the canon among the Kethubim corresponds with the place which Daniel occupied in the kingdom of God under the Old Testament; the alleged want of references to the book and its prophecies in Zechariah and in the [apocryphal] book of Jesus Sirach is, when closely examined, not really the case: not only Jesus Sirach and Zechariah knew and understood the prophecies of Daniel, but even Ezekiel names Daniel as a bright pattern of righteousness and wisdom.[95]

95 Keil and Delitzsch, *Commentary on the Old Testament: Ezekiel and Daniel* (Peabody, MA: Hendrickson, 2001), 507.

There are other internal issues that have concerned critics, such as the presence of Greek-influenced terms within the text, however archaeology (particularly in the remains of Nineveh) has evidenced that Greek influence was felt even before Daniel's time.[96] Also of concern is the seeming error of Daniel 1:1 which identifies Nebuchadnezzar's invasion as being in the third year of Jehoiakim, while Jeremiah 46:2 indicates it took place in Jehoiakim's fourth year. This is easily explained by the difference between the Jewish and Chaldean calendars, however, with Jeremiah writing from the perspective of the Jewish calendar, while Daniel wrote from the perspective of the Chaldean calendar. The book of Daniel is difficult for some to accept, as it describes the future of the world, it is communicated with precision and purpose, and finds its ultimate fulfillment in the Kingdom of Jesus Christ.

(4) Regarding the Gospels

Distinct characteristics tie Matthew, Mark, and Luke together, while John's Gospel stands alone in its context. The first three gospels handle many of the events of Christ's life in detail, while the fourth focuses on seven specific signs, demonstrating the deity of Christ. The first three provide a more detailed narrative of the events of Jesus' earthly ministry, while John states plainly that his intention is to record only

---

96 Ibid.

that information that would result in a saving belief in Christ:

> Many other signs therefore Jesus also performed in the presence of the disciples which are not written in this book; but these have been written that you may believe that Jesus is the Christ, the Son of God; and that believing you may have life in His name. (Jn. 20:30-31).

It is commonly suggested in modern times that Mark wrote first because his writing was shorter than Matthew's or Luke's, because much of the information in the Gospel of Mark can be found in Matthew and Luke as well, and because of apparent grammatical refinements in Matthew and Luke. It appears that Mark wrote between 50-60 AD; and while it is possible that he was the earliest author, it is not probable. Most who assume Mark's early authorship also assume that Matthew and Luke borrowed from him, due to the previously mentioned reasons.

Matthew was the only one of the first three Gospel writers to have been an eyewitness of Jesus. As one of the twelve disciples of Christ he would have been very acquainted with the teachings and doings of the Savior. It seems most logical that his nearness to Christ would have allowed him to compose an "original" Gospel – or at least from a human standpoint one who was with Jesus would not logically have to borrow information from one who was not. It is most probable that Matthew did indeed write first and that his information came from his own eyewitness, and the work of the Holy Spirit. This was also universally held in the very early church, and as a result has always been placed first in the New Testament.[97] Matthew could have written as early as 37-39 AD, but almost certainly no later than 45 AD, which would predate Mark's Gospel by at least several years.

Luke clearly did "borrow" information, as he states this emphatically in the early going of his Gospel (1:1-3), probably from Matthew, Mark and possibly the testimony of other disciples as well. He makes no apology for his use of sources to compile his Gospel. Even so, the authority of his writings is certainly not compromised, as he bore the authority of a companion of Paul at the very least, was a missionary in his own right, and bears the unmistakable brand of truth upon his Gospel.

John wrote his Gospel at least before the destruction of Jerusalem in 70 AD, in part due to a present tense reference to Jerusalem (5:2). It has become popular to assume that Matthew and Luke borrowed from Mark, but modern criticism extends farther and goes something like this:

According to the theory, Mark wrote the first Gospel, based upon the authority of Peter, and in parallel with the hypothetical source document referred to as "Q." Matthew then wrote, borrowing from unique sources, from Mark, and from Q. Finally, Luke wrote,

---

97 Jamieson, Fausset, and Brown, *Bible Commentary* (Peabody, MA: Hendrickson, 2002), 3:xxvii.

but did not use Matthew's unique sources; in fact he didn't use Matthew at all, but rather used Mark and Q, as well as his own unique sources.

This theory seeks to explain difficult similarities and likenesses in the Gospel account, but it creates more problems than it solves. First, it assumes that God did not inspire the words of these individual men as independent, but rather used human sources to glean their information; and while Luke proclaims his use of sources (which very well could have been the other Gospels, as well as other oral traditions of the apostles which were not recorded in the Gospels), Matthew and Mark do not, which makes the documentary hypothesis a speculative leap. Second, it assumes that an eyewitness of Jesus (Matthew) borrowed from someone who was not with Jesus (Mark), creating a logical inconsistency with this hypothesis. And finally, it introduces "other sources," including "Q," for which there is no historical or Biblical evidence, again too speculative and assuming, and in result attacking the authority of the text.

Considering Higher Criticism: The Relationship of Authenticity to Authority[98]

John Locke deftly identified the central problem of biblical authority: he explained that if all of holy writ

---

98 Reprinted with permission from Christopher Cone "Considering Higher Criticism: The Relationship of Authenticity to Authority" in *Journal of Dispensational Theology*, Vol. 16, No. 47 (Apr. 2012), 7-22.

is to be equally considered as inspired of God, then there is much to be questioned regarding the Christian faith;[99] however, if it is not to be so considered, then the authority of the text may be questioned and ultimately undermined, and thus the Christian faith is disintegrated.[100] It is quite a problem indeed that Locke unearthed. If the text is not authoritative then hermeneutic exercises are quite inconsequential for any purposes other than literary appreciation. Therefore, the authority of the text is central at this point. How then does biblical criticism influence the discussion? Furthermore, what can be said of authority after the text has been submitted to the critical processes?

Louis Wallis keenly summarized the rise of biblical criticism, observing correctly that it did not originate in the minds of German scholars, but instead enjoyed a more eclectic genesis. His comments traced progress from the twelfth to the eighteenth century, and their thoroughness and conciseness warrant their full representation here. He described the rise of biblical criticism as follows:

> . . . distinctly foreshadowed by a Spanish Jew, Ibn Ezra, the most eminent biblical scholar of the Middle Ages, far back in the twelfth century

---

99 E. S. de Beer, ed., *The Correspondence of John Locke,* 8 vols. (Oxford: Clarendon Press, 1979) 2:748-51.

100   John Marshall, *John Locke: Resistance, Religion and Responsibility* (Cambridge, MA: Cambridge University Press, 1994) 340.

A.D. The idea was taken up by the English scholar Hobbes, in his book, Leviathan, published in 1651; by the Frenchman L Peyrere, in his book Pre-Adamites, issued in 1655; and by the Jewish philosopher Spinoza, of Amsterdam, Holland, in Tractatus-Theologico-Politicus, which came out in 1670. In the meanwhile the Frenchman Louis Cappellus in 1650 published his Critica Sacra, demonstrating the imperfect and fallible condition of the Hebrew vowel points. In 1678, Richard Simon, another Frenchman, put forth a volume entitled Critical History of the Old Testament, showing that the Mosaic Law was compiled and edited centuries after the time of Moses. In 1753 appeared a work by Astruc, a French writer, identifying the so-called Jehovist and Elohist documents in Genesis. In 1800 was published the Critical Remarks of Alexander Geddes, a Scotchman, who denied the Mosaic authorship of the Pentateuch. And although German scholars in the nineteenth century did more for biblical interpretation than did the scholars of other countries, they were matched in critical acumen during that period by Renan of France, Colenso of England, and Kuenen of Holland.[101]

Notably, two of the earlier critics cited by Wallis (viz.

_____

101 Louis Wallis, "The Paradox of Modern Biblical Criticism," *The Biblical World* 52 (July 1918): 42-43.

Ibn Ezra and Spinoza), built upon earlier traditions. Fred G. Bratton suggested they borrowed from the Talmudists, "who called attention to scores of discrepancies and contradictions in the Old Testament."[102] Bratton provided a series of examples, citing observations "by one that the flood was not a world catastrophe but local in character, by another that Moses and Elijah did not ascend to heaven, and by a third that the birds which fed Elijah were human."[103]

In the ninth century, Hivi[104] considered Bible difficulties, resolving some of them in anticipation of "rationalistic exegesis."[105] Another scholar, whose name is unknown but whose eleventh century work Schecter described, gave attention to every perceived Old Testament discrepancy.[106] The earlier Talmudists, and these two later textual critics (in addition to Origen and his hermeneutic apologetics), demonstrate that biblical criticism is not simply a modern concern. Nonetheless, modernity gave impetus to such a degree of refinement in biblical criticism that the inspiration of the text—and consequently its authority as a moral support—has been widely doubted.

---

102 Fred G. Bratton, "Precursors of Biblical Criticism," *Journal of Biblical Literature* 50 (1931): 180.

103 Ibid. 180.

104 Talmudist as cited by ibid. 180.

105 Ibid.

106 Ibid.

Writing in the twelfth century, Abraham Ibn Ezra questioned Mosaic authorship of the Pentateuch based upon retrospective language that seemed well beyond the years of Moses' lifetime. Additionally, Ezra was the first to assert plural authorship of Isaiah, citing, for example, that references to Cyrus (as Israel's deliverer) could not have been penned by the eighth century Isaiah.[107] Despite his questioning of the text in these specific regards, he had great respect for it, considering it worthy of study. His precise understanding of the Hebrew language allowed him to offer clarifications where others had difficulty; this gave him such a high degree of credibility that he is perceived as having a vital relation between ancient and modern biblical scholarship.[108]

Hobbes resumed the discussion in 1651 in the thirty-third chapter of his Leviathan,[109] in which he questioned the authorship of Moses. He discussed a few specific cases which seem to cast doubt upon Moses' authorship of the Torah. He cited Deuteronomy 34, which includes the account of Moses' death (i.e. how he journeyed up a mountain to view the promised land which he was forbidden from entering due to a moment of rebellion, how he died, and how God dispensed with Moses' body and it was never discovered). Hobbes

---

107 Ibid. 181.

108 Ibid.

109 Thomas Hobbes, Leviathan, ed. Richard Tuck (Cambridge: Cambridge University Press) 260-68.

asserted that Moses could not have written his own death and burial account. He cited Genesis 12:6 which uses the phrase "while the Canaanites were in the land." During Moses' lifetime, the Canaanites were not in the land, and it was not until the conquest of Joshua's day that they began to be removed, thus Hobbes declared that Moses could not have written this passage. Furthermore, Numbers 21:14 references the Book of the Wars of the Lord, which Hobbes reckoned to be the writings of Moses, and thus Numbers was written after Moses' lifetime. Hobbes did not intend to demolish the authority of the text; however, he indicated that all that Moses is said to have spoken that he did indeed say, thus the text is not dishonest, Moses just did not author all that tradition assigns to him.

While Hobbes' motive was not to redefine God, Benedict Spinoza's was. He emphasized the immanence of God, holding that God was monistic and impersonal, and that he was revealed in the laws of nature and was to be understood by reason. Spinoza's critical method is apparent in his *Tractatus Theologico Politicus* (1670), and is characterized by a threefold hermeneutic process, which assumed that scriptures should be studied in the same way as would nature: in light of reason. *First*, he focused upon the linguistic analysis of the time of writing, which involved in-depth analysis of the Hebrew text and developments in the Hebrew language itself. *Second*, he promoted topical and systematic organizations of the text under headers, so that as interlocutors interpret they have other similar and related passages available to them. *Finally*, he concentrated intensely upon the method of textual formation. The final process constituted his primary achievement in biblical criticism as he considered the author's context, setting, motivation, limitation, education, and a multitude of other factors. Spinoza made textual formation a critical step in the process of ascertaining what the text meant.

As a result of his investigation, Spinoza rejected Mosaic authorship by taking into consideration what he considered retrospective passages and anachronism. He asserted that the Pentateuch, in addition to Joshua and Judges were the work of later redactors, including Ezra the scribe. Spinoza likewise considered Nehemiah to have been penned possibly in the second century BC, Proverbs to have been post-exilic, Chronicles to have been so unreliable as to be undeserving of being included in the canon, Jeremiah to have been the product of plural authorship, Job to have been initially a Gentile poem, and Daniel to have been inauthentic.[110]

Spinoza identified two kinds of scriptures: (1) prophetic theology, which was beyond reason and could be understood only from the Scriptures themselves; and (2) narrative, of which Spinoza was decidedly critical. He perceived the writers of narrative to have gravely mischaracterized God as essentially a secondary cause rather than the immediate efficient cause. Spinoza argued against the dualism of God and nature, suggesting there was no dichotomy and no distinction:

---

110 Bratton, "Precursors of Biblical Criticism," 183.

God and nature are one. Therefore, Spinoza also argued there is no beginning or end, that is, no teleology (i.e. no purpose and no cause), and thus his biblical criticism led to (or was based upon) a significant redefinition of God. Taking into consideration Spinoza's conclusions, Bratton credited him as having immeasurable impact upon the modern understanding of the Bible, particularly in his demonstrating "that the Bible is not one book but many, coming from different periods of history and exhibiting different degrees of inspiration."[111]

Spinoza's conclusion that the text is not univocal is of particular importance in the context of the present discussion, and if the argument is to be made for univocality and consequently for the authority of the text, then Spinoza's criticisms cannot be ignored.

Richard Simon wrote his *Histoire Critique de Vieux Testament* from Paris in 1678, which he published as a more complete version seven years later. His *Critique* consisted of three books, the first was a biblical criticism, focusing upon Jewish historical methods and Mosaic authorship; the second was an account of the various Old Testament translations (he relied upon the Masoretic text and the Greek Septuagint, perceiving previous Hebrew Old Testament manuscripts so obscure as to make *sola Scriptura* untenable); and, the third was an account of the major Old Testament commentators. Additionally, he completed three New Testament critiques, but for all

---

111 Ibid. 184.

his labor his primary unique achievement was in his theory that throughout Jewish history there was a tradition of historical recording and a continuous succession of annalists who fulfilled this task. Simon hypothesized that it was from this group that Moses and other biblical writers borrowed.[112]

Jean Astruc wrote his *Conjectures sur la Genèse* in 1753 to counter, in particular, Hobbes' and Spinoza's critiques of biblical reliability. Astruc used contemporary methods, including those of Eichhorn and Wilhelm de Wette (father of the historical critical school) in order to offer a biblical criticism of his own. He focused upon doublets (retellings of historical narratives) and the stylistic distinctions between passages that named God as YHWH and those that titled him Elohim, and concluded thusly that there were two authors of Genesis (one of whom was Moses).[113] Astruc's conclusions were formative for Wellhausen's documentary hypothesis which would be forthcoming over a hundred years later.

Julius Wellhausen proposed his documentary theory in his *Prolegomena zur Geschichte Israels.* Based upon Astruc's considerations of stylistic distinctions, Wellhausen's hypothesis is regarded as the JEDP theory, an acronym for the distinctive writers that Wellhausen perceived to be involved in the initial

---

112 Wallis, "The Paradox of Modern Biblical Criticism," 43.

113 Ana M. Acosta, "Conjectures and Speculations: Jean Astruc, Obstetrics, and Biblical Criticism in Eighteenth Century France," *Eighteenth-Century Studies* 35 (Winter 2002): 257-59.

transmission of the text. The J is for the Jahwist (JHVH the Latinized transliteration of YHWH), the E is for the Elohist, the D is for the Deuteronomist or the redactor (perhaps the one responsible for the many doublets), and P is for the priestly writer who penned Leviticus, etc. Wallis described Wellhausen's critique as so influential that "Bible study everywhere took a new start."[114]

Therefore, Hobbes' critiques find their fulfillment in Wellhausen's theory, and ultimately the prescriptive value of the text—based upon this theory —as anything more than a cultural and (somewhat) historical commentary can be legitimately questioned. While the approach answers one aspect of Locke's notions,[115] in so doing it ultimately undermines the authority of the text. Moreover, biblical criticism advanced beyond Wellhausen. Against the background of World War I, Willis interpreted the role of biblical criticism in the context of social development. In particular, Wallis regarded the biblical text—despite the allegations asserted against it by the textual critics —as a fundamental component in the development of a new social consciousness which would set a precedence, via a democratic mindset (removing interpretive power from the autocracy and giving it to the people), for that war-torn generation to   "move onward through the

---

114 Wallis, "The Paradox of Modern Biblical Criticism," 46.

115 Either the text is completely and equally inspired or not. Wellhausen's theory concludes it is not, and consequently takes the Bible's ethical value for granted.

flames of war"[116] into a brighter era. Wallis' optimism bears with it an internal contradiction that is notable. He suggested that one does not need orthodoxy but "a conservatism that maintains all the religious values enshrined in the Scriptures,"[117] yet the biblical criticism which he lauded creates a condition in which the boundaries between truth and falsity in a propositional sense are obfuscated at best.

W. R. Taylor diagnosed the problem, and attempted a remedy, and in so doing really only illustrated the problem. He suggested, "we should be ready to abandon the indefensible and to concentrate our attention on the essential qualities of the sacred oracles as time and research bring them into fuller relief."[118] Taylor's assessment invites several questions. Which values should be maintained, and which discarded? Which are indefensible and which are essential? Without a propositional approach—such as that employed by James Nash—this is a question impossible to answer with any certainty. Taylor suggested that biblical criticism has resulted in the demise of "the belief in verbal inspiration, the inerrancy of the Bible in all its parts in science and history, and its infallibility in morals and religion,"[119]

---

116 Wallis, "The Paradox of Modern Biblical Criticism,"49.

117 Ibid.. 49.

118 W. R. Taylor, "Biblical Criticism and Modern Faith," *The Journal of Religion* 23 (October 1943): 229.

119 Ibid. 230.

and that better conceptions of God are now possible.

Taylor's observation represents a supreme degree of inconsistency that requires a greater degree of faith to bear than is required for accepting the legitimacy of the text as a whole. He suggested that the Bible is not revelation but is simply the record of it.[120] However, where does the revelation end and the record begin? Taylor argued that though old ideas of what constitutes suitable warrant for authority have ceased, what has emerged should instill confidence in the reader. "In short, we can say that recent research has brought into high relief (a) the Bible's unique significance in the cultural process, (b) the qualitative superiority of the biblical literature comparatively, and (c) the Bible as a body of sincere and vital documents."[121]

Though his three ideas are commonly held, the issue of whether the text is worthy of confidence remains disputed, perhaps in part due to a pervasive inattention to detail on the part of textual-authority-apologists as illustrated further by Taylor's culminating exhortation: "we must be careful to show that the essential truths which we by our methods reach in the Scriptures can and must be made meaningful to our generation."[122] Unfortunately for Taylor's thesis, this generation—like any other—may

---

120 Ibid. 231.

121 Ibid. 239-40.

122 Ibid. 240.

have difficulty accepting essential truths from a source whose apparently non-essential ones are not truths whatsoever. It seems, then, only consistent (consistency being an important and deciding factor, in this author's estimation) to either abandon ideas of revelation altogether, and consequently the optimism and even the supposedly better conceptions of God derived from the text if the text itself is devalued, and dismiss the values enshrined in the text as not being suitably warranted from the text, or alternately to consider the text in a *prima facie* manner—interpreting it in the most plain or natural sense—and in response, one may consider the value of the content based upon not only the individual parts but also upon the sum of those parts. Such a consideration is not foreign to those represented in the Bible, and seems to be the expected response the writers sought from their readers.

The truth that Moses wrote the first five books, for example, is the representation of the Bible itself and is attested to by earliest interpretive tradition. Joshua 8:31-32 distinguishes between the law of Moses (v. 32) and the book of the law of Moses (v. 31), as the law generally referenced the entire body of the covenantal stipulations, including all six hundred and thirteen commandments (*the mizvot*), and was usually represented by the first ten.[123] Forms of the phrase *book of the law* are used some twenty-one times in the Hebrew Bible (Deut. 28:58; 28:61; 29:20; 30:10; 31:24;

---

123 Probably, it was this shorter list that Joshua wrote on the stones in the events of Joshua 8.

31:26; Josh. 8:31; 8:34; 23:6; 24:26; 2 Kgs. 14:6; 22:8; 22:11; 23:24; 2 Chr. 17:9; 34:14, 15; Neh. 8:1, 3, 18; 9:3), and notably the term does not appear until the concluding chapters of Moses' final book. Jesus later applies the term (Mk 20:26) when He referenced events in Exodus as being contained in the book of Moses and as "Scripture." Jesus directly recognized Exodus (cf. Mk. 7:10 and Ex. 20:12; also Mk. 12:26 and Ex. 3:6), Leviticus (cf. Mt. 8:4 and Lev. 13:49; 14:2ff.), Numbers (cf. Jn. 3:14 and Num. 21:9) and Deuteronomy (cf. Mt . 19:7-8 and Deut. 24:1-4) to be Mosaic, and referenced Genesis as genuine and legitimately included in the Hebrew Bible.[124]

Not only did Jesus consider Genesis genuine, but He also considered it Mosaic. He referred to the

---

124 Timothy Lin catalogued Jesus' affirmations as follows: "He confirmed the genuineness of the first two chapters of Genesis by testifying to the creation of Adam and Eve as a historical fact, and not a myth or legend (Mt. 19:4-6; Mk. 10:5-9). When He rebuked the scribes and Pharisees, He mentioned 'the blood of Abel' as the beginning of the Jews' guilt (Mt. 23:35). He confirmed that Noah's flood was a historical destruction (Mt. 24:37-39) and the devastation of Sodom and Gomorrah as God's judgment (Mt. 11:23-24). He described Lot's time in Sodom and the judgment of his wife as a historical warning regarding the last days (Lk. 17:28-32). In His preaching and teaching, He often spoke of Abraham (Jn. 8:37-40,56-58) and repeatedly He testified of Abraham, Isaac, and Jacob (Mk. 12:26) and their lives before God (Mt. 8:11; 22:32). The above references indicate that Christ testified to the truthfulness of essentially the entire book of Genesis" (Timothy Lin, *Genesis: A Biblical Theology*, 4th ed. (Carmel, IN: Biblical Studies Ministries International, 2002) 29-30).

Hebrew Bible as "the Law of Moses and the Prophets, and the Psalms" (Lk. 24:44), a structural parallel to the Masoretic text of *Torah* (law), *Nevi'im* (prophets), and *Ketuvim* (writings, of which Psalms is the first book). Also, in Luke 11:49-51, Jesus detailed a chronology of martyred prophets from the foundation of the world to that point. He referenced Abel as the first and Zechariah as the last. Abel's death occurs in Genesis (the first book of the Tanakh) and Zechariah's in Chronicles (the final book of the Tanakh). It seems rather certain that Jesus understood the entire Hebrew Bible to be genuine, and the individual books it contained to be organized as one observes in the Masoretic text. He understood that the Law (or Book of the Law) of Moses—the Torah—was both genuine and Mosaic.

Nevertheless, what of Wellhausen's refined multi-author theory? Emblematic of an influential tradition of biblical scholarship, Timothy Lin challenged the documentary hypothesis as fallacious and unworkable.

Lin's critique is potent and worthy of consideration here: "This hypothesis is far from being workable. For instance, in certain J passages 'Elohim,' which is characteristic of E, is present (3:1, 3, 5; 4:25; 7:9, 16; 9:27; etc.), and in certain E and P passages 'Yahweh,' which is characteristic of J, is found (17:1; 22:11; etc.). In order to cover this embarrassing situation, the critics cut some verses and clauses out of their context and assigned them to another document. They cut 5:29 out of P and assigned it to J, because the divine name 'Yahweh' (which is translated 'the LORD') is present. Yet they left 4:25 in J although 'Elohim' is in this verse. They separated 7:16b that has 'Yahweh' from the midst of P and assigned it to J. However, they left 9:26 and 16:13 undivided in J, but both have 'Yahweh' and 'Elohim.' Genesis 21:1 is a dilemma to the critics because both clauses have 'Yahweh.'

According to their theory of 'doublets' they should separate them. Yet according to their usage of divine names to designate different authors, they have to place the couplets together. To cut the knot they assigned 21:1a to J and 21:1b to P. How absurd! Genesis 21:33 was assigned to J, disregarding the presence of 'Elohim' in 33b. Genesis 22:11, 14 are both assigned to E, yet both have 'Yahweh.' Genesis 28:21 is assigned to E, yet 'Yahweh' is also found there. These examples are sufficient to show the fallacy of this hypothesis" (Gen. 27-28).

With detailed consideration of internal problems with the hypothesis, Lin argued that the analytic method the textual critics purport to use is not being consistently applied to these passages and that a consistent application of the method would not provide the basis for the multi-author conclusion. Gary Rendsburg critiqued the theory based upon the assertion that it fails to account for chiastic structure and other parallels found in the text,[125] though Marc Brettler, who believes Rendsburg's assertions fail to

---

125 Gary A. Rendsburg, *The Redaction of Genesis* (Winona Lake, IN: Eisenbraun, 1986) 104ff.

adequately resolve all the issues that the multi-authorship theory proposes, dismissed his argument.[126] The worthy considerations by both writers are emblematic of the present debate regarding the conclusiveness of the multi-author theory, that is, the matter is unresolved with regard to identifying what is the genuine outcome of the critical method.

Benjamin Mazar understood Genesis to be "a monumental historiographic composition, the product of rich and variegated material collected, combined, arranged, and worked into one harmonious tract, with the purpose of portraying both the beginnings of mankind and the origins of Israel in the spirit of the monotheistic concept, and with a didactic aim."[127] Mazar, not unlike Umberto Cassuto, based his criticism of Mosaic authorship not upon literary form but upon a number of historical factors that he recognized as anachronisms in the text and which he believed indicated a much later date than the roughly 1400 BC/BCE date demanded in the text itself.[128] His thesis is

---

126 Marc Brettler, "Rendsburg's The Redaction of Genesis," *The Jewish Quarterly Review* 78 (July-October 1987): 113-19.

127 Benjamin Mazar, "The Historical Background of the Book of Genesis," *Journal of Near Eastern Studies* 28 (April 1969): 74.

128 Mazar wrote, "It is within reason that Genesis was given its original written form during the time when the Davidic empire was being established, and that the additions and supplements of later authors were only intended to help bridge the time gap for contemporary readers, and had no decisive effect on its contents of its overall character" (ibid).

seemingly based in large part on a presupposition that there is no (divinely inspired) prophetic utterance (i.e. that the Hebrew prophets were not speaking on God's behalf and that there is no legitimate divine revelation). Note the following phrases used by Mazar: "it is within reason" (used twice);[129] "it is then in place to assume;"[130] "[O]ne may, apparently, also count among these. . . ;"[131] "it seems to me;"[132] "in my view, it is much more within reason;"[133] "[O]ne may find in the accounts. . . ;"[134] and, "there is no need . . . to assign it a later date."[135] Conjecture seems to be a significant influence in his assertions.

He also suggested that the ethnographic similarities between Genesis 16 and Psalm 83 (the date of which he says is reasonably understood to be during the end of the period of the Judges) suggest a later date for Genesis.[136] He noted that the characteristics of the Joseph account "are such as to make us think that the traditions and motifs joined together in this single

---

129 Ibid.

130 Ibid. 75.

131 Ibid. 76.

132 Ibid.

133 Ibid. 77.

134 Ibid. 78.

135 Ibid.

136 Ibid. 79.

tableau...were given their sophisticated novelistic literary form no earlier than the beginning of the Monarchy."[137] Perhaps most notably, though, he argued that the Genesis 49:10 blessing of Judah was not prophetic, but that it was a later developed apologetic for Judah's right to rule (a right that is prominently featured and defended during the early monarchy period).

While this is a significant instance of assumed anachronism (as there seems no other basis for it other than the non-prophetic presupposition), aside from these numerous defenses of Davidic kingship, Mazar cited several alleged anachronisms in Genesis. Notably, in context, most are related to Davidic right, and one might wonder if these would be anachronisms at all if Davidic right was indeed a result of prophetic utterance. Nonetheless, these would need to be addressed by any who would defend an early date consistent with Mosaic authorship, and Mazar suggested (without, in this context, any particular explanation of why) that those who have attempted to resolve these issues in light of various external sources (such as Akkadian sources, Mari documents, Nuzi tablets, and variously dated Egyptian sources) have "gone too far,"[138] though he admitted that there is "certainly room for thought and reconsideration of the conflicting views as to the dating of the "patriarchal

---

137 Ibid. 82-83.

138 Ibid. 76.

period" to the first, second, and third quarters of the second millennium B.C."[139]

To sumarize, Mazar's conclusions are not presented as necessary, though he did (of course) prefer them to the alternative. In any case, it is at least evident from Mazar's writing that—as is the case with the JEPD hypothesis—the late-date theory is far from a certitude. Also, it would seem that the late-date theory and JEPD seem based upon the presupposition that divine revelation and prophetic utterance are not legitimate possibilities.

Paul Minear recognized challenges for biblical criticism with regard to presuppositions and first principles.[140] Minear suggested, quoting Croce, that in this epoch the prevailing frame of reference, that is, "the heart and brain (of recent historiography) . . . is naturalism."[141] The pre-commitment to naturalism provides a set of guidelines that cannot be easily

---

139 Ibid.

140   Paul S. Minear observed, "The reflective historian must consciously orient his technical research with an articulate 'frame of reference,' a view of history which determines his presuppositions, defines his method and circumscribes his conclusions. Such orientation is particularly important in an epoch when perspectives of thought shift so rapidly. Each successive change in world-view stimulates new conceptions of history, raises new questions for the historian to answer, and provokes new assaults upon prevailing methodology" ("How Objective Is Biblical Criticism," *Journal of Bible and Religion* 9 [November 1941]: 217).

141 Ibid. 218.

discarded.[142] In particular, Minear suggested that biblical historians (few of whom are "avowed naturalists"[143]) utilize a method that is developed from, and, at least, implies naturalism. What result then is to be expected from a naturalistically based method? Certainly the tension between an assumed metaphysic and a method that negates the metaphysic is not conducive to a high degree of consistency in the end. Nevertheless, it is this tension that Locke (for example) acknowledged as present in the discussion.

Considering, for example, the Deuteronomy 34 account of Moses' death, one may note that Hobbes perceived this to be evidence against Mosaic authorship of the Pentateuch as a unit, yet there are two possibilities worthy of consideration and which may present a resolution to the issue. *First*, if this was indeed revelation, rather than the mere product of human invention, then theoretically God could have informed Moses of what would occur. Predictive prophecy (if such a possibility is allowed) accounts for nearly a third of the Hebrew Bible (if a plain or natural sense hermeneutic is consistently applied). To dismiss casually the possibility of divine revelation seems more

---

142 Minear suggested, "The historian's function is to establish generalizations applicable at all times and places. The test of his conclusions is their predictive accuracy. Novelty, particularity, becomes a scandal. Confronted by the unique, the historian can only stutter, 'It can't be!' Thus the history that is dictated by a naturalistic world-view ends by negating itself." (Ibid).

143 Ibid. 219.

based upon naturalistic presuppositions and an intention to de-mythologize the Bible than in unbiased textual criticism.

Second, nonetheless, it is not a necessity for genuineness that Moses wrote his own obituary. There might have been a separate writer (perhaps Joshua) who wrote the Deuteronomy epilogue, and this would not negate Mosaic authorship of the Pentateuch as a unit, much in the same manner that Jesus' reference to the *Ketuvim* (the Writings section of the Hebrew Bible) as "the Psalms" did not imply that the book of Psalms was the only component of the *Ketuvim*, and in the same manner that one may refer to the Epistle to the Romans as Pauline, though it claims, in fact, to have been penned by Tertius (as Paul's amanuensis) (Rom 16:22). The internal evidence of the Hebrew (OT) and Greek (NT) texts considered collectively leaves no doubt that if the texts are themselves genuine, they argue for genuineness and Mosaic authorship of Genesis. The early external evidence likewise introduces no doubt.

The second-century BC pseudoepigraphical Book of Jubilees presents a creation account similar (though not identical) to that of Genesis, but unlike Genesis, Jubilees contains a preface affirming the authorship of the creation story.[144] The Jubilees account not only asserts Mosaic authorship, but also narrates how he came to write the creation account. In similar fashion, Philo of Alexandria, a notable first-century AD Jewish philosopher, understood Genesis to be of Mosaic origin, extolling, for example, the philosophic prowess Moses demonstrated in beginning his laws with a creation account.[145] To understand that Philo recognized Mosaic

---

144 Jubilees 2:1 reads as follows: "And the angel of the presence spake to Moses according to the word of the Lord, saying: 'Write all the words of the creation, how in six days the Lord God finished all His works and all that he created, and rested on the Sabbath day and hallowed it for all ages, and appointed it as a sign for all His works'" (R. H. Charles, "A New Translation of the Book of Jubilees. Part I," *The Jewish Quarterly Review* 6 (October 1893): 187).

145 Philo commented: "But Moses . . . made the beginning of his laws entirely beautiful, and in all respects admirable, neither at once declaring what ought to be done or the contrary, nor (since it was necessary to mould beforehand the dispositions of those who were to use his laws) inventing fables himself or adopting those which had been invented by others. And his exordium, as I have already said, is most admirable; embracing the creation of the world, under the idea that the law corresponds to the world and the world to the law, and that a man who is obedient to the law, being, by so doing, a citizen of the world, arranges his actions with reference to the intention of nature, in harmony with which the whole universal world is regulated. . . . Since, then, this world is visible and the object of our external senses, it follows of necessity that it must have been created; on which account it was not without a wise purpose that he recorded its creation, giving a very venerable account of God. . . . And he says that the world was made in six days. . . ." (Philo, "On the Creation," in *The Works of Philo*, ed. C. D. Yonge [Peabody, MA: Hendrickson, 1993] 3).

authorship is important not just as a consequence of his philosophical assessment of Moses' motivations, but also because Philo was a pioneer of biblical criticism. He was an important developer of the allegorical hermeneutic, which he utilized frequently in order to resolve aspects of the text that he perceived to be inconsistent with the Hellenistic philosophy of his time. Philo, it would seem, did not consider Mosaic authorship to be troublesome whatsoever. On the contrary, he considered it to be an important fact, and one that connected cosmology with ethical theory.

Though his objectivity as a historian has been questioned,[146] Josephus nonetheless offers an important first-century AD Jewish perspective on many aspects of Israel's history. He discussed (similarly to Philo) Moses' unique approach to legislation, recognizing the acumen with which Moses directed minds to God before directing attention to laws.[147] He also spoke of the creation account as being

---

146   For a thoroughgoing discussion of Josephus' apologetic designs, see Louis H. Feldman, "Josephus' Portrait of Moses," *The Jewish Quarterly Review* 82 (January-April 1992): 285-328.

147 Josephus wrote, "Now when Moses was desirous to teach this lesson to his countrymen, he did not begin the establishment of his laws after the same manner that other legislators did; I mean, upon contracts and other rites between one man and another, but by raising their minds upwards to regard God, and his creation of the world; and by persuading them, that we men are the most excellent of the creatures of God upon the earth" (Flavius Josephus, Antiquities of the Jews, in *The Works of Josephus*, trans. William Whiston [Peabody, MA: Hendrickson, 1987] "Preface," 21).

entirely Mosaic.[148] In summarizing verse-by-verse the Genesis 1 creation account, Josephus asserted Mosaic authorship no less than four times ("Moses said," 1.1.29; "Moses says," 1.1.33; "Moses...begins to talk philosophically," 1.1.34; and, "Moses says further," 1.1.37).[149]

Josephus, Philo, and the Book of Jubilees represent early external evidence complementing the biblical assertions of Mosaic authorship of Genesis, and they are not inconsistent with more recent views. Moses Maimonides (twelfth century), for example, was unapologetic about Mosaic authorship. He included, as one of his Thirteen Principles, the following: "I believe with perfect faith that the entire Torah that we have now is that which was given to Moses."[150] One mainstream contemporary Jewish encyclopedia argues in favor of singular authorship and challenges certain premises of the documentary hypothesis, including alleged anachronisms, historiographic principles, and

---

148 Josephus commented briefly, "I shall now betake myself to the history before me, after I have first mentioned what Moses says of the creation of the world, which I find described in the sacred books after the manner following" (ibid. 26).

149 Josephus, *Antiquities*, 1.1.29-37.

150 Moses Maimonides, *Commentary on the Mishnah, Tractate Sanhedrin*, trans. Fred Rosner (New York: Sepher- Hermon Press, 1981) ch. 11, principle 8.

doublets.[151] Furthermore, the encyclopedia directly counters textual criticism on seven points: (1) there is no external proof of compilation; (2) interpretations of so-called internal evidence to that end is "unstable and deceptive;" (3) the process leading to the compilation conclusion is complex beyond consistency; (4) even if alleged contradictions and repetitions existed, they would not prove plural authorship, just as this process applied to other single author works would be met with equal failure; (5) the theory is unnecessary and based on multiple misunderstandings of ideas, tendencies, and themes; (6) arguments based on variations of language are circular; and, (7) exegetical mishandling is necessary for the compilation understanding.[152]

Though the internal and external evidence presented here may not satisfy some readers of the certainty of Mosaic authorship, perhaps there has been shown enough evidence to warrant reasonable consideration of the mere possibility that Genesis is genuinely Mosaic. If the reader is willing to grant this much, then the possibility that the text provides some binding ethical foundation remains. If not, then the

---

151 "Anachronisms such as various critics allege in Genesis do not in reality exist; and their assumption is based on a misunderstanding of the historiographic principles of the book. . . . Nor are there any repetitions or unnecessary doublets" (Benno Jacob and Emil Hirsch, "Genesis, The Book of" [article online] [The Jewish Encyclopedia, 1912, accessed 30 January 2010] available from http://www.jewishencyclopedia.com/articles/6580-genesis-the-book-of).

152 Ibid.

discussion needs progress no further, as the Bible would offer nothing of any real ethical value beyond what one might expect from a fable or a legend. As Isaac Abravanel argued, if the biblical text (and the Torah in particular) is presumed to be authoritative, then it must be believed in its entirety and not doubted.[153]

To assert that the Genesis account is not genuine requires that one dismiss its ethical contribution as authoritative. Therefore, if one would discuss the book as potentially authoritative, one must consider it as, at least, *potentially* genuine, and if one cannot assent to this potentiality (at least), one may rely upon Callicott's warning not to miss the point that many Jews and Christians consult the biblical text for ethical guidance.[154] One will find, then, that the text is either ethically authoritative, or, at least, a significant

---

153 Abravanel suggested, "it is not proper to postulate principles for the divine Torah, nor foundations in the matter of beliefs, for we are obligated to believe everything that is written in the Torah. We are not permitted to doubt even the smallest thing in it. . . ." (Isaac Abravanel, *Principles of Faith*, Rosh Amanah, trans. Menachem Kellner [Oxford: Littman Library of Jewish Civilization, 2000]195).

154 J. Baird Callicott reminded his readers: "Contemporary Jews and Christians, searching for meaningful advice about how to live in the world in which today they find themselves, will consult the Bible and will inevitably ponder what they read (in translation) in light of their contemporary concerns, their personal experience, and their own locale" ("Genesis Revisited: Murian Musings on the Lynn White, Jr. Debate," *Environmental History Review* 14 [Spring-Summer 1990]: 85).

number of people perceive that it is—whether with proper warrant or not—and those people will seek to follow the meaningful advice found within its pages. As Henry Morris reminded his readers, Genesis is the foundation of all the biblical books, and is thus the most critical portion of the book "that has exerted the greatest influence on history of any book every produced."[155]

Some Elements of Lower Criticism

Because we do not possess the original manuscripts of Scripture, and the copies that we have contain variances, the primary purpose of lower criticism (or textual criticism) is to reconstruct the original wording of the original Biblical text.[156] The objective credibility of the manuscripts of Scripture as revealed by textual criticism suggests that we have a Bible over 99% accurate, and that there are bridges that deal with any purported gaps. Yet there needs be attention given to the transmission and translation of the text over the years to understand how we can have confidence in the Word of God as it has been passed down through the generations.

---

155   Henry M. Morris, *The Genesis Record: A Scientific and Devotional Commentary on the Book of Beginnings* (Grand Rapids: Baker, 1976) 17.

156   Richard Soulen, *Handbook of Biblical Criticism*, (2nd Ed., Atlanta, GA: John Knox Press, 1981), 192.

TRANSMISSION

There are several eras of transmission for the Old Testament Manuscripts: The Talmudic era (300 BC-500AD) includes the Dead Sea Scrolls (167 BC-133AD) – which serve to confirm the accuracy of the Masoretic Texts. The Masoretic era (500-1000AD) continued reverence for the text, rules for approaching it, and also developed the vowel system. The Greek translation of the Old Testament, known as the Septuagint (LXX), came later (250 BC) and was often but not exclusively referred to by Jesus and His disciples.

Likewise, the New Testament Manuscripts also saw periods of evolution and development. The first three hundred years give tremendous evidence for the accuracy of the text we possess today. Constantine's legalization of Christianity throughout the fourth and fifth centuries increased copies of manuscripts, while the sixth century brought less careful but more voluminous reproduction. After the tenth century manuscripts increased rapidly.[157]

The early church copied manuscripts on codexes, two sided papyrus pages bound in book style. Initially, and until the 9th century the New Testament was copied in all capital letters with no spacing or punctuation. These manuscripts are called uncials. Later manuscripts, which demonstrate development in the writing style, are known as miniscules. Likewise,

---

157 Geisler and Nix, 354-355.

initially, the Hebrew Old Testament had no vowels until the Masoretic Text of the 10th century. The Masoretic text came to be the received text of the Hebrew Old Testament, differing to some degree with the Septuagint rendering, yet validated by Dead Sea Scrolls manuscripts from a thousand years earlier.

Some Important Manuscripts

Papyrus *46* (P46), 200 AD, provided an early testimony to the Epistles of Paul, including much of Romans, 1 and 2 Corinthians, Ephesians, Galatians, Philippians, Colossians, and 1 and 2 Thessalonians. P46 also included the Book of Hebrews (for this reason some recognize it as Pauline, despite internal evidence to the contrary). *Papyrus 66* (P66), 200 AD, included much of John's Gospel. *Papyrus 72* (P72), roughly 200 AD, includes Jude, and 1 and 2 Peter. *Papyrus 75* (P75), 175-225 AD, includes John and the earliest known copy of Luke.

Codex *Vaticanus* (identified as "B") is an early 4th century uncial, containing much of the LXX and a significant portion of the New Testament. *Vaticanus* provides the greatest manuscript evidence for the authenticity of the NT. *Codex Sinaiticus* (commonly identified simply as "א," the Hebrew letter, aleph) is a 4th century uncial which contained the Greek text of much of the Old Testament and all of the New, along with some extra biblical writings (including the Epistle of Barnabus and sections of the Shepherd of Hermas). *Sinaiticus* is second only to *Vaticanus* in its importance. *Codex Alexandrinus* (identified as "A") is a mid-5th century uncial from Alexandria, provides along with *Vaticanus* and *Sinaiticus* significant evidence for NT authenticity. *Alexandrinus* contains nearly all of the OT (with only tiny portions missing) and most of the NT.

Translation

There are numerous notable surviving translations even from fairly early in the church's history. Origen produced the Hexapla (240-250), a parallel Bible with the following six-columns: Hebrew, Hebrew transliterated into Greek, Aquila's literal translation, Symmachus' revision, Origen's revision of the LXX, and a Greek revision of Theodotian. By the sixth century a Syriac NT was complete.

From about 200 AD, came a defective Latin translation from the LXX.

Jerome was the first early church father to be fluent in Hebrew and Greek, ultimately recognized the Hebrew text as the final authority. His translation varied in some instances from the Septuagint, due to his appeal to the Hebrew, causing quite a stir among many, including Augustine, who were concerned that the authority of the Septuagint was being threatened. Despite the early controversy, Jerome's Latin Vulgate (382-405) became the popular translation. Thus what Jerome sought to accomplish – a return to the authoritative original languages – was ironically hampered by a dependence on his own Latin translation.

Partial English versions between the fifth and fifteenth centuries include those of Caedmon, Aldhelm, Egbert, Venerable Bede, Alfred the Great, Aldred, Aelfric, Ormin, William of Shoreham, and Richard Rolle all translated portions of the Bible into early English. John Wycliffe translated the NT (1380) and the OT (1388) from the Vulgate. John Purvey, Wycliffe's secretary revised Wycliffe's version in 1395.

Erasmus, in 1516, published a Greek-Latin (not from the Vulgate, but his own) parallel NT; he sought to correct errors of the Vulgate. His translation represented a break with established tradition and a return to the original languages. Erasmus' translation and later editions, including Robert Stephanus' 1550 (3rd) edition, Beza's editions (published from 1565 - 1611) and the Elzivir text of 1624-1633 were seen as the *Textus Receptus*[158] from which would stem the Authorized Version (KJV). Ironically, like Jerome, he sought to restore the Biblical languages, yet his translation later became the standard to the extent that any alternative translations would be challenged, much like Erasmus challenged Jerome's.

William Tyndale translated a printing of the NT from Greek (1525), and the Pentateuch (1530), and book of Jonah (1536) from the Hebrew. Miles Coverdale, assistant and proofreader to Tyndale, completed the first printed edition of the English Bible

---

158   Latin, received text, from Bonaventure's and Elzivir's comment "Textum ergo habes, nunc ab omnibus receptum", which references the text which "all now receive".

in 1535, though not directly from Hebrew and Greek. Thomas Matthew, another assistant of Tyndale, combined Tyndale's and Coverdale's versions (1537). Richard Taverner in 1539 revised Matthew's Bible. The Great Bible, by Coverdale (1539) became the standard authorized version for churches.The Geneva Bible, (NT 1557, revised NT and OT, 1560), more closely followed the Hebrew and introduced the verse divisions. Rheims-Douay Version (1589, 1609) relied exclusively on the Latin Vulgate.

The King James Version (1611) actually was a translation (a work created from the original languages, as opposed to a version, which is a revision of a translation into a different receptor language), followed Erasmus' Greek text, among others. The recent New King James Version (1979) retains much of the *Textus Receptus* base while updating a large portion of the English terminology.

Despite the popularity of the *Textus Receptus*, which relied on a small number of later manuscripts, the need for a more critical approach to manuscript verification was brought to the forefront by B.F Westcott and J.F.A. Hort, who identified the history of the transmission of the New Testament as a primary justification for the necessity of textual criticism:

> The books of the New Testament have had to share the fate of other ancient writings in being copied again and again...Every transcription of any kind of writing involves the chance of the introduction of some errors...repeated

transcription involves multiplication of error; and the consequent presumption that a relatively late text is likely to be a relatively corrupt text is found true on the application of all available tests....[159]

Westcott and Hort took direct aim at the *Textus Receptus*, which was based primarily on Erasmus' 1516 edition, citing his haste to be the first publisher as leading to a "strange carelessness"[160] in the handling of the text. Their resultant alternative approach is the critical method, establishing a series of internal and external evidences for the validity of their *Critical Text*, (first published in 1881) which for the most part appealed to the oldest and fewest of the manuscripts as the most reliable.

In recent years, as an alternative to the *Textus Receptus* and *Critical Text* approaches, the *Majority Text* approach has come into view. While the *Textus Receptus* utilizes few and later manuscripts, and the *Critical Text* utilizes a more eclectic approach, considering all but generally relying on the older, less numerous manuscripts, the *Majority Text* relies on the greatest plurality of all the Greek manuscripts, and in so doing finds itself most often in agreement with the *Textus Receptus* (since the greatest plurality is generally found in the later manuscripts), much more

---

159 BF Westcott and FJA Hort, *Introduction to the New Testament in the Original Greek* (Peabody, MA: Hendrickson, 1988), 4-6.

160 Ibid., 11.

so than with the *Critical Text*. In 1982, Hodges and Farstad published a Greek New Testament based upon the Majority Text, and founded upon two methodological premises:

> (1) Any reading overwhelmingly attested by the manuscript tradition is more likely to be original than its rival(s)...(2) Final decisions about readings ought to be made on the basis of a reconstruction of their history in the manuscript tradition. This means that for each New Testament book a genealogy of the manuscripts ought to be constructed.[161]

Robinson and Pierpont also have produced an MT based Greek New Testament (1991, revised in 2005).

From the *Critical Text*, several English translations have arisen, developed primarily from two basic methods: verbal equivalence and dynamic equivalence.

The American Standard Version (1901) achieved a high level of fidelity to the original languages through *verbal equivalence* (the representation of each word in the original text with the most comparable word in the receptor language – this is, inasmuch as is possible, the word-for-word approach), and was later revised to become the New American Standard Bible (originally

---

161 Zane Hodges and Arthur Farstad, *The Greek New Testament According to the Majority Text* (2nd Ed., Nashville, TN: Thomas Nelson, 1985), xi-xii.

published in 1971 and further updated in 1995), which the Lockman Foundation[162] suggests (without argument from this writer) is the most literally accurate translation from the original languages.[163] Despite the sometimes unwieldy wording of the NASB, because of the commitment to verbal equivalence, the translation is quite reliable.

In 1946 (New Testament) and 1952 (Old Testament), the Revised Standard Version[164] was published and later updated (1971), and was the springboard for the English Standard Version[165] (2001). The RSV and ESV for the most part utilize verbal equivalence, but of the two, the ESV is more respected for being, as its publisher claims, an "essentially literal translation."[166]

Utilizing dynamic equivalence (the representation of each concept or idea in the original text with the most comparable concept or idea in the receptor language, this is a phrase-for-phrase approach) is Zondervan's New International Version (NT, 1973; OT, 1978), which, while in many cases communicates overall concepts more clearly than the

---

162 The Lockman Foundation holds the copyright on the NASB.

163 See http://www.lockman.org/nasb/.

164 The National Council of Churches holds the copyright on the RSV.

165 Published by Crossway Books.

166 See http://www.esv.org/about/intro.

verbal equivalents, seems to this writer inadequate because of the greater role of interpretation in the translating process and the inevitable omission of key words which of necessity are the derivation of key concepts. In addition, further evolutions (specifically gender neutralization) in the NIV have further distanced it from accuracy in translation.

In addition to the translating methodologies of verbal and dynamic equivalence, a third type of text is the paraphrase, which is really no translation at all. The paraphrase craze was begun (perhaps unintentionally) in 1971 when Kenneth Taylor (and Tyndale House) produced the Living Bible (primarily from the ASV) with the honorable intention of helping to facilitate reading to his children – and therefore also that of other parents to their own children.[167] Taylor's Bible steadily increased in popularity and later served as at least the conceptual basis of the later New Living Translation (1996), a paraphrase from the original languages. These (and other) paraphrases admittedly make no attempt to accurately represent the *words* of the Bible, and constitute a concerning trend in Bible transmission.

---

167 Harold Myra, "Ken Taylor: God's Voice in the Vernacular," *Christianity Today*, October 5, 1979.

PILLAR #3

NATURAL-MAN'S INCAPACITY
TO COMPREHEND GOD'S REVELATION

Once one has a proper perspective and understanding of the reality of God, he can begin to have a proper understanding of himself. As man is a reflection of his Creator, he cannot successfully grasp his own nature without having first ascertained that of his Creator; thus the understanding of natural man's incapacity to comprehend God's revelation must come after first the recognition of the Biblical God, which of course presumes the authority of Scripture. How does man respond to Scripture? How *can* he respond to the Divine Revelation?

THE PURPOSE OF LANGUAGE *(Gen. 1)*

God used language to communicate with Himself before man was created. He blessed creation (1:22), thereby using language to reveal Himself to creation. He gave imperatives (1:24, etc.), and finally He communicated with man. Human language does not have human origin, but rather originates with God, and for His purposes. The whole earth spoke His language (11:1) until He confused the language (11:9). Terry presents the basic argument of the origin of language:

The origin of human speech has been a fruitful theme of speculation and controversy. One's theory on the subject is likely to be governed by his theory of the origin of man. If we adopt the theory of evolution according to which man has been gradually developed, by some process of natural selection, from lower forms of animal life, we will very naturally conclude that language is a human invention, constructed by slow degrees to meet the necessities and conditions of life. If, on the other hand, we hold that man was first introduced on earth by a miraculous creation and was made at the beginning a perfect specimen of his kind, we will very naturally conclude that the beginnings of human language were of supernatural origin.[168]

Once again, presuppositions impact the argument early on. There does exist arguments against the efficacy of language to serve as an effective vehicle of God's truth. Packer identifies four such arguments as:

[1] A widespread sense of the inadequacy of all language as a means of personal communication... [2] widespread doubt as to whether language can convey transcendent realities at all...[3] the widespread unwillingness of Christian teachers to

---

168   Milton Terry, *Biblical Hermeneutics* (Grand Rapids: Zondervan, 1976), p. 69.

allow that in and through the teaching of scripture God is informing us about Himself... [4] the widespread influence of Eastern religious ideas, all stressing that God is inexpressible by man.[169]

However, God's usage of language is perhaps the greatest single evidence for the usefulness of language in accomplishing the purpose of communicating with absolute clarity of meaning God's truth. These arguments against the efficacy of language sharply contradict, at least in a logical sense, God's own ability to communicate. As God used language to communicate Himself to man it is clear that He intended His revelation to be understood – even creating the very vehicle He would use to carry His truths.

First, in the cognitive sense man has understood God's general revelation (Rom. 1:18-23). There is no doubt here that man's failure is not one of lacking understanding of the character of God, rather it is lacking the proper response to submission to Him *as* God. The cognitive fundamental of His existence has been resisted by the fallen human mind, and has been replaced by worship of the creation itself, the failure here not being a lack of understanding, but a lack of fearing Him *as* God, and thus man possesses ultimately an innate inability to arrive at wisdom.

Second, in the cognitive sense man has understood God's special revelation through Scripture.

---

169   J.I. Packer, "The Adequacy of Human Language," in *Inerrancy*, Norman Geisler, editor, 202-205.

As revealed using the tools of language, Scripture is grammatically understood by the unbeliever (although with remarkably increasing difficulty), yet the unbeliever understands the self authenticated truths to be foolishness (1 Cor. 2:14) and thus fails to respond positively,[170] ultimately rejecting the claims of Scripture.

Third, in the cognitive sense man has understood God's personal revelation in Christ Jesus. Every man has been enlightened by the incarnation of Christ (Jn. 1:9) – Christ has explained the Father, and while understood cognitively,[171] He is not received, for darkness is preferred by humanity over the light He provides (Jn. 3:19).

Why then does man, while understanding cognitively the revelations of God, consistently fail to grasp them in the personal sense without His divine aid?

THE NOETIC EFFECTS OF SIN

The death promised in Gen. 2:17 was a result of disobedience to the command not to eat of the tree of the *knowledge* of good and evil. The epistemology of the human race was changed at the moment Adam ate,

---

170   Although there are varying levels of understanding with varying usages/misusages (Neh. 8:8; Mt. 21:45; Lk. 20:19; Php. 1:15-17; 1 Ti. 1:6-7; 2 Tim. 3:5-7; Jam. 1:22; Jude 4).

171   Note that His opponents clearly understood His claims, yet failed to acknowledge them as truth (Jn. 5:18,39-40; 8:57-59).

accompanied by the spiritual death – the separation of man from fellowship with God. This change in the mind was certainly not for the better, despite Satan's promise that the offenders would be like God, knowing good and evil. Satan was half right – as humanity from that point forward would indeed know evil, yet would be fully incapable of grasping good.

Roughly fifteen hundred years after Adam's sin, God described the thoughts of the human heart as "only evil continually" (Gen. 6:5). Later, God characterizes the human heart as more deceitful above all else and desperately sick (Jer. 17:9). The Satanic promise of *knowing good* proved to be a deception - the following of which left humanity without the capacity to rightly think and appraise reality. The spiritually dead man was no longer able (as the pre-fall Adam surely seemed to be, Gen. 2:16, 19) to understand, appraise, or respond positively to God's revelation (1 Cor. 2:14). Although creation pours forth truth and revelation of God (Ps. 19), that truth, being understood and clearly seen in natural revelation (Rom. 1:19), has been suppressed (Rom. 1:18) by the human mind.

The noetic effects of sin result in more than simply the lack of ability to appraise "spiritual things" (1 Cor. 2:14-16); there is, in the human mind, a bent to suppress and reject the truth of God, as men love the darkness rather than light (Jn. 3:19). As a result, God has given the ungodly over to a depraved mind (Rom. 1:28), and further, the minds of the perishing are blinded by Satan (2 Cor. 4:3-4), continuing the contrast between the natural mind and the regenerated mind (Jam. 3:13-18). The freedom of neutrality that Satan seemed to offer was nothing of the sort; rather it proved to be bondage to faulty thinking, as none are disposed to fear God (Rom. 3:18), and since the fear of the Lord is the beginning of knowledge (Prov. 1:7), there are none who can claim a right epistemology without the intervention of God. The supplementing of human reason with divine revelation is not effective for bringing about the positional knowledge[172] of God. Rather, as Van Til notes, the fundamental conclusions of the fallen mind (as suppressing the truth of God) must be reversed.[173]

This is why the four pillars (the fourth yet to be identified), if employed by the unbeliever, will not and cannot translate of their own accord to saving faith. The right use of the four prerequisites by the unbeliever can only allow perhaps a mere glimpse of the unity and beauty of God's revelation, and therefore the unbeliever's need to receive it, and therefore an awareness of his need of Divine assistance in doing so. Van Til explains that the only way to see is to first believe:

[T]his God cannot be proved to exist by any other method than the indirect one of presupposition. No proof for this God and for the truth of His revelation

---

172 The term *ginosko* as defining a relationship involving eternal life in Jn 17:3 in contradistinction to the *ginosko* of Rom. 1:21.

173 Cornelius Van Til, *An Introduction to Systematic Theology*, (Philipsburg, NJ: Presbyterian and Reformed, 1974), 15-16.

in Scripture can be offered by an appeal to anything in human experience that has not itself received its light of the sun for the purposes of seeing by turning to the darkness of a cave.[174]

So how then does the incapable natural man believe in order to see? How then does God communicate in special revelation His truth to the human mind? For who can rightly appraise His revelation? His ways are higher, yet His word accomplishes what He desires, namely the revelation of Himself to those who are lower, despite their inherent limitations (Is. 55:8-9). How then does He overcome the effects of sin? Blaise Pascal in his *Penses (Thoughts) #60* captured the essence of this issue:

First part: Misery of man without God. Second part: Happiness of man with God. Or, First part: That nature is corrupt. Proved by nature itself. Second part: That there is a Redeemer. Proved by Scripture.[175]

Man is separated from God by a wide chasm of depravity and ungodliness. But praise be to God that He acts to vanquish the chasm.

---

174 Van Til, *The Defense of the Faith*, 109.

175 Blaise Pascal, *Thoughts* (New York: PF Collier and Son, Co., 1910), 23.

THE WORK OF THE FATHER, SON, AND SPIRIT

Based on His choosing (Rom. 9:15-16), the Father draws to Himself those whom He wishes (Jn. 6:44). None can come of personal volition, and even if any could, they would not, for there is none who seeks after Him (Rom. 3:12-18). He has chosen those whom He will draw, even before the foundations of the world (Eph. 1:4-6), and His drawing work is efficacious, ultimately resulting in the glorification of those whom He has chosen (Rom. 8:30). His drawing work seems best equated with His calling work (Gal. 1:4-6, 15), and refers to His active involvement in bringing man to Himself, creating in man the ability to respond positively to His revelation. Also note Mt. 16:15-17 – the truth regarding Jesus Christ is revealed by the Father – Jesus is the Logos, the Word, the very Idea of God (Jn. 1:1-5) and Jesus Christ reveals the Father.

By virtue of His relationship with the Father, only Christ can adequately explain or reveal Him (Jn. 1:18). There is no other who possesses this divine relation (as only begotten God), and there is therefore no other to whom humanity can look for the explanation of God's character. Christ claimed to be the only access to the Father (Jn. 14:6). His revelation of the Father is both representative (as the very image of God, Col. 1:15; as the exact representation, Heb. 1:3), and hortatory (in teaching about the character of the Father, Jn. 16;12; 17:4-8). As the revelation of the Father, Christ is the primary topic of special revelation (Lk. 24:27, 45; Jn. 5:39). Without His revealing work, man would have no enlightenment (Jn. 1:9), no explanation of the Father (1:18).

The Spirit guides into all truth (Jn. 16:7-11, 13). He is given to the believer so that[176] the believer will have comprehension[177] of that given by God (1 Cor. 2:12). Chafer emphasizes on this point that "...in so far as He opens the understanding to the Scriptures, He unveils that which He has originated."[178] By virtue of the anointing of the Holy Spirit, which every believer possesses, He is the Divine Teacher of the believer (1 Jn. 2:27). Without Him the individual is simply "worldly-minded" (Jude 19). Without His convicting work (Jn. 16:8) and divine enablement (1 Cor. 12:3) the individual would be fully incapable to respond with repentance leading to the knowledge of the truth (2 Tim. 2:25).

Importance
John Whitcomb identified a significant flaw in certain apologetic approaches, saying,

> ...it must be admitted that Christians have too often been guilty of building systems of apologetics on *other foundations than the one set*

---

176 Note the *hina* purpose clause of 1 Cor. 2:12.

177 *eidomen* rather than *ginoskomen*, highlighting accurate cognitive rather than experiential understanding, reversing enslavement to the noetic effects of sin, providing the believer with the mind of Christ (1 Cor. 2:12-16).

178 Chafer, *Systematic Theology*, 6:37.

forth in Scripture. Instead of giving the impression that men are eagerly waiting for proof that Christianity is true, the Bible exposes men's hearts as sealed shut against any and all finite pressures for conversion.[179]   (emphasis mine).

Whitcomb's characterization is also applicable to theological method. If the apologetic foundations are flawed, then by virtue of the apologetic relation to theological method, the theological foundations are equally flawed. Both methodologies – apologetic and theological – must find their base, form, and function in Scripture.

Man's incapacity cannot be overcome by an achievement of the mind. The great chasm between man and God can only be bridged by the hand of God through His work, both allowing and enabling man to respond in faith. Yet, as He revealed Himself with the tools of language, He does not work in counteraction to the basic principles of language (i.e., hermeneutic principles). Therefore, there is dual responsibility borne in developing proper apologetic and theological method: (1) God's part: He must reveal Himself to and illuminate those whom He has chosen to know Him (positionally), and (2) the believer's part: the believer must be dependent upon God's divine guidance and

---

179 John C. Whitcomb, "Contemporary Apologetics and Christian Faith, Part 1," *Bibliotheca Sacra* 134 (April-June 1977): 104.

diligent to rightly utilize the tools of language in order to understand His revelation.

PILLAR #4

A CONSISTENT HERMENEUTIC

The word *hermeneutics* is derived from the Greek *hermeneia* (interpretation). Hermeneutics here refers to the discipline (both art and science) of Biblical interpretation. It is science in that rules and methods must be followed, and it is art in that the depth of meaning in communication often exceeds the bounds of rules and methods.

This Biblical theology assumes the vital need and therefore the practice of a consistent hermeneutical approach to the entirety of Scripture. The hermeneutic chosen cannot contradict any of the previous three prerequisites. The chosen system of hermeneutics must allow for the keeping of, in particular, the second prerequisite: that God has revealed Himself authoritatively in Scripture. To fail at this requirement is at its heart the adaptation of the non-Christian interpretive principle which places the interpreter above the very Revelation of God (the Scriptures themselves), ultimately, if taken to the logical conclusion, denying the very existence of the Creator, and thus replacing Him with the creature. It is therefore a matter of great importance the hermeneutic used in approaching God's self-revelation. It will become evident that only one hermeneutical approach will suffice for the task at hand.

Lockhart, in defense of his rule demanding that we "interpret communications of all kinds by the same general principles,"[180] makes this observation:

> There is a limitless variety of the kinds of matter to be interpreted in the world...all must be studied somewhat differently, so that it will be necessary to consider the character of the work before interpreting it; nevertheless, the same laws are to be followed and the same rules are to be applied.[181]

The previous prerequisites require that God, rather than man, is the authority over revelation. In light of this, the specific aim of the hermeneutic process must be then the knowledge of God - in this context, the proper understanding of His revelation of self-disclosure resulting in a proper understanding of Him, which is a significant factor in the working of the Holy Spirit, who convicts and enables a proper response to Him. The hope here is that the interpreter will move from the knowledge of God (*ginosko*) possessed by those in Romans 1:21 who did not honor Him as God, to the knowledge of God (*ginosko*) which is by very definition eternal life in John 17:3, i.e., the establishment, by the power of God, of a personal relationship with God. While this cannot, of course be accomplished simply by

---

180 Clinton Lockhart, *Principles of Interpretation* (Delight: AR: Gospel Light, 1915), 35.

181 Ibid., 33.

hermeneutical process, the hermeneutical process rightly applied to Scripture allows for proper understanding of the message as authored by the Holy Spirit, and thus provides a springboard, if you will, for His working.[182]

Some, like coventalist John Gerstner, suggest that it is impossible to maintain a consistently literal hermeneutic, particularly in approaching Biblical prophecy,[183] and that dispensationalists are therefore inconsistent in their hermeneutic approach. However, an examination of the various methods of interpretation demonstrates that the only method which consistently recognizes this foundational truth in practice is the literal grammatical historical approach, and thus not only is necessary, but by virtue of its necessity (for one) it is certainly possible.

A consistently spiritualizing or allegorical approach destroys objectivity, and ultimately the authority of the Scriptures themselves, as the interpreter, in this hermeneutical approach, ultimately usurps authority over the text. A consistently literal approach to the whole of Scripture – specifically the literal grammatical historical approach– will result in certain idiosyncratic and even exclusive conclusions.

---

182 See Acts 8:28-38, the Ethiopian eunuch, after being guided rightly into understanding the meaning of Scripture, responds rightly to God.

183 John Gerstner, *Wrongly Dividing The Word Of Truth* (Morgan, PA: Sole Deo Gloria, 2000), 93, 96, and 110.

CONSISTENTLY LITERAL APPROACH RESULT #1: SUBMISSION TO THE AUTHORITY OF SCRIPTURE

If Scripture bears this brand of authority, the interpretive approach to Scripture should be exegetical not eisegetical. It must be primarily inductive (beginning with the text to find the theology) rather than primarily deductive (beginning with the theology in order to determine the text).

> Individual believers must therefore test their experience in the light of common witness, and submit to its authority. We have been warned that there are spiritual forces at work which will seek to pervert the truth, and so it is only as we reform our own opinions according to the collective witness that we will be preserved from error.[184]

On the infallibility and authority of Scripture, even in light of the current lack of original manuscripts, Van Til's reasoning is important:

> It is impossible to attain to the idea of such a God by speculation independently of Scripture. It has never been done, and is inherently impossible. Such a God must identify Himself. Such a God and only such a God, identifies all

---

184   Gerald Bray, *Biblical Interpretation Past and Present* (Downers Grove: Intervarsity Press, 1996), 15.

the facts of the universe. In identifying all the facts of the universe He sets these facts in relation to one another. Such a view of God and of human history is both presupposed by, and in turn presupposes, the idea of the infallible Bible; and if such a God is presupposed then it is not a matter of great worry if the transmissions are not altogether accurate reproductions of the originals...God in His providence has provided for the essentially accurate transmission of the words of the original.[185]

If Scripture indeed bears this level of accuracy and authority, the necessity of humility on the part of the reader, in submitting to the authority of the Biblical record, is inescapable and a necessary result of a literal interpretation.

CONSISTENTLY LITERAL APPROACH RESULT #2: RECOGNITION OF CUMULATIVE REVELATION

This is a major point of departure for non-dispensational and progressive dispensational theologians, whom, while insistent of their utilization of a consistently literal hermeneutic, raise questions as to how literal interpretation should actually be conducted. Of significant importance in this question is the relationship of the Old Testament to the New. John Feinberg identified the central issues as: (1) relation of

---

185 Cornelius Van Til, *A Christian Theory of Knowledge*, 28.

cumulative, or progressive, revelation to the priority of one Testament over the other; (2) recognition and ramifications of the New Testament's utilization of the Old Testament; and (3) how to approach typology.[186]

The hermeneutic of non-dispensationalism and progressive dispensationalism disregards cumulative revelation in general, in part because of its resultant Old Testament priority in regard to definition of key ideas and terms (the New Testament holds priority in respect to providing a complete theology). Feinberg's observations are again helpful:

> Nondispensationalists begin with NT teaching as having priority and then go back to the OT. Dispensationalists often begin with the OT, but wherever they begin they demand that the OT be taken on its own terms rather than reinterpreted in the light of the NT.[187]

The recognition of cumulative revelation is intrinsically vital for the consistent application of literal interpretation. As a result of a literal interpretation this recognition arises, as one would obviously begin with the earliest revelation and advance in kind to the most recent. Stallard confirms

---

186 John S. Feinberg, "Systems of Discontinuity," in *Continuity and Discontinuity: Perspectives on the Relationship Between the Old and New Testaments*, ed. John S. Feinberg (Wheaton, IL: Crossway, 1988), 73-74.

187 Ibid., 73.

this as a paramount principle in his four steps[188] of theological method: (1) recognition of one's preunderstanding; (2) formulation of Biblical theology of the Old Testament from a literal grammatical historical interpretation of the Old Testament; (3) formulation of Biblical theology of the New Testament from a literal grammatical historical interpretation of the New Testament; and (4) production of systematic theology by harmonizing input from 2 and 3. Note the priority that Stallard places on the Old Testament vs. the New, simply as a product of recognizing cumulative revelation. Ryrie declared this recognition "an imperative"[189] without which will be raised "unresolvable contradictions."[190] The Biblical evidence for Ryrie's conclusion is strong. Ryrie further asserts the reality of cumulative revelation as a definitive aspect of Biblical theology, saying,

> Biblical theology studies revelation in the progressive sequence in which it was given. It recognizes that revelation was not completed in a single act on God's part but unfolded in a series of successive stages using a variety of people. The Bible is a record of the progress of

---

188   Adapted from Mike Stallard, *Literal Hermeneutics, Theological Method, and the Essence of Dispensationalism,* unpublished.

189 Charles Ryrie, *Basic Theology,* 114.

190 Ibid.

revelation, and biblical theology focuses on that.[191]

Christ illustrated the cumulative revelation principle in His approach to handling Old Testament revelation in His appearance to the two on the road to Emmaus: "And beginning with Moses and with all the prophets, He explained to them the things concerning Himself in all the Scriptures" (Lk. 24:27). His listeners later described His process as "explaining the Scriptures" (24:32). Christ makes reference to this order within Scripture on other occasions as well, and His characterizations are not simply acknowledgments of the commonly held structure of the OT revelation.

It is significant that in order to explain the Scriptures, Christ Himself started at the beginning. Again, we see that Christ Himself, as the personal revelation of God, is the apex of cumulative revelation, as He is identified as that revelation of God in the last days Who is "the radiance of His glory and the exact representation of His nature" (Heb. 1:2-3). At his earliest proclamations regarding Christ, John appeals to the beginning (Jn. 1:1), then to the law of Moses (1:17), and again, to the prophets (1:19-25). Christ is the culmination of a cumulative revelation. Note 1 Kings 17:1 and 18:41 later expounded on in Luke 4:25 and James 5:17.

---

191 Charles Ryrie, *Basic Theology* (Wheaton, IL: Victor Books, 1986), 14.

The progressive dispensational and non-dispensational position has been characterized by an acknowledgment of a sometimes literal hermeneutic, yet one that interprets the Old Testament in light of the New.[192] However, even postmillennial A.H. Strong,[193] who admittedly strays from the literal hermeneutic in prophecy,[194] recognizes the cumulative, or progressive, nature of Scripture.[195] Berkhof, however seems to admit that a cumulative understanding would certainly be a verification of the premillennial perspective, as he refers to the premillennial understanding of the thousand year reign in Rev. 20:1-6, saying that

> the only Scriptural basis for this theory is Rev. 20:1-6, after an Old Testament content has been poured into it.[196]

Unfortunately, inconsistency is evident as he continues, saying,

---

192 Robert Saucy, *The Case for Progressive Dispensationalism* (Grand Rapids, Zondervan, 1993), 20.

193 A.H. Strong, *Systematic Theology* (Philadelphia, Judson Press, 1947), 1008.

194 Ibid., 1012.

195 Ibid., 175.

196 Louis Berkhof, *Systematic Theology* (4th revised and enlarged edition, Grand Rapids: Eerdmans, 1941), 715.

> This passage occurs in a highly symbolic book
> and is admittedly very obscure...The literal
> interpretation of this passage...leads to a view
> that finds no support elsewhere in Scripture.[197]

Yet he admits that by reading the passage through the
eyes of the OT the literal interpretation is plausible.
The predisposition against the cumulative nature of
revelation is evident here. The amillennialist Kuyper
seems to argue for the cumulative nature, saying

> The Old Testament is to us the fixed point of
> support, and the New cannot legitimate itself
> other than as the complement and crown of the
> Old, postulated by the Old, assumed and
> prophesied by Christ....[198]

If the NT is postulated by the OT, as Kuyper suggested,
by logical conclusion the NT must be interpreted on the
basis of the revelation given in the OT.

Finally, O.T. Allis, while distorting the
dispensational emphasis on cumulative revelation,
recognizes that the basic idea is a prerequisite of literal
interpretation:

> A further important result of the claim of
> Dispensationalists that prophecy must be

197 Ibid.

198   Abraham Kuyper, *Principles of Sacred Theology* (Grand
Rapids, Baker Book House, 1980), 461.

interpreted literally, that so understood it is perfectly intelligible and if unconditional must be literally fulfilled, is the tendency to exalt the Old Testament at the expense of the New Testament, to insist that its predictions stand, we may say, in their own right, and are in no sense dependent upon the New Testament for amplification, illumination, or interpretation... The assumption that underlies these statements is that anything but literal fulfillment would be tantamount to abrogation or modification.[199]

While there is inconsistency regarding the acknowledgment of the cumulative nature of revelation among those of non-literal persuasion, there should be none for those holding to a literal hermeneutic.

CONSISTENTLY LITERAL APPROACH RESULT #3: AWARENESS OF DOXOLOGICAL CENTRALITY

An examination of a few basic works of God coupled with a literal interpretation of the creation account demonstrates the centrality of God's doxological purpose, as the major works of God revealed in Scripture *all* serve the doxological purpose: (1) God's predestining and calling works, Eph. 1:5-12; 2 Pet. 1:3; (2) The ministry of Christ (including His

---

199 O.T. Allis, *Prophecy and the Church* (Philipsburg, NJ: 1945), 48.

resurrection), Jn. 13:31-32; 17:1-5; 21:19; 2 Cor. 1:20; Heb. 13:21; (3) the keeping of His word, Rom. 3:1-7; (4) Salvation, Ps. 79:9; Rom. 15:7;16:25-27; Eph. 1:14; 1 Tim. 1:15-17; 2 Tim. 4:18; Jude 24-25; (5) the church, 1 Cor. 10:31; 2 Cor. 4:15; Eph. 1:12; Php. 1:11; 2 Thes. 1:11-12; 1 Pet. 4:11,16; (6) fruitfulness of believers, Jn. 15:8; 1 Cor. 10:31; (7) the kingdom, Php. 2:11; 1 Thes. 2:12; Rev. 1:6; (8) sickness, death, and resurrection, 1 Sam. 6:5; Lk. 17:11-18; Jn. 9:1-3; 11:4; (9) Judgment, Rom. 3:7; Rev. 14:7; (10) deliverance of Israel, Is. 60:21; 61:3; (11) the fulfilling of covenants and summing up of all things, Is. 25:1-3; 43:20; Lk. 2:14; Rom. 4:20; 15:8-9; 2 Cor. 1:20; 2 Pet. 1:3-4; Rev. 19:7; (12) creation is identified as a primary work, Ps. 19; Is. 40; Rev. 4:8-11.

He created as an expression of His glory (Rev. 4:11). He reveals Himself to His creation that it might be filled with His glory (Num. 14:21) and that all will ascribe to Him the glory due His name (1 Chr. 16:28-29; Ps. 29:1-2; 96:7-8). The existence of all things serves the purpose of divine Self-expression, i.e., Self-glorification (Rom. 11:36), in perhaps the same manner as the symphony reflects the skill of the composer, the masterpiece reflects the brilliance of the painter, and the piercing words reflect the heart of the poet.

What Is at Stake?

If the literal creation account is denied, the necessary result is that the other works of God must also be denied.

(1) God's Predestining and Calling Works- Eph. 1:4 tells us of His choosing before the foundation of the world, yet if Scripture speaks without authority and in ignorance of the foundation of the world, how is it to be trusted in this regard?

(2) The Ministry of Christ – God asserts that Christ is the Creator (Jn. 1:1-3; Col. 1:13-16; Heb. 1:1-3). If He is not, then on what basis can any other ministry of Christ be trusted? If Jesus has no rights as Creator, on what authority could He raise Himself from the dead (Jn. 2:19)?

(3) The Keeping of His Word- How valuable is His word if He claims to be the Creator Who created in a precise manner if He is not and did not?

(4) Salvation – If He has no rights over creation as the Creator, what right would He have as Savior? Without His creative work He would possess no authority to redeem.

(5) The Church – Dependent on Christ for its existence as the body of Christ, yet Christ's identity and ministry would already have been by virtue of denial of the creation account rendered ineligible.

(6) Fruitfulness of Believers- (Jn. 15:1-11) Demonstrates the fruitfulness of the believer as deriving from abiding in Christ, and through the

predetermined choosing work of God (Eph. 2:8-10). These bases, since assumed false would be fruitless.

(7) The Kingdom –The rulership and authority of the Kingdom is by virtue of the rights of Creator (Col. 1:13-16). God would otherwise have no right to rule.

(8) Sickness, Death, and Resurrection – (Jn. 9:1-3; 11:4) If there is no authority as Creator, there is no authority over creation.

(9) Judgment – (Rom. 1:19-20) Man is held accountable for his failure to acknowledge God's natural revelation. Where is God's authority and justice if He did not reveal Himself in this way?

(10) Deliverance of Israel - Rom. 9:6 tells us that God's future plan of deliverance for Israel is dependent on His word, which would have been rendered false by the "errant creation account."

(11) The Fulfilling of Covenants and Summing up of All Things – If He didn't start it He can't finish it (e.g., Rev. 22:10). The beginning and the end go hand in hand.

To sum up:
  (1) God's revealed purpose in all things is to glorify Himself.
  (2) God's works serve this purpose.
  (3) Creation is identified as a primary and foundational work upon which the other works to

some degree depend. A fully literal interpretation of the creation account (Gen. 1-2) necessarily results in a six-day creation duration (*Biblical Creationism*).

(4) If the literal six-day creation account is denied, the necessary result is that the other works of God must likewise be denied.

(5) If His works are denied, His worthiness and glory are denied, ultimately exalting the creation (i.e. man) and thus accomplishing Satan's deceptive plan (Gen. 3:1-6). However if we acknowledge His works, we will recognize His worthiness to be praised (Rev. 4:8-11)

CONSISTENTLY LITERAL APPROACH RESULT #4: NORMATIVE DISPENSATIONAL CONCLUSION

A truly Biblical dispensational theology is *not* a hermeneutic method; rather it is the *result* of a consistently applied literal grammatical-historical hermeneutic method. Even those who disagree with the conclusions of dispensational theology readily admit that dispensational conclusions are generally the necessary result of a literal interpretive approach: Gerstner explains that dispensationalism results from a more consistently literal method, saying,

We should not accuse the dispensationalists of being absolute literalists nor should they accuse non-dispensationalists of being spiritualizers. We all are literalists up to a certain point. At the point where we differ, there is a tendency for the dispensationalists to be literalistic where the non-dispensationalist tends to interpret the Bible figuratively.[200]

Berkhof admits that certain premillennial (dispensational) conclusions are

based on a literal interpretation of the prophetic delineations of the future of Israel and the Kingdom of God, which is entirely untenable.[201]

Allis notes that literal interpretation is a hallmark of premillennial dispensationalism:[202]

One of the most marked features of Premillennialism in all its forms is the emphasis which it places on the literal interpretation of Scripture.... Dispensationalists are ardent literalists whose canon of interpretation like that of other Premillenarians may be expressed by the words, "literal wherever possible" (H. Bonar) or "literal unless absurd" (Govett).[203]

---

200 John Gerstner, 93.

201 Louis Berkhof, *Systematic Theology*, 712.

202 It should be noted that he also accuses dispensationalists of inconsistency, particularly in regard to typology. This will be discussed later.

203 O.T. Allis, 16, 18-19.

Ryrie succinctly asserts that the system results from the method:

> Classic dispensationalism is a result of consistent application of the basic hermeneutical principle of literal, normal, or plain interpretation. No other system of theology can claim this.[204]

Change the method and the resultant theology will necessarily be altered. Attention to methodology is obviously quite important.

Basic Variations of Eschatological/Theological Conclusions

Historically there have been (and remain) a number of distinct theological systems identified primarily by their eschatological idiosyncrasies. One key identifier is the chronology of the return of Christ and the institution of His kingdom. There are three germane views: postmillennialism, amillennialism, and premillennialism.

Postmillennialism holds that the church will be victorious on the earth, instituting the millennium, with Christ returning *after* this tremendous victory has been accomplished. Defining elements of this view were found in Augustine's writings, but were later developed by Daniel Whitby (1638-1725) and others. Kenneth

---

204 Charles Ryrie, *Dispensationalism*, Revised and Expanded (Chicago, IL: Moody Press, 1995), 85.

Gentry identifies four cornerstones[205] of support for the postmillennial position: (1) Creation – God's purpose in creation would be thwarted if the earth were to be destroyed and remade; (2) Covenant – the promises of an "unshakeable kingdom" and earthly blessings require that this earth remain, and that the kingdom is the apex of human existence; (3) Prophecy – it is suggested here that prophecy requires the gradual and ultimate progress of man toward peace and prosperity; and (4), Kingdom – based on Gentry's interpretation of 1 Corinthians 15:24, he suggests that the kingdom is the culminating factor in history.

Amillennialism is the belief that there will be no literal 1000 year reign of Christ upon the earth. This view is also associated with Augustine, who held to a spiritual interpretation of Revelation 20, identifying that the kingdom was fulfilled in the church. He also recognized a literal kingdom (in the current age), suggesting that Christ's return would come afterwards – utilizing a recapitulation interpretation (that ch. 20 precedes ch. 19 chronologically) of the passage. Augustine's observations contain elements of and provide the springboard for both the postmillennial and amillennial views. Berkhof claims that amillennialism is the historic faith of the church, having in mind Augustine's view.[206]

---

205 Kenneth Gentry, Jr., *Postmillennialism: Wishful Thinking Or Certain Hope?* (from www.cmfnow.com, access date unknown).

206 Louis Berkhof, *Systematic Theology*, 708.

Premillennialism asserts that Christ's second coming will precede the literal fulfillment of the 1000 year reign of Christ on the earth. Ryrie claims that Premillennialism is the historic faith of the Church,[207] having in mind a literal interpretation of Scripture, and thus appealing to authority predating the post-apostolic fathers from whom developed the non-literal approach and the amillennial and postmillennial viewpoints. Erickson, likewise, observes that premillennialism was the dominant teaching during the church's first three centuries.[208]

Covenant/Reformed Theology
This system has three basic tenets, or identifying factors: the covenant of works, one people of God, and an inconsistent hermeneutic.

(1) Covenant of works/ covenant of grace
God entered into a covenant with Adam. Adam broke it. God then began the covenant of grace, offering eternal life through faith. The Westminster Confession identifies these two covenants:

Man by his fall having made himself incapable of life by that covenant, the Lord was pleased to make a second, commonly called the covenant of

207 Charles Ryrie, *The Basis of the Premillennial Faith* (Neptune, N.J.: Loizeaux Brothers, 1953), 17.

208 Millard Erickson, *Christian Theology* (Grand Rapids, MI: Baker, 1983), 1213.

grace: wherein he freely offered unto sinners life and salvation by Jesus Christ, requiring of them faith in him, that they may be saved, and promising to give unto all those that are ordained unto life, his Holy Spirit, to make them willing and able to believe.[209]

Neither of these covenants are ever mentioned or so called in Scripture. This approach seeks to unify Scripture, rescuing it from the supposed disjointed results of a literal interpretation; emphasizes one people of God, denying the distinction between Israel and the church; places modern day believers in the age of law, and admittedly utilizes allegorical hermeneutics particularly in prophetic passages.

Covenant theologian Berkhof admits the newness of the covenant system:

In the early church fathers the covenant idea is seldom found at all, though the elements which it includes, namely, the probationary command, the freedom of choice, and the possibility of sin and death, are all mentioned.... In the scholastic literature and in the writings of the Reformers, too, all the elements which later went into the construction of the doctrine of the covenant of

---

209 Westminster Confession, 7:3.

works were already present, but the doctrine itself was not yet developed.[210]

While Heinrich Bullinger is often identified as the father of covenant theology, Coccaeus developed the threefold covenant system of works, redemption, and grace, but held to such sharp distinction between Old and New Testaments that he could hardly be seen as a true "covenant theologian." The covenant of redemption speaks of the Father's covenant with the Son regarding the redemptive plan, and therefore the redemptive plan becomes the unifying issue of Scripture.

(2) One people of God

The New Testament saints share the same basic identity, positions, and citizenships as the Old Testament saints – Israelite believers (OT) and church age believers (NT) are essentially the same body.

(3) Inconsistent hermeneutic

Where there is difficulty in the conclusions of the literal hermeneutic, the allegorical hermeneutic is applied, particularly in regard to prophecy.

Within the system, there are three basic eschatological conclusions: Covenant Postmillennialism looks for a fulfillment of Old Testament prophecy through a golden age of the church after which time the second coming of the Lord

---

210 Louis Berkhof, *Systematic Theology*, 211.

occurs;[211]   Covenant Amillennialism denies a literal reign of Christ on earth,[212] although generally acknowledging a literal return of Christ to the earth; and Covenant Premillennialism recognizes a literal return of Christ to institute His eternal kingdom on earth, however, not in the context of a 1000 year reign. It only differs from amillennialism in verbiage.[213]

Ultra Dispensationalism

Sometimes this view is referred to as hyper dispensationalism or Bullengerism - because this system was popularized with doctrines delineated in the notes of E.W. Bullinger's Companion Bible. H.A. Ironside identified six definitives or distinctives of Ultra Dispensationalism.[214] (1) The Gospels have no real message for the church; (2) Acts is transitional between dispensation of law and dispensation of mystery, and deals with a "different church" than does Paul in his epistles; (3) Paul didn't receive revelation of the mystery of the body until his imprisonment in Rome, and therefore, his earlier epistles deal with the same transitional "church" as Acts; (4) the entire book

---

211   J. Marcellus Kik, *An Eschatology of Victory* (Nutley, NJ: Presbyterian and Reformed, 1975), 4.

212   John Walvoord, *The Millennial Kingdom* (Grand Rapids, MI: Academie, 1959), 6.

213 As promoted by George Eldon Ladd.

214 summarized from H.A. Ironside, *Wrongly Dividing the Word of Truth*, 4th Ed.(Neptune, NJ: Loizeaux Brothers, 1989), 9-10.

of Revelation deals with future events – the seven letters are for seven Jewish churches in the tribulation; (5) the body of Christ is distinct from the bride of the Lamb, the latter supposed by Bullinger to be Jewish in nature; (6) baptism and the Lord's Supper, being revealed before Paul's prison epistles, do not pertain to the present church age. Other more moderate ultra-dispensationalism perspectives are elucidated by Cornelius Stam.[215]

Progressive Dispensationalism (PD)

Proponents of this recently developed system (Saucy, Blaising, Bock, et al, roughly 1993) characterize the system as a mediating position between dispensationalism and covenant theology, but in fact PD bears more resemblance to the covenant system than the dispensational one. PD consists of seven basic tenets that define it in practice as non-dispensational, and lead Ryrie to suggest that PD is very closely related to covenant premillennialism:[216]

(1) The kingdom of God is the unifying factor of OT and NT.

---

215 See Cornelius Stam, *Things That Differ* (Chicago, IL: Berean Bible Society, 1959).

216 Charles C. Ryrie. "Update on Dispensationalism," in *Issues in Dispensationalism*, edited by Wesley R. Willis, John R. Master, and Charles C. Ryrie, (Chicago, Il: Moody Press, 1994), 23.

As the theme of Biblical history, the kingdom is that program through which God affects his lordship on the earth in a comprehensive salvation within history.[217]

(2) Four dispensations of Biblical history: Patriarchal, Mosaic, Ecclesial (church), and Zionic (kingdom). These four are derived by a fairly straightforward three-pronged methodology as follows (most notable is the first of the three):

> ...(1) begin with the structure of New Testament Dispensationalism; (2) keep the basic dispensational scheme as simple as possible; and (3) be flexible with the notion of a dispensation so as to be able to see greater simplicity or greater differentiation than the working dispensational scheme allows....[218]

(3) Christ is currently on the throne of David - The Davidic covenant pertains both to Israel and the church. Christ is at the right hand of God, which, as asserted by PD, is the Davidic throne.[219]

---

217 Robert Saucy, *The Case For Progressive Dispensationalism*, 27-28.

218 Craig A. Blaising and Darrell L. Bock, *Progressive Dispensationalism* (Grand Rapids: Baker Books, 1993), 120.

219 Saucy, *The Case for Progressive Dispensationalism*, 73.

(4) the New Covenant is already inaugurated, though not fully realized yet.[220]

(5) Distinction between Israel and the church overemphasized in classical dispensationalism.[221]

(6) Complementary hermeneutic — while there is no outright denial of literal grammatical-historical interpretation, it is asserted that the NT makes complementary changes to the OT. Blaising and Bock define this saying,

> The additional inclusion of some in the promise does not mean that the original recipients are thereby excluded. *The expansion of promise need not mean the cancellation of earlier commitments God has made.*[222]

They refer to this principle as the "complementary principle.[223] This complementary approach is seen as a necessary and natural refinement of literalism.

---

220 Bruce A. Ware, "The New Covenant and the People(s) of God," in *Dispensationalism, Israel, and the Church*, edited by Craig A. Blaising and Darrell L. Bock, (Grand Rapids, MI: 1992), 84-97.

221 Saucy, 27-29.

222 Blaising and Bock, *Progressive Dispensationalism*, 103.

223 Ibid.

(7) An already not yet approach – the covenants are progressively being fulfilled (hence the name progressive dispensationalism), and are thus finding fulfillment both now and in the future.[224]

Normative Dispensationalism

Key elements of normative dispensational theology include those identified by Guer:[225]   (1) literalism (the basic hermeneutic principle); (2) diversity of classes in the body of the redeemed (distinction between Israel and the church); and (3) the literal usage of *day* in prophecy. Perhaps the most effective characterization of foundational elements are found in Ryrie's *sine qua non*:[226] (1) distinction between Israel and the church; (2) consistent use of a literal hermeneutic; (3) doxological purpose of God at the center.

Dispensational divisions provide an important structural tool in outlining the unfolding plan of God. While there are a number of different approaches to outlining these divisions, three of these approaches are particularly of value in the estimation of this writer, and calculate the dispensations respectively as three, seven, and twelve:

---

224 Blaising and Bock, *Progressive Dispensationalism*, 96-100.

225   as identified by Mike Stallard, *Literal Hermeneutics, Theological Method, and the Essence of Dispensationalism.*

226 Charles C. Ryrie, *Dispensationalism Today* (Chicago: Moody Press, 1965), 43-47.

Dispensation Divisions (AC Gaebelein)[227]

(1) The Age of Preparation – beginning in Gen. 3:15, and including the calling of Israel; (2) the Age of Participation beginning in Acts 2 at Pentecost and ending with the rapture of the church (1 Thes. 4:17-18); (3) the Age of Consummation – beginning at the return of Christ after the tribulation, encompassing the Millennial Kingdom, and ushering in eternity.

Gaebelein acknowledged other possibilities, yet maintained the essential elements of these three particular dispensations.[228]

Dispensational Divisions (based on C.I Scofield)

(1) Innocence – Gen. 1:3-3:6; (2) Conscience – Gen. 3:7-8:14; (3) Government – Gen. 8:15-11:9; (4) Promise – Gen. 11:10-Ex. 18:27; (5) Law – Ex. 19:1-Jn. 14:30; (6) Grace[229] – Acts 2:1 – Rev. 19:21; (7) Millennium – Rev. 20:1-5.

---

227 AC Gaebalein, "The Dispensations" *Our Hope* 37 (Dec. 1930), 341-346.

228 Mike Stallard, *The Theological Method of AC Gaebelein*, a Dissertation, 1992, 204.

229 Although Scofield originally communicated his dispensational soteriology with some confusion (see *Scofield Reference Bible*, 1917, p. 1115), dispensationalists agree that salvation has always been by faith, with the content varying by dispensation – namely some looked forward in time to redemption through the Messiah, others look back.

Twelve Dispensational Divisions[230]

(1) Planning: Eternity Past[231] – Jn. 17:24; Eph. 1:4; 1 Pet. 1:20; (2) Prelude: Innocence of Man - Gen. 1:1-3:5; (3) Plight: Failure of Man – Gen. 3:6-6:7; (4) Preservation and Provision: Common Grace and Human Government – Gen. 6:8-11:9; (5) Promises Pronounced – Gen. 11:10-Ex. 18:27; (6) Prerequisite Portrayed: The Broken Covenant: The Tutor – Ex. 19:1- Mal. 4:6; Gal. 3:24-25; (7) Promises Proffered: The Kingdom Offered – Mt. 1:1-12:45; (8) Postponement and Propitiation: The Kingdom Postponed and New Covenant Ratified – Mt. 12:46-Acts 1:26; (9) Participation: The Church Age – Acts 2:1- Rev. 3:22; (10) Purification: The Tribulation, Jacob's Trouble – Rev. 4:1-19:10; (11) Promises Performed: The Kingdom Initiated – Rev. 19:11- 20:6; (12) Postscript: Eternity Future – Rev. 20:7 – 22:21.

---

230 Held to by this writer, based on a synthetic overview of Scripture, uniting soteriological and kingdom elements under the doxological purpose.

231 Most dispensational divisions do not include eternity past or future. Dispensations, however, are not limited to periods of time, but rather to delineations of varying economies within God's purpose and plan. Therefore, neglecting dispensations outside of time (i.e., eternity past and future) seems to focus too much on man – nearly leaning toward a redemptive center, or at least a man-centered one – rather than focusing on God's eternal and doxological purpose. In order to rightly perceive the eclectic economies within the framework of time, it seems most necessary to acknowledge events taking place in the eternities which bring the very planning and fulfillment of the time-divided economies. See later discussion on definition and delineation of dispensations.

Normative Dispensationalism has remained distinct and identifiable, with slight development, particularly in the following aspects: Classical Dispensationalism – viewed the church as an interruption (parenthesis) in God's earthly plan with Israel; Revised Dispensationalism – viewed the church as an integral part of God's plan, with more of a heavenly center, thus seeing the unity of the message of Scripture; Presuppositional Dispensationalism – normative dispensationalism in the revised sense, built upon the foundations of a presuppositional epistemology. This approach hopes to most suitably ground dispensational theology with the proper moorings.

CONSISTENTLY LITERAL APPROACH RESULT #5: CLEAR DISTINCTION BETWEEN ISRAEL AND THE CHURCH

Perhaps the simplest litmus test for consistency in hermeneutic method is the resultant view regarding distinction between Israel and the church (or the lack thereof).

Replacement Theology
Based on the understanding that Israel has been superseded by the church due to Israel's rejection of her Messiah has arisen the perspective known as *replacement theology*. This approach sees the church as "true Israel" which replaces "unfaithful Israel," and thereby inherits the Old Testament promises made to

Israel. Grudem represents this view, saying with clarity,

> ...the church has now become the true Israel and will receive all the blessings promised to Israel in the Old Testament.[232]

Scofield correctly diagnosed the impact of this misunderstanding on the church in particular. His analysis is sobering:

> I believe that the failure of the Church to see that she is a separated, a called-out Body in the purposes of God, charged with a definite mission limited in its purpose and scope, and the endeavor to take from Israel her promises of earthly glory, and appropriate them over into this Church dispensation, has done more to swerve the Church from the appointed course than all other influences put together. It is not so much wealth, luxury, power, pomp, and pride that have served to deflect the Church from her appointed course, as the notion, founded upon Israelitish Old Testament promises, that the Church is of the world, and that therefore, her mission is to improve the world. Promises which

---

232 Wayne Grudem, *Systematic Theology* (Grand Rapids, Mi: Intervarsity Press, 1994), 863.

were given to Israel alone are quoted as justifying what we see all about us today.[233]

And again he says,

> It may safely be said that the Judaizing of the church has done more to hinder her progress, pervert her mission, and destroy her spiritually than all other causes combined. Instead of pursuing her appointed path of separation from the world and following the Lord in her heavenly calling, she has used Jewish Scriptures to justify herself in lowering her purpose to the civilization of the world, the acquisition of wealth, the use of an imposing ritual, the erection of magnificent churches, the invocation of God's blessing upon the conflicts of armies, and the division of an equal brotherhood into "clergy" and "laity."[234]

The superimposition of the church into Israel's framework has brought significant consequences throughout the history of the church, including (to at least some degree) various persecutions of Jews, the

---

233 C.I. Scofield, *The Biggest Failure of the Church Age*, from http://www.biblebelievers.com/scofield/scofield_church-age.html, access date unknown.

234 C.I. Scofield, *Rightly Dividing the Word of Truth* (New York: Loizeaux Brothers, Inc., 1896), 12.

crusades, the inquisitions, Hitler's holocaust, etc.[235] Church and world history are littered with these consequences of theological inaccuracy.

Replacement theology finds its presuppositional foundation in the necessity of Israel's dismissal, while its hermeneutic method must necessarily be allegorical. On the consequences of such allegorical thinking, Ronald Diprose comments,

> The logic of replacement theology required that much of the Old Testament be allegorized. Only in this way could the church be made the subject of passages in which the nation of Israel is addressed. This led to the virtual abandonment of the Hebrew worldview and concept of God and the adoption of a framework of thought which had its roots in Greek philosophy. All of this fostered an attitude of contempt toward ethnic Israel and led to the exclusion of Israel as a subject of theological reflection.[236]

The literal hermeneutic, however, destroys any perceived legitimacy of the replacement approach, as

---

235 For a perspective (certain aspects of which this writer does not agree) on these issues worthwhile of consideration, see Gerard S. Sloyan's essay "Christian Persecution of the Jews over the Centuries."

236 Ronald Diprose, *Israel and the Church, The Origin and Effects of Replacement Theology* (Waynesboro, GA: Authentic Media, 2004), 169-170.

admittedly the literal approach results in a necessary distinction between Israel and the church. God has a grand purpose for Israel, and one that is distinct in many ways from his plan for the church. It is evident that one's perspective of Israel is symptomatic of one's worldview, and that one's worldview is impacted dramatically by one's hermeneutic.

Points of Distinction

Fruchtenbaum identifies six particular evidences for the distinction between Israel and the church: (1) the church's birth at Pentecost via Spirit baptism (Acts 1:5; 2:1-4; 11:15-16; 1 Cor. 12:13; Col. 1:18); (2) certain events of Christ's life were prerequisite to the genesis of the church: His death (Mt. 16:18, 21), His resurrection (Eph. 1:20-23), and His ascension (Eph. 4:7-11); (3) the four mystery (refers to something not previously revealed in the Old Testament) aspects of the church (Eph. 3:3-5, 9; Col. 1:26-27): Jew and gentile united in one body (Eph. 3:1-12), Christ indwelling the believer (Col. 1:24-27; 2:10-19; 3:4, 11), the church as the bride of Christ (Eph. 5:22-32), and the rapture (1 Cor. 15:50-58); (4) the church as the one new man (Eph. 2:11-3:6) – distinct from Israel and the Gentiles; (5) the three groups are distinct from one another (1 Cor. 10:32); (6) the term Israel is never used of the church.[237]

---

237   Arnold Fruchtenbaum, *Israelology* (Tustin, CA: Ariel Ministries Press, 1989), 680-683.

Chafer references the distinction between Israel and the church as an "inexhaustible field of investigation,"[238] noting in particular twenty-four specific areas of distinction.[239]

While there is overwhelming evidence for such a distinction, three specific points stand out: (1) the covenants literally applied demand the distinction; (2) the relation of Christ to Israel as Messiah and King and to the church as Husband and Head demand the distinction; (3) the scope of blessing for the two groups demand the distinction.

THE BIBLICAL HERMENEUTIC METHOD
(An Old Testament Analysis)

The Biblical approach (meaning that of the Scriptural writers who were called upon to interpret special revelation of God) to hermeneutics has always fallen in the category of literal grammatical historical – a normal understanding of words used in context. Scripture, as quoted by the Biblical writers always was understood to have a literal meaning except where clearly identified.

---

238 Chafer, *Systematic Theology*, 4:47.

239 Ibid., 4:47-53.

Literal Hermeneutics in the Historical Narrative and Complementary Books

If any had occasion for a non-literal hermeneutic, it would have been Noah. God approached him with instructions that had seemingly no historical contextual relevance or precedent in that Noah had probably never even seen rain,[240] or at least if he had,[241] it was nothing like that which God was describing in the context of a worldwide flood, see Gen. 2:5-6; yet Noah took Him literally and he did "according to all that God had commanded him, so he did" (6:22, also 7:5).

Abram also was approached by God with an unusual request (that of going forth from his country and from his relatives and from his father's house, 12:1a); yet he, like Noah, took God literally, and demonstrated such by going forth "as the Lord had spoken to him" (Gen. 12:4a). Again, Abram took God literally when He promised Abram a son (15:6) — so much so, in fact, that he tried to manufacture a method for God to keep His word *literally* (Gen. 16). A third time (at least), Abraham demonstrates a literal hermeneutic, as God gives an imperative with no precedent: "take now your only son, whom you love, Isaac, and go to the land of Moriah; and offer him there

---

240 John Whitcomb and Henry Morris, *The Genesis Flood* (Grand Rapids, Baker Book House, 1961), 241-242.

241 H. C. Leupold, *Exposition of Genesis*, (1942 reprint, Grand Rapids: Baker Book House, 1987), 1:113-114.

as a burnt offering...." (22:2). Abraham's response was calculated: he did exactly as he was commanded (22:3), until the Angel of the Lord amended the command. Abimelech interpreted what "God said to him in the dream" (20:6) as literal, and he acted with precision in obeying it.

Jacob interpreted self-revelation of God through prophetic dreams as literal (28:10-22; 31:3-13). Joseph interpreted his own dreams of divinely appointed authority as pictorial of literal and certain truth – as evidenced by his father's response: "Shall I and your mother and your brothers *actually* [emphasis mine] come to bow ourselves down before you to the ground?" (37:10b) Joseph interpreted the dreams of the cupbearer and the baker also as pictorial (40:9-23), yet it is important to note that these were not revelations of self-disclosure by God, nor were they hortatory presentations of doctrine. The dreams were "visions" of pictorial nature, and of these, the interpretation belongs to God (40:8).

Likewise, Joseph interprets Pharaoh's dream as pictorial of God's plan, saying, "God has told Pharaoh what He is about to do" (41:25b). Pharaoh's recognized that Joseph was "discerning and wise" (41:39b) in his approach to God's divine plan, as the nature of the dreams was, in a very common sense way, clearly pictorial. Tan makes the distinction regarding revelational dreams between those using "familiar objects and concepts" and those using unfamiliar objects or concepts - in the cases of the latter, often language of analogy is used, i.e., the beasts of Dan.7.[242]

Dreams were an important part of Old Testament revelation particularly; and while they are usually pictorial, those that were self-disclosure of God were always to be taken literally. Those that were not the latter type of direct revelation of God were often analogy, but were to be interpreted literally with the simplest understanding of grammar in the historical context.

In view of dreams bearing the light of revelation, Deut. 13:1-5 makes evident the fact that simple verification of a predictive dream (or sign or wonder) by its unfolding or coming true did *not* provide the sum of verification. The relation of the prophet or dreamer, in this case, to God and the message about God was equally as important if not more so (13:2). Therefore, the commissioning of the dreamer, interpreter, or prophet becomes an important cog in the wheel of understanding the veracity and authority of the revelatory dream.

Moses demonstrates the literal hermeneutic in his response to the Lord's words from the burning bush by putting himself in a life-threatening situation (bearing exceedingly unpleasant news to Pharaoh) and by afterward doing *just as the Lord commanded* him in regards to the Mosaic covenant (Lev. 8:4; Num. 27:11,22). He sought no deeper meaning, but rather

---

242 Paul Lee Tan, *The Interpretation of Prophecy* (Dallas: Bible Communications, Inc., 1993), 83-84.

understood the words of God to be soundly grammatical and historical in context, and thus intended to be taken literally. Note that even Pharaoh used a literal hermeneutic – he did not question God's words (As Moses repeatedly said "Thus says the Lord"), rather he hardened his heart against them (Ex. 8:32; 9:34-35). Moses, in his charge to Joshua, is emphatic that Joshua should be careful to do all that is written in the Law (Josh. 1:8).

The phrase *it is written* appears seventy five times in Scripture, and demonstrates by its context and usage a literal grammatical historical approach utilized and expected. Joshua used the phrase to appeal to Mosaic Law and to demonstrate a literal keeping of it (Josh. 8:31). The Angel of the Lord appeals to His own word to Israel, reminding them that they had been unfaithful. Israel's response (they wept loudly) demonstrated a literal understanding both of His original command, and the words He spoke to them at that moment (Jud. 2:1-5). The historical narrative of Ruth is built upon the literal understanding and application of redemptive marriage (from Deut. 25:5-10). Saul's failure as king and consequent judgment by God was based upon a failure to keep, literally and precisely, the command of the Lord (1 Sam. 15). David responds to God's promise (the Davidic Covenant) by saying 'Thy words are truth" (2 Sam. 7:28), and adding that there would be a literal fulfillment – that his house would be blessed forever (7:29).

The literal fulfillment of Nathan's message of judgment from God (the death of David's and Bathsheba's son because of adultery and murder) came just seven days after its pronouncement (2 Sam. 12). It is notable that in this case, a figure was used to illustrate the literal truth and fulfillment. David again recognizes literal fulfillment (1 Kgs. 2:2-4) as he charges Solomon to obey with caution all that God had revealed, so that God would keep His promise of 2 Samuel 7:25. God reiterates the same to Solomon in 1 Kings 9:1-9. Solomon's personal decline is associated with his failure to carefully, literally and precisely, keep the mandate God had previously given regarding the conduct of kings in Deuteronomy 17.

Literal Hermeneutics in the Psalms
    The Psalms also provide a broad sample of literal hermeneutic applications:

Ps. 33:11 – The counsel of the Lord stands forever. It does not evolve as do hermeneutic theories.

Ps. 37:31 – The law of his God is, in his heart. God's law is propositional and transferable – that is it can move from the page to the heart, as it communicates a clear and understandable message, resulting in delight to do His will (Ps. 40:7-8, where the writer – David – interprets his own writings literally).

Ps. 44:1 – The sons of Korah heard with their ears the works of the Lord, from the days of their fathers. They received what they heard as historical narrative.

Ps. 62:11-12 – David sums up two important truths gleaned from God's word: that both power and lovingkindness belong to God, and that He recompenses according to deeds. In God's word propositional and absolute truths regarding God are available.

Ps. 78:5 – God established a testimony and a law to be taught to the next generation. This also presupposes the usefulness of language in a natural sense for the purpose of transference of knowledge. The verses following provide a poetic yet historical narrative of God's working with Israel from the deliverance from Egypt to the kingdom of David.

Ps. 85: 8 – The sons of Korah will hear what God the Lord will say – He will speak peace to His godly ones. Here is a summarization of His dealings with those who fear Him, that He communicates truth to them.

Ps. 89:19 – Even when speaking in visions, God's message is propositional.

Ps. 102:18 – Truth will be written in order that a later generation will respond to it and praise the Lord. The nature of truth is static, and useful for all generations.

Ps. 103:20 – His word is to be obeyed from generation to generation, and thus to be understood from generation to generation as well.

Ps. 105:8-10 – God remembered His covenant, His word, His oath, and He confirmed it. His word is unalterable.

Ps. 106 – Here is a poetic and historical narrative of Israel's failures, demonstrating a literal hermeneutic approach to the chronological books of the Old Testament.

Ps. 108 – Note the usage of Ps. 60, almost identical verbiage.

Ps. 112 – The man who delights in His commandments is blessed. Delighting in His commandments is tied here to the fear of the Lord, which is the beginning of knowledge and wisdom (Pr. 1:7; 9:10). This kind of delight results from a true understanding of His word. True understanding is both possible and necessary.

Ps. 117:2 – His truth is everlasting.

Ps. 119 – This entire chapter is a profound testament to the validity and necessity of His word, as well as the transferability from the pages to the mind and heart. David references God's word as propositional truth at least 177 times in this Psalm (word – 36, law – 25, testimonies – 22, statutes – 22, precepts – 21, commandments – 21).

Ps. 132:11-12 –David understands the promise of 2 Sam. 7 to be quite literal.

Ps. 135 – The psalmist recounts as literal historical narrative the events surrounding Exodus 7-11.

Ps. 136 – The psalmist recounts as literal the creation account and the events of the exodus.

Literal Hermeneutics in the Prophetic Books
Note the many literal fulfillments in prophecy – McDowell highlights twelve key prophecies and their historical fulfillments (Tyre - Ezek. 26; Sidon -Ezek. 28; Samaria – Hos. 13; Gaza-Ashkelon – Amos 1, Jer. 47, Zeph. 2; Moab-Ammon – Ezek. 25, Jer. 48-49; Petra and Edom – Is. 34, Jer. 49, Ezek 25 and 35; Thebes and Memphis – Ezek. 30; Nineveh – Nah. 1-3; Babylon – Is. 13-14, Jer. 51; Chorazin, Bethsaida, Capernaum – Mt. 11; Jerusalem's enlargement – Jer. 31:38-40; and Palestine – Lev. 26, Ezek. 36).[243] He further observes,

[prophecy illustrates] the power of God through fulfillments of seemingly impossible predictions

---

243 Josh McDowell, *Evidence That Demands a Verdict* (San Bernadino, CA: Here's Life Publishers, 1979), 1:267-320.

directly grounded in the course of human events.[244]

Equally as impressive are the precisely fulfilled prophecies of Daniel - four kingdoms of Nebuchadnezzar's statue (ch. 2) already witnessed literally by history; the literal fulfillment of Nebuchadnezzar's humiliation (ch. 4); the end of the Babylonian empire (ch. 5); the rise and fall of Greece (ch. 8; 11:3-4); the already fulfilled seven and sixty-two sevens of 9:25-26a.

The fulfillments of prophecy found in Daniel are so marvelous, that Sir Robert Anderson sees no alternative but reasonably founded belief,

> To believe that the facts and figures here detailed [particularly in Dan. 9] amount to nothing more than happy coincidences involves a greater exercise of faith than that of the Christian who accepts the book of Daniel as Divine. There is a point beyond which unbelief is impossible, and the mind in refusing truth must needs take refuge in a misbelief which is sheer credulity.[245]

---

244 Ibid., 267.

245 Sir Robert Anderson, *The Coming Prince* (Grand Rapids, MI: Kregel, 1984), 129.

In addition, Floyd Hamilton confirms 332 specific Old Testament prophecies fulfilled literally by Christ.[246] If these prophecies are not to be taken literally, then why did God choose to fulfill them literally? Is He using a faulty hermeneutic? Inarguably, His hermeneutic is a literal one. Anderson comments also on the Messianic prophecies:

> Two thousand years ago who would have ventured to believe that the prophecies of Messiah would receive a literal accomplishment! "Behold a Virgin shall conceive and bear a son." [Is. 7:14] "Behold thy King cometh unto thee: He is just, and having salvation; lowly, and riding upon an ass, and upon the colt the foal of an ass." [Zech. 9:9] "They weighed for my price thirty pieces of silver;" "And I took the thirty pieces of silver and cast them to the potter in the house of the Lord." [Zech. 11:12-13; Mt. 27:5,7] "They part my garments among them and cast lots upon my vesture." [Ps. 22:18; Jn. 19:23-24] "They pierced my hands and my feet." [Ps. 22:16] "They gave Me vinegar to drink." [Ps64:21] "He was cut off from the land of the living; for the transgression of my people was He stricken." [Is. 13:8] To the prophets themselves, even, the meaning of such words was a mystery [1 Pet. 1:10-12]. For the most part, doubtless, men

---

246 Floyd Hamilton, *The Basis of Christian Faith* (New York: Harper and Row, 1964), 160.

regarded them as no more than poetry or legend. And yet these prophecies of the advent and death of Christ received their literal fulfillment in every jot and tittle of them.[247]

With significance equal to that of demonstrating God's sovereignty, fulfilled prophecy demonstrates inarguably the literal implications of Biblical prophecy. After examining all the evidence, Anderson concludes that literalness is paramount, saying that literalness of fulfillment may therefore be accepted as an axiom to guide us in the study of prophecy.[248]

A BRIEF HISTORY OF HERMENEUTIC METHOD

The origin of faulty hermeneutics can be traced back to Satan's approach in the garden to God's revelation. He introduces five errors: (1) He questions God's word, Gen. 3:1; (2) misrepresents it 3:1; (3) questions God's motives, 3:5; (4) redefines the purpose for revelation, 3:5; and (5) completely contradicts the original message of revelation, 3:4. Eve is deceived, and thus the relationship between sin and the mishandling of God's revelation becomes very apparent.

Later, as the writing of the Hebrew Bible commenced during Moses' day (1500BC) those who received God's word seemed to interpret it literally

---

247 Anderson, 147-148.

248 Ibid., 148.

based on the common usage of the language of the day. Human response to God's word, as recorded in the Old Testament, is a significant witness to the necessity and expectation that interpretation and understanding of the text be in the literal sense.

However, during the intertestamental period, as the Greek culture flourished, no such authority as the Hebrew God was recognized. Conflict developed between the philosophical traditions and the religious ones, as "the religious tradition had many elements which were fanciful, grotesque, absurd, or immoral."[249] The Greek pantheon of Homer and Hesiod was in need of moral rescuing, and this redemption was accomplished by the allegorizing of the Greek religious literature. And, although Tate believes the motivation of Greek allegorism to be more positive and exegetical, he does present a traditional example of the apologetic tendency, saying

> Pythagoras and Xenophanes had accused Homer, and Theagenes of Rhegium came to the rescue by showing how the Battle of the Gods could be understood as a conflict partly between forces of nature and partly between warring passions in the human breast.[250]

---

249 Ramm, *Protestant Biblical Interpretation*, 25.

250 J. Tate, "On the History of Allegorism," *Classical Quarterly* 28 (1934): 105.

The Jewish interpreters of the Alexandrian school, most notably Philo (20 BC-50 AD) were influenced by the Greek system – both apologetically, attempting to reconcile Biblical revelation with Greek philosophy, and exegetically, seeking to enhance the meaning of the text. Origen (185-254) followed in Philo's interpretive footsteps, developing a threefold approach to Old Testament interpretation, identifying literal, ethical (or spiritual), and allegorical. He saw the literal as "the body not the soul."[251] The spiritual found Christ at the center (Jn. 5:39). The allegorical was primarily typological.

Justin Martyr (100-165) in his dialogue with Trypho demonstrates the impact Greek allegorism had on Biblical exposition as early as the second century, in his typological comparisons:

> When the people...waged war with Amalek, and the son of Nave (Nun) by name Jesus (Joshua), led the fight, Moses himself prayed to God, stretching out both hands, and Hur with Aaron supported them during the whole day, so that they might not hang down when he got wearied. For if he gave up any part of this sign, which was an imitation of the cross, the people were beaten, as is recorded in the writings of Moses; but if he remained in this form, Amalek was proportionally defeated, and he who prevailed prevailed by the cross. For it was not because

---

251 Ibid., p. 32.

Moses so prayed that the people were stronger, but because, while one who bore the name of Jesus (Joshua) was in the forefront of the battle, he himself made the sign of the cross. For who of you knows not that the prayer of one who accompanies it with lamentation and tears, with the body prostrate, or with bended knees, propitiates God most of all? But in such a manner neither he nor any other one, while sitting on a stone, prayed. Nor even the stone symbolized Christ, as I have shown.[252]

Here, and throughout the *Dialogue*, the intensive non-apologetic allegorism is evident. This represents the dawning of an age of spiritualization in the church.

In the early third century Origen (185-254) continued the allegorical tradition, carrying spiritualization to greater heights. Abandoning the commonly held premillennial view of Christ's return, Origen allegorized Jesus' second coming as personal spiritual experience and the immanency of his return was representative simply of the reality of death. Origen held that the Bible

...contains three levels of meaning, corresponding to the threefold Pauline (and Platonic) division of a person into body, soul and

---

252 Justin Martyr, Dialogue with Trypho, Chapter XC in *The Ante-Nicene Fathers*, edited by Alexander Roberts and James Donaldson (1885 reprint, Grand Rapids: Eerdmans, 1989), 1: 244.

spirit. The bodily level of Scripture, the bare letter, is normally helpful as it stands to meet the needs of the more simple. The psychic level, corresponding to the soul, is for making progress in perfection....[253]

Passages which seemed to disagree with Origen's eschatological conclusions he either discarded or spiritualized.[254]

In the fourth and fifth centuries Augustine of Hippo (354-430) held strongly to an allegorical approach, but he did not apply it universally; rather he relegated his allegorism to the prophetic passages. As Tan explains Augustine introduced a dualistic method that would make allegorism more palatable to future generations of interpreters:

> Augustine modified allegorism by confining it to the prophetic Scriptures...he interpreted the non-prophetic Scriptures literally and the prophetic Scriptures allegorically....Augustinian dualism was accepted without much debate into the Roman Catholic Church, and later also by the Protestant reformers.[255]

---

253 Joseph W. Trigg, *Origen*. (London: SCM Press, 1983), 120.

254 Many examples of this are present in *On First Principles*, Book 4.

255 Tan, *The Interpretation of Prophecy*, 50.

The allegorical approach had profound impact on church history, as Ramm observes:

> The allegorical system that arose among the pagan Greeks, copied by the Alexandrian Jews, was next adopted by the Christian church and largely dominated exegesis until the reformation, with such notable exceptions as the Syrian school of Antioch and the Victorines of the Middle Ages.[256]

Allegorism enabled the church fathers to develop a new unifying theme of Scripture. Based on a spiritualization of John 5:39, Christology was placed at the center, further bolstering allegorical method and enabling the spiritualizing of difficult passages. This is notably a misuse of the passage, as in it Christ reveals the Father and the doxological purpose as the unifying theme. Bray adds to the discussion here:

> The early Christians accepted the Jewish Scriptures as divinely inspired, but interpreted them in a completely different way. They did not regard the Old Testament as a prelude to Christianity, which the new revelation in Christ augmented or displaced.... Christians generally believed that the Old Testament spoke about Jesus Christ, not merely prophetically but in types and allegories which the Spirit revealed to

---

256 Ramm, *Protestant Biblical Interpretation*, 28.

Christians... In all probability, the first Christians looked on every part of Scripture as Christological, and were prepared to see Christ in it by whatever exegetical means would produce the desired result. It did not worry them if the literal meaning of the text seemed somewhat distant from this concern, since in that case it was plain that the passage in question contained a revelation of Christ which was more difficult to grasp than simpler texts.[257]

After an almost millennium long intercalation of church-dogmatic hermeneutics, the reformers of the sixteenth century returned to the literal approach except when dealing with prophecy and Israel – thus following Augustine's dualistic method. Luther rejected allegorical interpretation and recognized the supremacy of the Biblical languages; yet, he could not maintain consistency regarding prophecy and Israel. Calvin did likewise.

Within just a few years of the reformation rationalistic views of the Bible became prominent. Ramm characterizes the rationalistic perspective as "whatever is not in harmony with educated mentality is to be rejected."[258] This later leads to a redefining of the

---

257 Gerald Bray, Creeds, *Councils and Christ: Did the Early Christians Misrepresent Jesus?* (1984, Fearn, Ross-Shire: Mentor, 1997), 49 and 51.

258 Ramm, *Protestant Biblical Interpretation,* 63.

supernatural, and an application of the concept of evolution to the Scriptures.

In the early twentieth century, Karl Barth (1886-1968), the father of neo-orthodoxy, denied infallibility and inerrancy, and rejected the Bible as prepositional revelation, characterizing it rather as witnessing revelation. Barth concluded that truth can be found within the Bible, but truth does not encompass it. In essence, Barth's neo-orthodoxy is existential at its heart, emphasizing that revelation becomes revelation as it is experienced in the human response.

The latter twentieth century and the early twenty-first century have been characterized by postmodernism, a most deliberate hermeneutic approach in its own right, and one in opposition to the literal approach. It is at this point notable that the literal method was used to varying degree widely throughout the history of the church, exclusively in the first generation of the church, and later with consistency in the realm of prophecy and consequently Israel with the arrival of John Bale (1495-1563) and Joseph Mede (1586-1638).[259]

---

259 Mal Couch, ed., *An Introduction to Classical Evangelical Hermeneutics* (Grand Rapids, MI: Kregel, 2000), 108-127.

BASIC CONTEMPORARY APPROACHES

Postmodernism: Probability and Cultural Response Hermeneutics

Postmodernism is a way of doing science – an epistemological framework for processing information, and thus a hermeneutic base. Several defining characteristics are evident: (1) neither universal authority nor absolute truth exists, (2) reality and value are relative and based upon the experiential rather than the rational, and (3) meaning is relative and is reconstructed by the subculture of the interpreter.

Because of the inherent impact of the context and perspective of the interpreter, determining authorial intent becomes less an objective task and more a probabilistic one. Certainty cannot be achieved, and probability is the endgame. Shockley uses variant interpretations of Rev. 20:1-6 to illustrate the postmodern argument:

> Three evangelical theologians were gathered together examining Revelation 20:1-6. Each of them were "led by the Holy Spirit" and "followed literal hermeneutics." However, all three of these Christian scholars arrived at different conclusions, mainly, amillennialism, postmillennialism, and premillennialism. The professor may ask, "How does one account for these striking differences?" After hearing a few responses, the scholar asserts that the

preconditions affected the interpretation; preconditions will always force interpreters to prescribe meaning to the Scriptures (consciously or unconsciously) to the degree that their perception of God's revelation (no matter if God's revelation is objective truth) is distorted. Further, the work of the Holy Spirit is limited to conviction, that is, volition, never cognition. In addition, the idea of being able to employ literal, plain, normal hermeneutics is itself a modernistic bias derived originally from "Scottish Common Sense." Therefore, this method of interpretation is a precondition as well.[260]

Of concern to the postmodern here is not the *correct* interpretation of the passage, but rather the perspective of the interpreters. The authority no longer belongs to the text itself but to the interpreter. Ironically postmodern hermeneutic method[261] seeks not to achieve greater authority for the interpreter, but rather a new level of humility in interpretation supposedly not found in previous Cartesian/ rationalistic approaches (such as the literal hermeneutic). This approach argues the futility and inefficacy of rationalistic approaches to determine

---

260 Paul Shockley, "The Postmodern Theory of Probability on Evangelical Hermeneutics" *Conservative Theological Journal*, 4/11 (March 2000), 70.

261 Or at least the "positive postmodernism" of Westphal, et al.

objective truth (such as authorial intent), and resultantly emphasizes the interpreter's perspective and experiencing of the text as of greatest import in the interpretive process. A focus on broader cultural/theological referents has contributed to the neglect of detailed analysis of what the Bible actually teaches. The postmodernist emphasis on cultural relevance produces a theology developing from the outside in – from cultural response as a hermeneutic key to understanding the textual base.

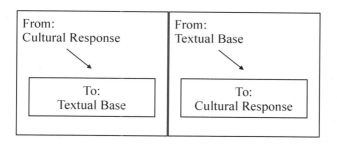

Lynn White, in his groundbreaking 1967 article demonstrates this *response* hermeneutic, when he makes such statements as:

> God planned all of this [creation] explicitly for man's benefit and rule; no item in the physical creation had any purpose save to serve man's purposes.... Christianity is the most anthropocentric religion the world has ever seen...[and] Christianity made it possible to

exploit nature in a mood of indifference to the feelings of natural objects....[262]

These conclusions can be drawn from a near-historical cultural response hermeneutic, but stand in contradistinction to necessary conclusions of the literal grammatical-historical hermeneutic (applied to such passages as Ps. 24:1; Is. 2:22; 40:15-17, 26; Jn. 3:30; Rom. 1:20; Col. 1:16, etc.).

White's claims are significant to his major argument that the (failed) modern idea of progress is "rooted in and indefensible apart from Judeo-Christian teleology" and it serves as a justification for his thesis:

> We shall continue to have a worsening ecologic crisis until we reject the Christian axiom that nature has no reason for existence save to serve man.[263]

Inarguably this is a hermeneutic issue the impact of which is truly monolithic.

The postmodernist perspective is characterized by an impassioned rejection of certain foundations of the modern era. The problems (real and perceived) of the present world are placed at the footstep of the modern era. White describes his solution to ecological crisis, saying

---

262 Lynn Townsend White, Jr., "The Historical Roots of Our Ecological Crisis," *Science* 155/3767 (March 10, 1967).

263 Ibid.

As a beginning we should try to clarify our thinking by looking, in some historical depth, at the presuppositions that underlie modern technology and science. Science was traditionally aristocratic, speculative, intellectual in intent; technology was lower-class, empirical, action oriented. The quite sudden fusion of these two towards the middle of the 19th century, is surely related to the slightly prior and contemporary democratic revolutions which, by reducing social barriers, tended to assert a functional unity of brain and hand. Our ecological crisis is the product of an emerging, entirely novel, democratic culture. The issue is whether a democratized world can survive its own implications. Presumably we cannot unless we rethink our axioms.[264]

Presuppositions and foundational axioms are to blame, and of course White ties these to the Judeo-Christian foundation, which therefore must be dismissed and replaced with something more effective at dealing with such problems as the ecological one.

Additionally, globalization has brought a heightened awareness of diverse belief systems, as interaction with dissimilar religious systems becomes more feasible due to technological advance and ease of travel, and more necessary for the maintenance of the

---

264 Ibid.

manufactured jungle.[265] The dialogue is not complete without a plurality of voices. As Ott argues in his discussion on the importance of peer review in theological consensus building,

> Not only will the results of a theology forged in global dialogue be potentially richer, but the community of believers is likely to be better served by such a theology.[266]

Presumably, in the ever globalizing marketplace of ideas theology should serve its constituency. It should solve problems – at the very least it should not contribute to them. (But in a *revelation* centered theology, the theology must simply follow that which is revealed. Such things as constituency and problem solving are not in view – once again, the nature of revelation is a pivotal issue.)

From this pluralizing of authoritative voices in theological matters has arisen an important byproduct: the identification and the characterization of fundamentalism. Those voices which seem to reject the shift to postmodernity, and consequently globalization, are categorized as fundamentalist due to their desire to resist change and hold fast basic tenets of their particular belief systems, and are summarily dismissed as valued voices in the marketplace of ideas. Evidently

---

265 Giddens' term akin to new world disorder.

266 Craig Ott and Harold Netland, *Globalizing Theology* (Grand Rapids, MI: Zondervan, 2006), 331.

it is not simply plurality of voice that is desired, but rather plurality of voice sharing a particular degree of diversity and nonresistant to the particular changes that come with a postmodernist/globalization program. Certain voices are unwelcome in the public square – misrepresented or not.

Authority and pedagogy are heavily impacted. In Friere's critique of the banking concept[267] of education he offers a definition which gives impetus for a new pedagogy:

> Implicit in the banking concept is the assumption of a dichotomy between human beings and the world: a person is merely *in* the world, not *with* the world of others; the individual is spectator, not re-creator. In this view, the person is not a conscious being (*corpo consciente*); he or she is rather the possessor of *a* consciousness: an empty "mind" passively open to the reception of deposits of reality from the world outside.[268]

Friere decries the narrative approach, instead preferring a problem-posing approach,[269] which, he

267   The teacher narrates, depositing information in the unquestioning and imaginationally unchallenged.

268   Paulo Friere, *Pedagogy of the Oppressed* (New York: Continuum, 2002), 75.

269 This approach makes the student a co-investigator, dialoguing with the educator.

claims, serves as a liberating praxis, overcoming such undesirables as authoritarianism, elite intellectualism, and false perceptions of reality. Friere's emancipatory pedagogy serves as a launching pad of sorts for postmodernist pedagogical methodologies. The answers lie in the process of continually asking questions.[270] Dialogue within a cultural context is paramount, and narration is de-emphasized.

With growing epistemological and pedagogical emphasis on *culture,* the question of authoritative basis must be addressed – particularly the relationship between revelation and culture. Ott identifies three differing approaches to this question: (1) revelation and culture are in opposition, (2) revelation and culture are equals, (3) revelation is determinative and culture is reflective.[271] Ott prefers the third, saying

> In this process, ideally, all will reflect together the glory of God and realize the mission of God in ways, greater, clearer, and brighter than possible from merely a single cultural reference point. Globalizing theology in this sense is not a homogenizing but a harmonizing of local expressions and an amplification of the overarching concern.[272]

---

270   Robin Usher and Richard Edwards, *Postmodernism and Education* (New York: Rutledge, 1994), 213.

271 Ott and Netland., 324-326.

272 Ibid., 325.

In postmodernist thought, cultural elements of context carry the greatest weight and as such "revelation" is dismissed as premodern superstition. Globalization reveals many worldwide traditions that would seem to justify such a dismissal. Pedagogical methodologies and foundations increasingly reflect this perspective on authority. Theology as a result moves away from dealing in matters of authority and becomes a vehicle for quasi cultural enrichment and pedagogical application.

Trajectory / Redemptive Hermeneutic

This hermeneutic operates under the basic presupposition that the text is gradually to be redefined (even improved) as cultural circumstances warrant. In promoting this view, William Webb suggests an XYZ approach.[273] X represents the cultural perspective, Y, the Biblical statement in its present stage of development (relative to X), and Z is God's ideal to which Y points. Thus on an issue such as slavery, the trajectory could be illustrated as follows:

---

273 William J. Webb, *Slaves, Women and Homosexuals* (Downers Grove: InterVarsity Press, 2001), 31.

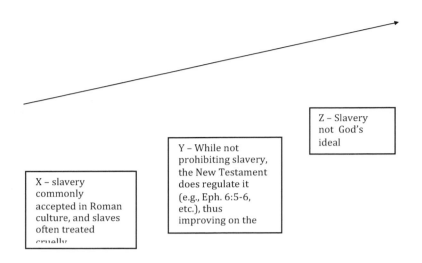

The trajectory is critical primarily between Y and Z, as Y must be altered (improved) to move more effectively toward Z. In other words, Y is a kind of ethical snapshot or even compromise – meeting culture where it is - and does not provide the ideal but rather a stepping stone leading toward the ideal. Y therefore must be seen as a foundation upon which the interpreter must build in order to continue the trajectory progressing toward Z. To ignore this is a significant failure in Webb's view, as he says

> To stop where the Bible stops (with its isolated words) ultimately fails to reapply the redemptive spirit of the text as it spoke to the original audience. It fails to see that further reformation is possible.... we should take that redemptive

spirit and move to an even better, more fully-realized ethic today.[274]

While the trajectory hermeneutic does attempt to deal with some important ethical questions (such as gender equality, social equality, etc.), by its (at least) inferential denial of the sufficiency of Scripture it defeats the ethical authority of the text. In this view, the Biblical text serves as a guide or intermediary beyond which the interpreter must advance. The Bible does not contain ethically ideal commands, but rather the redemptive spirit behind the commands is ideal.

It is also worthy of note that proponents of this kind of hermeneutic often fail to distinguish between the economies of Mosaic law and the church, creating unnecessary and unintended ethical dilemmas which seem to find their resolutions only through the application of the redemptive hermeneutic. In this, the hermeneutic error does not begin with the trajectory/redemptive process, but rather it begins with the failure to realize distinctions easily detected with the plain sense approach.

Finally, as trajectory/redemptive regards "stopping where the Bible stops" as a failure, perhaps it is appropriate to remind those to whom this hermeneutic appeals of Paul's warning to the Corinthian church not to go beyond what is written (1 Cor. 4:6).

---

274 Ibid., 247.

Allegorical Hermeneutic

First finding popularity with Alexandrian Jewish philosophers/theologians, the allegorical hermeneutic was a justification of perceived inconsistencies within the Old Testament regarding, in particular, how God related and communicated HImself to humanity (anthropomorphisms and theophanies). The Greek philosophies which influenced the Alexandrian Jews, including the dualism of Gnosticism, made it virtually impossible for a literal rendering of the text. However, by allegorizing the text – as simply the embodiments of spiritual or moral lessons – congruence could be found without violating the Greek philosophic principles.

The allegorical method, then, in origin, was a submission of the Divine Text to the pervading philosophies of the day in order to justify the Text with the perceived world around it. Rather than leaning solidly upon the words of Scripture to provide an interpretive base for understanding epistemology and philosophy, this method provided a means whereby current epistemological approach (specifically that of the Greeks) could go unchallenged.

Examples of the allegorical hermeneutic can be seen frequently in Philo (commonly recognized as the father of the allegorical hermeneutic). Philo saw Moses as having "reached the very summits of philosophy,"[275]

---

275 Philo, *The Works of Philo*, translated by C.D. Yonge (New Updated Version, Peabody, MA: Hendrickson, 1993), 3.

characterizing the creation account as Moses having "manifestly set before us incorporeal ideas"[276] rather than propositional truths, and presenting "five most beautiful lessons"[277] rather than expressing the simple narrative of origin. Philo's approach is evident in his discussion of Moses' identification of the four rivers in Genesis 2:10-14:

> In these words Moses intends to sketch out the particular virtues. And they also are four in number, prudence, temperance, courage, and justice. Now the greatest river from which the four branches flow off, is generic virtue, which we have already called goodness; and the four branches are the same number of virtues. Generic virtue, therefore, derives its beginning from Eden, which is the wisdom of God; which rejoices and exults, and triumphs, being delighted at and honoured on account of nothing else, except its Father, God, and the four particular virtues, are branches from the generic virtue, which like a river waters all the good actions of each, with an abundant stream of benefits.[278]

---

276 Ibid., 18.

277 Ibid., 24.

278 Philo, 32.

The allegorical approach functions in the world of ideas rather than in the realm of words, resulting in numerous interpretations of any particular verse, rejecting the literal sense whenever there is perceived philosophical contradiction. Ironside makes us of the multiple interpretation approach in his notes on Song of Solomon:

> Therefore we may think of the book from four standpoints. Looking at it literally, we see the glorification of wedded love. Looking at it from a dispensational standpoint, we see the relationship between Jehovah and Israel. Redemptively, we find the wonderful relationship between Christ and the Church. And studying it from the moral or spiritual standpoint, we see it as the book of communion between an individual soul and the blessed, glorified, risen Lord.[279]

While he acknowledges the literal sense, he sees deeper meaning through allegorical and spiritual usage.

Keil and Delitzsch acknowledge the problems created by the allegorical approach to the Song of Solomon, suggesting that this approach

> in spite of two thousand years' labour, has yet brought to light no sure results, but only

---

279 H.A. Ironside, *Proverbs and The Song of Solomon* (Nepture, NJ: Loizeaux Brothers, 1989), 11.

numberless absurdities, especially where the Song describes the lovers according to their members from head to foot and from foot to head.[280]

Fruchtenbaum explains that he

prefers the literal interpretation view, since it is the most self-consistent view and does not allow for runaway imagination. This view interprets the book normally, as the love relationship between a man and a woman.[281]

Regarding the prophecy of Haggai 2:5-9,[282] Augustine identifies the fulfillment not in a literal sense (reasoning that God's glory never filled the post-exilic temple), but rather its fulfillment came in the

---

280 Keil and Delitzsch, *Commentary on the Old Testament, Ecclesiastes and Song of Solomon* (Peabody,MA: Hendrickson, 1989), 2.

281 Arnold Fruchtenbaum, *Biblical Lovemaking* (Tustin, CA: Ariel Ministries Press, 1995), 2.

282 "As for the promise which I made you when you came out of Egypt, My Spirit is abiding in your midst; do not fear! For thus says the Lord of hosts, ' Once more in a little while I am going to shake the heavens and the earth, the sea also and the dry land. And I will shake all the nations and they will come with the wealth of all nations; and I will fill this house with glory', says the Lord of hosts."

church of Christ.[283] He didn't consider the possibility of a third and future temple (a plain sense meaning suggested by the future tense in the passage).

Regarding Ezekiel 37-48, John Taylor identifies the symbolic Christian interpretation, saying that this interpretation was "favored by many older commentators. They held that this vision had its fulfillment symbolically in the Christian church."[284]

On Matthew's reference to the kingdom of heaven in Matthew 4:17, Augustine equates the kingdom of heaven as the church,[285] and defends his view with an allegorical interpretation of Revelation 20:1-6, stating

> But while the devil is bound, the saints reign with Christ during the same thousand years, understood in the same way, that is, of the time of His first coming...the Church could not now be called His kingdom or the kingdom of heaven unless His saints were even now reigning with Him.[286]

---

283 Augustine, *City of God*, 18:48.

284 John Taylor, *Ezekiel* (Downers Grove, IL: Intervarsity Press, 1969), 252.

285 Augustine, *City of God*, 20:9.

286 Ibid.

Interpreting Revelation 12:1-6, Matthew Henry presents these verses as Satan's attempts to thwart the church:

> The church is represented, (1) as a *woman*, the spouse of Christ, and the mother of the saints. (2) As *clothed with the sun.* Having put on Christ, who is *the Sun of righteousness,* she shines in his rays. (3) as having *the moon under her* feet. Her heart and hope are not set upon sublunary things, but on the things that are in heaven, where her head is. (4) As having on her head *a crown of twelve stars,* that is the doctrine of the gospel preached by the twelve apostles. (5) As in travail and now in pain, to bring forth a holy progeny to Christ.[287]

On the interpretation of Revelation 20:1-6, C.H. Little illustrates the allegorization of the millennial kingdom, first by criticizing chiliasm (premillennialism):

> It is with this thousand years' bondage of Satan that the Chiliasts start spinning out their millenarian theories. Taking the thousand years as a literal number, they maintain that during this period Satan is absolutely bound...that Christ and His saints during this period reign peaceably and without interruption on the earth;

---

287 Matthew Henry, *Commentary on the Whole Bible,* edited by Leslie F. Church (Grand Rapids: Zondervan, 1961), 1979.

and that the Jews will be converted, and everything will be lovely as long as the thousand years last....[288]

He then offers the allegorical solution:

As a matter of fact, the thousand years in this chapter of Revelation begin with the binding of Satan or in other words, with the advent of Christianity, when Satan's power was curbed, so that he could no longer deceive the nations with the success that was his previous to the proclamation of the glorious Gospel of human salvation.[289]

The non-literal interpretation is here substantiated by "the imagery with which it [the 1000 year number] is surrounded."[290] The non-literal approach is here to be taken because other references in this context are also non-literal. And how is the non-literal approach to the context substantiated? The basis is a circular reasoning employed here to curtail what is identified as "certain Jewish opinions"[291] which are unacceptable to the writer.

---

288 C.H. Little, *Explanation of the Book of Revelation* (St. Louis: Concordia, 1950), 202.

289 Ibid., 203.

290 Ibid., 202.

291 Ibid.

The same type of circular reasoning is seen in Berkhof's approach to the same passage. Berkhof argues against the literal millennium, saying that

> The only Scriptural basis for this theory is Rev. 20:1-6, after an Old Testament content has been poured into it. This is a very precarious basis for various reasons. (1) This passage occurs in a highly symbolic book and is admittedly very obscure, as may be inferred from the different interpretations of it. (2) The literal interpretation...leads to a view that finds no support elsewhere in Scripture, but is even contradicted by the rest of the New Testament.[292]

Again, the literal approach is said to be implausible due to 'obscurity' of the passage. Yet the passage is only obscure due to an allegorical presupposition.

Berkhof argues that the "Old Testament Church" is found in Isaiah 49:14; 51:3; 52:1-2; and that "the term passes right over into the New Testament, Gal. 4:26; Heb. 12:22; Rev. 3:12; 21:9."[293] Using an allegorical approach to the Old Testament passage creates opportunity for the same approach in the New, but the motivation is a clear replacement of Israel with the church. The Augsburg Confession of A.D. 1530,

---

292 Berkhof, *Systematic Theology*, 715.

293 Ibid., 713.

based on these principles speaks strongly, condemning those

> who are spreading certain Jewish opinions, that before the resurrection of the dead the godly shall take possession of the kingdom of the world, the ungodly being everywhere suppressed.[294]

A popular contemporary application of allegorical method is preterism. From the Latin *praeteritus*, meaning *past*, preterism is an allegorical interpretive approach which sees prophetic events of Scripture as already having occurred in the past. Moderate preterism asserts, for example, that most of the Book of Revelation (and consequently all other Biblical prophecy) was fulfilled in 70 AD with the destruction of Jerusalem, yet it does leave room for a literal second coming of Christ. Moderate preterism is usually postmillennial. Radical preterism asserts that all prophecy has been fulfilled in the past.

Preterism, in general, emphasizes the genre of apocalyptic literature as characterizing Revelation in particular. Perhaps the key passage used to justify preterism is Matthew. 24:34, being understood to reference the generation (i.e., the disciples) present when these words were spoken (in light of the contextual reference of Mt. 23:36). It is notable that

---

294 'Article XVII,' *The Augsburg Confession* (St. Louis, MO.: Concordia Publishing House, 2006),.17.

'this generation' is used in Scripture of generations not pertaining to the specific audience of the writing (Heb. 3:10), and that the Matthew 24:34 passage taken in the immediate context of 24:4-31 and interpreted literally requires a futurist understanding. If a hermeneutic system has as its logical conclusion the de-emphasizing of Israel in God's plan and ultimately the degradation of the Jewish people, naturally one would have to question the motivation behind the hermeneutic. Particularly in light of Revelation 12, this approach is quite disturbing. The undermining of Scriptural authority through faulty hermeneutic process has uniquely profound impact on perspective regarding Israel.

Spiritualization/Mystic Hermeneutic

Although closely related to the allegorical hermeneutic, the spiritualization hermeneutic differs in motivation. Whereas the allegorical hermeneutic seeks at its heart to resolve textual difficulties arising from literal interpretation, the spiritualization hermeneutic seeks a deeper meaning in the text, and uses allegorical methods to accomplish that end.

Clement of Alexandria demonstrated a mystical hermeneutic in approaching Mosaic law, understanding a fourfold sense (threefold in addition to the natural): natural, mystical, moral, and prophetical:

> The sense of the law is to be taken in three ways,
> - either as exhibiting a symbol [mystical], or
> laying down a precept for right conduct [moral],

or as uttering a prophecy [prophetic].... For the whole Scripture is not in its meaning a single Myconos, as the proverbial expression has it; but those who hunt after the connection of the divine teaching must approach it with the utmost perfection of the logical faculty.[295]

Origen believed Scripture held three meanings: literal, moral, and spiritual. During the Middle Ages, the spiritual was divided into allegorical and anagogical, thus rendering a fourfold sense. Tan illustrates this fourfold meaning as applied to Genesis 1:3 ("Let there be light...") during the Middle Ages:

Medieval churchmen interpreted that sentence to mean (1) Historically or literally – An act of creation; (2) Morally – May we be mentally illumined by Christ; (3) Allegorically – Let Christ be love; and (4) Anagogically – May we be led by Christ to glory.[296]

Swedenborg identified three levels based on the three heavens: natural (the lowest), spiritual (the middle), and celestial (the highest). Note the ranking of the ultra spiritual as paramount, with natural at the lowest rung.

---

295 Clement of Alexandria, Miscellanies 1:28 in *The Ante-Nicene Fathers*, edited by Alexander Roberts and James Donaldson (1885 reprint, Grand Rapids: Eerdmans, 1989), 2: 341.

296 Tan, *The Interpretation of Prophecy* , 53.

Kant believed that the value of Scripture was found in the moral improvement of mankind, and therefore, if a literal understanding of a passage unveiled no particular moral truth, the literal interpretation was to be de-emphasized in favor of an allegorical approach from which would arise a moral truth.

While the spiritualization process utilizes an allegorical approach, due to the distinction in motivation the spiritualization can also stem from an ultra-literalistic hermeneutic. Overemphasis of words themselves have brought nearly a ritualistic approach to the spiritualization hermeneutic. Bible code, theomatics, and overemphasized typology are examples of a spiritualization or mystic hermeneutic.

Dispensational theology has traditionally placed large emphasis on types, and has often been criticized for doing so. O.T. Allis is justifiably critical of this approach:

It is a singular anomaly, which cannot fail to impress the careful student of Dispensational teaching, as represented, for example, in the Scofield Reference Bible, that it emphasizes and carries to such extremes these two distinct and in a sense opposite principles in interpreting Scripture. In dealing with the Old Testament history its treatment is highly figurative. Indeed, we sometimes receive the impression that the events of that history have little meaning for us in themselves; it is their typical meaning, a meaning which only those "deeply taught" in Scripture are able to appreciate, that is the really important thing about them. In dealing with prophecy, its treatment is marked by a literalism....[297]

Genre / Literary Form Hermeneutic

Genre, or literary form, hermeneutics sees recognition of literary form as the overriding factor in the hermeneutic process. By redefining the structure of various books, genre hermeneutics provides a means whereby the literal grammatical historical approach can be abandoned.

Marshall Johnson states his defining principle of genre hermeneutics (my term, not his) that

---

297 Allis, *Prophecy and the Church*, 22.

all writings must have had a meaning for their first readers, or at least, the author must have thought so.[298]

This is a key mistake, as it is evident that in some instances the writers of Scripture had no understanding of what they were writing, and thus would not have had the expectation that their readers would have had any additional wisdom with which to process the information, but due to obedience, they simply wrote as they were told. Even covenantalist interpreters agree that prophets were not always aware of the meaning of their prophecies.[299]

Ironically we see this in the two books which are most often mischaracterized by genre hermeneutics, Daniel (12:8-9), and Revelation (22:8-11). Note that by Revelation 22, John had already written the bulk of the "book of this prophecy," yet, he didn't know how to respond to it or what to do with it. The angel had to explain to him the purpose of the book and how to properly respond to it. It is very clear that John had no particular audience in mind, especially in chapters 4-22. From 1:11, it is clear that John received his imperative and the content of His writing from Christ. It was not up to John to make His writing "understandable" to his audience.

---

298 Marshall D. Johnson, *Making Sense of the Bible* (Grand Rapids: Eerdmans, 2002), 2-3.

299 See Gerstner, *Wrongly Dividing The Word of Truth*, 105.

Although influenced partly by prophetic and wisdom traditions, apocalyptic literature as it emerged after the Babylonian exile is unique in several respects and should not be confused with either of those predecessors[300].

Note the writer's humanization of the text – he is emphasizing cultural influences rather than the inspiration of God. This is the mistake of genre hermeneutics, and results in tremendously flawed conclusions about the nature of the text, and therefore about its message.

Virkler identifies the apocalyptic purpose as "the revealing of what has been hidden, particularly with regard to the end – times."[301] He further suggests that non-canonical literature shares commonality with the canonical, and identifies sections of Daniel, Joel, Amos, Zechariah and Revelation as apocalyptic.

Johnson says that Daniel writes "in typically apocalyptic style."[302] He also identifies Revelation 4-22 as apocalyptic literature,[303] resting his argument on John's use of the word *apokalupsis* in 1:1. This is a failure to understand the fact that John characterizes his writing as prophecy (22:18-19, etc.) by the definition

300 Ibid., 73.

301 Henry Virkler, *Hermeneutics* (Grand Rapids: Baker Book, 1981), 192.

302 Johnson, *Making Sense of the Bible*, 74.

303 Ibid., 77.

of Christ Himself (22:7), and not as apocalyptic literature; and that the 1:1 reference to *apokalupsis* is a literal reference to the unveiling of Christ – referring to the entire program of the prophetic book as culminating with Christ's final appearing in glory.

Cate likewise recognizes elements of Daniel as apocalyptic, saying,

> ...apocalyptic material may be somewhat strange. Apocalyptic material is visionary and highly symbolic. Examples in the Bible are parts of Daniel in the Old Testament and revelation in the New Testament, along with a few passages from other books in both Testaments.[304]

The difficulty is not so much in the use of the word *apocalyptic*. The problem arises when the term is used to override the internal description of the book. Daniel is a book of history, visions, and fulfillments. And it is notable that every fulfillment which took place in the book (i.e., Nebuchadnezzar's humiliation in chapter 4, and Belshazzar's death in chapter 5) is a literal fulfillment (with obvious acknowledgment of metaphor within the specific prophecies). Even those prophecies within the book which have still yet future fulfillments are very specific and require very precise fulfillment. Some characterize Daniel as *apocalyptic*

---

304 Robert Cate, *How to Interpret the Bible* (Nashville: Broadman, 1983), 33.

prophecy.[305]   Others are able to handle Daniel archaeologically and linguistically without seeing re-categorizing his prophecy as apocalyptic.[306]   A.C. Gaebelein is emphatic regarding the prophetic impact of Daniel, identifying it as a great prophetic forecast:

> It is the key to all prophecy; without a knowledge of the great prophecies contained in this book the entire portion of the word of God must remain a sealed book....The great prophetic portions of the New Testament, the Olivet discourse...and...the Book of Revelation, can only be understood through the prophecies of Daniel.[307]

By overriding the internal identifications and characterizations of Daniel with an apocalyptic genre, the entire prophetic message of Daniel can be veiled. And as Gaebelein pointed out, New Testament prophecy is so intertwined with Daniel, and Daniel with the Old Testament covenants, that in one fell

---

305 LaSor, Hubbard, and Bush identify Daniel as "a different kind of prophecy, in many respects, from that seen in the Prophets. Nevertheless it is prophecy." William Sanford LaSor, David Allan Hubbard, and Frederic William Bush, *Old Testament Survey* (Grand Rapids: Eerdmans, 1982), 661.

306 A.C. Gaebelein, John C. Whitcomb, John Walvoord, Leon Wood, etc.

307 A.C.Gaebelein, *The Annotated Bible Volume V Daniel to Malachi* (New York: Our Hope), 6.

swoop of genre override, God's prophetic forecast becomes inaccessible to the interpreter.

The book of Revelation likewise does not fall into an apocalyptic category, as it makes repeated self-characterization as prophecy (1:3; 11:6; 22:7,10, 18,19). It is prophecy regarding *apokolupsis.*

The literal interpretation of Genesis 1-11 is increasingly challenged on a literary form basis. Note Bierlein's characterization:

> The Bible contains an excellent illustration of the binding power of civic myth, as well as what happens when the myth breaks down. To be a Jew in ancient Israel meant to accept the king and the Torah as the moral, civic, and religious authorities. One had to identify with the sacred history of the Jewish people and accept that nationhood was defined by a covenant with God. The Old Testament sets forth that Israel prospered when the nation was faithful to the covenant; when that covenant was abandoned and the people worshipped the gods of neighboring peoples, society broke down and the Jews were sent into exile. This is the power of myth in action.[308]

Van Til accurately identifies a key consequence of a faulty approach to Genesis:

---

308 J. F. Bierlein, *Parallel Myths* (New York: Ballantine, 1994), 21.

If we deny the historicity of the Genesis
narrative we shall be compelled to reduce man's
responsibility for sin so drastically that in reality
nothing remains of it.... [Men] who virtually
reduce the Genesis narrative to the status of
myth, find themselves compelled to deny also the
historic Christian views of sin, of Christ, and of
the atonement.[309]

What the genre hermeneutic begins in Genesis is not
complete until the entire authority of Scripture is
undermined, placing the interpreter above the
revelation, and thus placing the creature above the
Creator (thus violating prerequisite #2: God has
revealed Himself authoritatively in Scripture).

Leupold describes some elements of
preunderstanding on the part of the genre interpreters
of Genesis:

Strong dogmatic presuppositions are too
definitely displayed by these scholars: miracles
are considered as practically impossible; so is
plenary inspiration; Israel's history can rise to no
higher levels than the Babylonian or the
Egyptian; an arbitrary evolutionary standard is

---

309 Van Til, *The Defense of the Faith* , 211.

to be employed in measuring historical evidence.[310]

For these few presuppositions there are even more counters in support of the historicity of Genesis:

The following facts of Israel's history are overlooked: a) the utter dissimilarity of the Genesis record and the legends of the nations... b) the clear distinction preserved by Israel's sacred records of the successive stages of revelation...c) the accuracy of Israel's historical tradition...d) distinct efforts by the patriarchs to perpetuate the remembrance of events of outstanding religious importance...e) the sober tone displayed in recording the most exalted revelation...f) the utter impartiality displayed in recording the history of those who are the patriarchs and fathers of tribes.... A proper evaluation of the facts enumerated above leads definitely to the conclusion that Genesis gives a sober, accurate, historical account of the events..."[311]

Literary form is indeed a consideration in the hermeneutic process, however two principles preside over literary form: (1) literary form should not be a

---

310 Leupold, *Exposition of Genesis*, 1:, 11.

311 Ibid., 11-12.

reason to avoid the literal hermeneutic. Regardless of the genre, the text is to be interpreted literally. (2) The Scriptures are unique and therefore the identification of literary form should not be based upon secular documentation such as myth and apocalyptic literature.

The five basic literary forms of Scripture are self-evident, with some overlap:

(1) *Primary Historical Narrative* – historical narrative which carries forth in deliberate fashion the chronology of Biblical history: includes Genesis, Exodus, Numbers, Joshua, Judges, 1 and 2 Samuel, 1 and 2 Kings, Ezra, Nehemiah, The Gospels, and Acts.

(2) Complementary Historical Narrative - Books of historical narrative which complement (inasmuch as they are contemporaries of) the primary historical narrative. This category includes Job, Leviticus, Deuteronomy, Ruth, 1 and 2 Chronicles, and Esther.

(3) Poetry and Praise – includes Psalms, Proverbs, Ecclesiastes, Song of Solomon, Lamentations

(4) Prophecy – interspersed with historical narrative and poetry, this form presents, usually, God's revelation of judgment and restoration. Isaiah, Jeremiah, Ezekiel, Daniel (although not included in the Nebi'im section of the Hebrew Old Testament, its form is prophetic and complementary historical), and the twelve minor prophets.

(5) Epistles – letters including Pauline and General (Hebrews, James, 1 and 2 Peter, 1, 2, and 3 John, and Jude).

Within these various forms are uses of allegory, symbolism, type, parables, and other figures of speech; and it is important to recognize the basic context in which these literary tools are used in order to understand them in their most natural sense and how they contribute to the overall meaning of the writing.

Canonical Hermeneutic
Canonical hermeneutics are distinguishable in at least two strains: (1) canonical in respect to the canon or dogma of church, and (2) canonical in respect to the canon of Scripture. The canonical dogmatic hermeneutic is the preunderstanding of Scripture which relies on previously stated church doctrine as the primary interpretive factor. While there are certainly other examples, Catholicism exemplifies this approach prominently. Ramm explains:

> The Catholic interpreter obediently accepts whatever the Catholic Church has *specifically* said about matters of Biblical introduction, and authorship of the books of the Bible.
> ...The Catholic interpreter accepts all verses which the Church has officially interpreted.[312]

---

312 Ramm, *Protestant Biblical Interpretation*, 39-40.

The Catechism of the Catholic Church underscores the principle cause behind Ramm's observation:

> Read the Scripture within "the living Tradition of the whole Church." According to a saying of the Fathers, Sacred Scripture is written principally in the Church's heart rather than in documents and records, for the Church carries in her Tradition the living memorial of God's Word, and it is the Holy Spirit who gives her the spiritual interpretation of the Scripture ("according to the spiritual meaning which the Spirit grants to the Church").[313]

This can also be demonstrated by adherence to various confessions and councils over and above allowing the text to speak for itself. Chafer emphasizes that this is a significant problem:

> One of the greatest errors of the Church of Rome is that of making the church, and not the Bible, the immediate and final authority in all matters of divine revelation....
>
> She argues that there were many things which Christ and the apostles taught which were not recorded in the Bible...but these...have been

---

313 *The Catechism of the Catholic Church*, 113.

preserved by the church and are as binding as are those precepts which are written.[314]

The canonical process hermeneutic represents a constant redefining in Scripture – an overemphasized and slightly altered understanding of cumulative revelation. Waltke defines it as follows:

> By the canonical process approach I mean the recognition that the text's intention became deeper and clearer as the parameters of the canon were expanded. Just as redemption itself has progressive history, so also older texts in the canon underwent a correlative progressive perception of meaning as they became part of a growing canonical literature.[315]

Seemingly, this view sounds compatible with the literal hermeneutic and the necessary idea of cumulative revelation; however, Waltke reads cumulative revelation into the earlier revelation, thus interpreting the Old Testament in light of the New, rather than vice versa. The result is, for example, the conclusion of replacement theology; particularly that Israel's covenants are fulfilled ultimately in the church.

---

314 Chafer, *Systematic Theology*, 1:14.

315 Bruce Waltke, "A Canonical Process Approach to the Psalms" in *Tradition and Testament*, ed., John Feinberg and Paul Feinberg (Chicago, IL: Moody Press, 1981), 7.

Bock and Blaising utilize this approach also (in essence it is quite related to their complementary hermeneutic): They suggest that the canonical-systematic level of reading the Biblical text

> takes the passage in light of the whole, either through all of an author's writing, through the lens of a given period, or, most comprehensively, in light of the whole of the canon.[316]

Here, as in Waltke's approach, the New Testament is read back into the Old, thus distorting cumulative revelation (a stated result they would surely not agree with). Brevard Childs demonstrated the approach as he insisted that the Old Testament is given new meaning by the entirety of the completed canon.[317] Ladd communicates well the issues at stake:

> Here then is the basic watershed between a dispensational and a nondispensational theology. Dispensationalism forms its eschatology by a literal interpretation of the Old Testament and then fits the New Testament into it. A nondispensational eschatology forms its theology from the explicit teaching of the New Testament. It confesses that it cannot be sure how the Old

---

316 Blaising and Bock, *Progressive Dispensationalism* , 101.

317   Paul Noble, *The Canonical Approach: A Critical Reconstruction of the Hermeneutics of Brevard S. Childs* (New York: EJ Brill, 1995), 26.

Testament prophecies of the end are to be fulfilled, for (a) the first coming of Christ was accomplished in terms not foreseen by a literal interpretation of the Old Testament, and (b) there are unavoidable indications that the Old Testament promises to Israel are fulfilled in the Christian church.[318]

Complementary Hermeneutic

Identifying the non-dispensational (covenant theology) hermeneutic, Saucy suggests that the approach is basically the same as that of the dispensationalist:

An analysis of non-dispensationalist systems... reveals that their less than literal approach to Israel in the Old Testament prophecies does not really arise from an a priori spiritualistic or metaphorical hermeneutic. Rather it is the result of their interpretation of the New Testament using the same grammatical-historical hermeneutics as that of dispensationalists.[319]

Saucy further understates the distinction between the non-dispensational and dispensational hermeneutic, in

318 George E. Ladd, "Historic Premillennialism" in *The Meaning of the Millennium: Four Views*, ed. Robert G. Clouse (Downers Grove, IL, Intervarsity Press, 1977), 27.

319 Robert Saucy, *The Case For Progressive Dispensationalism*, 20.

characterizing the most fundamental difference between dispensationalists and non-dispensationalists as, "neither a basic hermeneutical principle nor the ultimate purpose of human history.[320]

To ensure no misunderstanding on the part of his readers, he emphasizes later,

> We do not retract our earlier assertion that the basic hermeneutical procedure, especially in its beginning principles, is essentially the same for both dispensational and non-dispensational scholars. Both affirm a historical-grammatical hermeneutic.[321]

Saucy refers to this approach as the "natural understanding."[322] This is a description he echoes in a later treatise as a general principle of Biblical interpretation.[323] Gerstner asserts the same premise:

> In spite of all contentions that the dispensationalists are the consistent literalists, they start out in their biblical interpretation

---

320 Ibid.

321 Ibid., 29-30.

322 Ibid., 29.

323 Robert Saucy, "Is the Bible Important Today?" in *Understanding Christian Theology,* Charles Swindoll and Roy Zuck, editors, 131.

pretty much where everyone else does. They follow inductive, grammatical, historical method just as others do.[324]

An example of the progressive dispensationalist 'natural understanding' is evident in Saucy's understanding of the right hand of God in Ps. 110 and Acts 2:

> The entire Psalm, therefore, fits the picture of the Old Testament messianic hope, the reign of the Messiah on earth. The "right hand of God" is the position of messianic authority. Taking "throne" in its metaphorical sense as a "symbol of government," the right hand of God is also the Messiah's throne. It is probably in this sense that we are to understand Peter's reference to Christ as having been raised to sit on the throne of David."[325]

The certainty of the position is made clear in this statement: "The meaning of the 'right hand of God' in Psalm 110:1 and Acts 2:33 is, therefore, the position of messianic authority. It is the throne of David.[326]

---

324 John Gerstner, *Wrongly Dividing The Word Of Truth*, 91-92.

325 Robert Saucy, *The Case For Progressive Dispensationalism*, 71.

326 Ibid., 72.

This example of "natural understanding" is clearly not the literal grammatical historical approach utilized by classic dispensationalism. So then what is it? The writer explains,

> The outworking of the Old Testament prophetic hope necessarily involves some new aspects not clearly seen earlier. What was portrayed in the Old Testament as on single messianic movement was divided in the New Testament into two phases of fulfillment. The ascension of the Messiah during the first phase was therefore not plainly evident in the Old Testament. But this reality does not cancel out a future fulfillment in the full sense of the psalm.[327]

This is the concept that the NT makes complementary changes to the OT. Blaising and Bock further explain the concept, saying,

> The additional inclusion of some in the promise does not mean that the original recipients are thereby excluded. The expansion of promise need not mean the cancellation of earlier commitments God has made.[328]

---

327 Ibid., 71.

328 Blaising and Bock, *Progressive Dispensationalism*, 103.

They refer to this principle as the "complementary principle."[329]

Those holding to the complementary hermeneutic may at times seem baffled by distinctions in exegetical conclusions, attributing the differences to other factors (such as the interpreter's personality[330]), but in reality there is clearly a different hermeneutic in play here.

If Saucy is reticent to admit a difference in hermeneutical approach, Blaising and Bock seem a bit proud of the distinction, identifying the system as perhaps more refined than the literal grammatical historical approach:

> It should be noted that progressive dispensationalism is not an abandonment of "literal" interpretation for "spiritual" interpretation. Progressive dispensationalism is a *development* [emphasis mine] of "literal" interpretation into a more consistent historical-literary interpretation.[331]

Bock elaborates,

> When progressives speak of a complementary relationship between Old Testament and New

---

329 Ibid.

330 Ibid., 20.

331 Blaising and Bock, *Progressive Dispensationalism*, 52.

Testament texts, they are claiming that a normal, contextually determined reading often brings concepts from the Hebrew Scriptures together in the New Testament in a way that completes and expounds what was already present in the older portion of God's Word.[332]

While the progressive dispensation system affirms strongly such ideas as one stable meaning in texts, dual authorship, and progress of revelation,[333] it is evident nonetheless, as Elliott Johnson observes, that "what is affirmed is cast into question by what is done with texts."[334] And that which is achieved by the position falls far short of that which is stated.[335]

Theological Hermeneutic

While by necessity there must be a certain degree of preunderstanding in the hermeneutic process, elements which should be preunderstood are those regarding the text itself (i.e., words have meaning based on their historical grammatical usage) and how

---

332 Darrell L. Bock, "Hermeneutics of Progressive Dispensationalism," in *Three Central Issues in Contemporary Dispensationalism,* edited by Herbert W. Bateman IV (Grand Rapids: Kregel, 1999), 89.

333 Ibid., 94.

334 Elliott E. Johnson, "Response [to Darrell L. Bock," in Bateman, 101.

335 Ibid., 105.

to approach the text (the hermeneutic method), but this preunderstanding should not extend to *a priori* doctrinal conclusions.

It is noteworthy that the prerequisites forming the pillars of the theological method employed in presuppositional dispensationalism are not inconsistent with a non-theological hermeneutic. These prerequisites stem from a literal grammatical-historical hermeneutic and form the *a posteriori* basis as a *sine qua non*, or more specifically – the identifying conclusions of the theological system.

The *theological hermeneutic* in this context references an eisegetical grid used as the overriding factor in the hermeneutical process. John Calvin, dealing with the New Covenant of Jeremiah 31 demonstrates theological eisegesis when he explains the reason for his interpretive conclusion regarding the nature of the covenant:

> We hence see that this passage necessarily refers to the kingdom of Christ, for without Christ nothing could or ought to have been hoped for by the people, superior to the Law; for the Law was a rule of the most perfect doctrine. If then Christ be taken away, it is certain that we must abide in the Law.[336]

---

336 John Calvin, *Commentaries on the Book of the Prophet Jeremiah and the Lamentations*, translated by John Owen (Grand Rapids: Baker, 1989), 4:124-125.

Note his use of the word *we*, including the church in submission to the Law, in contrast to the literal reading of Jer. 31, which indicates that the Old Covenant (and the New) was made with Israel. Calvin's theological hermeneutic takes the form of *a priori* replacement theology – the view that the church has replaced Israel.

The theological hermeneutic is the basis of the Roman Catholic hermeneutic (the canonical dogmatic). The theological preunderstanding in this specific case deals with the belief that the church is mediatorial in the revelatory process:

> The theologian will appeal first to the presence of the revelatory Christ-event in her or his life. Thus does he or she say and mean, "I believe in Jesus Christ." Second, this personal faith is also recognized as mediated to an individual through the church community (both a concrete, local community and the abstract, centuries-old community of Christian tradition).[337]

Other Hermeneutic Considerations

The hermeneutic circle refers to the idea that in order to understand any single aspect of revelation, the whole must be understood. In the diagram below, in

---

337   Robert Grant and David Tracy, *A Short History of the Interpretation of the Bible* (Philadelphia: Fortress, 1985), 182.

order to rightly interpret #1, #4 must be understood; in order to understand #2, #3 must be grasped.

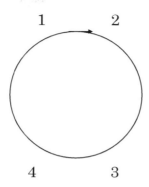

In Biblical hermeneutics the hermeneutic circle is a legitimate consideration, and would relate to the idea of cumulative or progressive revelation, underscoring the need to allow Scripture to interpret Scripture and to consider all parts when considering the whole, and the whole when considering the parts. The circle does not make interpretation impossible, but it does illustrate the need for grammatical-historical considerations to be made.

An intensification of issues related to the hermeneutic circle results in the hermeneutic spiral - here the hermeneutic circle is extended infinitely, as the meaning of the parts continuously changes as the whole is understood.

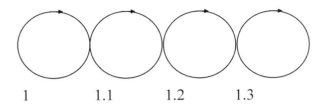

1   1.1   1.2   1.3

In the first go around the meaning of #1 is altered by the understanding of the whole to become #1.1. This then affects the whole differently, causing it to reflect in the second go around #1.2, which likewise affects the new understanding of the whole, thus altering it to be #1.3, ad infinitum.

As a result there is no final meaning or interpretation, for the meaning is constantly being changed to accommodate elements of perspective, preunderstanding, dialogue with the material, etc. In Biblical interpretation we do not find this principle present. The spiral assumes that attaining meaning is ultimately impossible, and this assumption is contradictory to the assertions of Scripture (1 Cor. 14:10-11; 2 Pet. 1:20-21, etc.).

The Literal Grammatical-Historical Hermeneutic

There are a number of challenges presented in the interpretation of the Bible. None so great as the fact that we are presently far removed from the cultural and linguistic settings of Biblical times. It is thus paramount that we understand the words of Scripture in proper context. This is the heart of the literal grammatical historical hermeneutic. Milton Terry offers a very worthy definition:

The grammatico-historical sense of a writer is such an interpretation of his language as is required by the laws of grammar and the facts of history. Sometimes we speak of the literal sense, by which we mean the most simple, direct, and ordinary meaning of phrases and sentences. By this term we usually denote a meaning opposed to the figurative or metaphorical. The grammatical sense is essentially the same as the literal, the one expression being derived from the Greek, the other from the Latin. But in English usage the word grammatical is applied rather to the arrangement and construction of words and sentences. By the historical sense we designate, rather, that meaning of an author's words which is required by historical considerations.[338]

This type of interpretation, therefore is grammatical in that it properly understands the utilization of words, phrases, sentences, etc., and is historical in that it properly understands the context in which the words, phrases, and sentences are used.

Again with clarity Terry further identifies the fundamental task of the grammatical-historical method as:

to gather from the Scriptures themselves the precise meaning which the writers intended to

---

338 Milton Terry, *Biblical Hermeneutics*, 203.

convey. It applies to the sacred books the same principles, the same grammatical process and exercise of common sense and reason, which we apply to other books.[339]

What did the words mean at the time they were written? Who wrote them? To whom were they written and why? What did the author mean by the use of his words? These are a few of the questions that the following principles seek to provide a method for answering.

To answer these questions, this writer suggests eight general principles for interpreting the Bible.

(1) God's word in its entirety is authoritative propositional truth.

(2) Everyone bears personal responsibility to study all of it.

(3) The study of God's word should affect lives, not simply increase knowledge (2 Tim. 3:16).

(4) Man cannot appraise Scripture without the aid of the Holy Spirit and the mind of Christ.

(5) Scripture is written in common language, bearing one meaning (univocal), and should be understood in its normative (literal historical grammatical) sense.

---

339 Ibid., 173.

When the plain sense makes sense seek no other sense. Regarding single meaning, Ames said,

> ...there is only one meaning for every place in Scripture. Otherwise the meaning of Scripture would not only be unclear and uncertain, but there would be no meaning at all – for anything which does not mean one thing surely means nothing.[340]

Milton Terry was also emphatic on single meaning:

> A fundamental principle in grammatico-historical exposition is that words and sentences can have but one signification in one and the same connection. The moment we neglect this principle we drift out upon a sea of uncertainty and conjecture.[341]

This is *exactly* why a consistent hermeneutic is prerequisite to a truly *Biblical* theology. Only one hermeneutic can be consistently applied, and only one hermeneutic stands firmly in practice upon single meaning, and that is the literal grammatical historical approach.

---

340   William Ames, *The Marrow of Theology*, ed. and trans. John D. Eusden (Boston: Pilgrim, 1968), 188.

341   Milton Terry, Biblical Hermeneutics, 205.

Terry further identifies the single meaning approach as being fairly straightforward and usually readily identifiable:

> Hence that meaning of a sentence which most readily suggests itself to a reader or hearer, is, in general, to be received as the true meaning, and that alone.[342]

The figurative sense should only be so identified when it is the plain sense or when specifically delineated by use of figures of speech or specifically symbolic language.

(6) Context determines the meaning of words, including the verses immediately surrounding the text, the paragraph and chapter, the whole book, the historical and cultural setting, and the literary form.

(7) Cumulative revelation determines context. It is God's word, and, therefore, He decides what it means; therefore, use Scripture to explain Scripture, rather than placing outside sources (church doctrine, theological conclusions, personal experience, etc.) above the authority of Scripture.

(8) There is distinction between primary and secondary application, and we must be sure not to confuse the two.

---

342   Ibid.

Others have stated axioms for governing Biblical interpretation:

Fruchtenbaum's / Cooper's Rules[343]
(1) The Golden Rule – When the plain sense makes common sense, seek no other sense.
(2) Law of Double Reference – Not to be confused with double fulfillment – simply stated, this law deals with prophecy referring to two separate events with no distinguishable separation in the immediate context. (e.g., Zech. 9:9-10)
(3) The Law of Recurrence – repetition of prophecy with added detail in the recurrent prophecy. (e.g., Gen. 1-2; Is. 30-31)
(4) The Law of Context
(5) The Law of Non-Contradiction –   (e.g., 1 Cor. 1:10-17 and 1 Pet. 3:21; 1 Jn. 1:8 and 3:9)

Hodge's Rules
(1) Words are to be taken in their plain historical sense.[344]
(2) Scripture is the work of one Mind (non-contradiction).

---

343   Adapted from Fruchtenbaum, who credits David Cooper. Arnold Fruchtenbaum, *Footsteps of the Messiah* (San Antonio: Ariel Press, 2004), 3-6.

344   Charles Hodge, *Systematic Theology* (Grand Rapids: Eerdmans, 1977), 1:187. However, in approaching the interpretation of prophecy, Hodge violated his own rule #1.

(3) Guidance of the Spirit is needed.

Benware's Rules of Interpreting Prophecy[345]
(1) Interpret the prophetic passage literally.
(2) Interpret by comparing prophecy with prophecy.
(3) Interpret in light of possible time intervals.
(4) Interpret in light of double reference (with great caution).
(5) Interpret figurative language Scripturally.

> Though the Bible is largely written in factual style to be interpreted as a normal, factual presentation, the Bible, like all other literature, uses figures of speech, and they should be recognized for their intended meaning. All forms of biblical literature ultimately yield a factual truth.[346]

Kaiser's Principles of General Hermeneutics[347]
(1) The Bible is to be interpreted by the same rules as other books.
(2) The principles of interpretation are as native and universal to man as is speech itself.

---

345   Paul N. Benware, *Understanding End Times Prophecy: A Comprehensive Approach* (Chicago: Moody, 1995), 21-30.

346   John Walvoord, *The Prophecy Knowledge Handbook* (Dallas: Dallas Seminary Press, 1990), 13.

347   Walter Kaiser, "Legitimate Hermeneutics," in *Inerrancy*, edited by Norman L. Geisler (Grand Rapids, MI: Zondervan, 1980), 118-122.

(3) My personal reception and application of an author's words is a distinct and secondary act from the need to first understand his words.

BASIC INTERPRETIVE PROCESS

The interpretive process described here is comprised of four basic steps: (1) observation –the gathering of data; (2) interpretation – the hypothesis based on the data; (3) correlation – verification of the data; and (4) application – the correct use of the data. Notably, prayer is not included as a separate step in the interpretive process, simply due to the necessity of prayer and fellowship in every step of Biblical interpretation. Therefore, prayer is an intrinsic and necessary aspect for the entire process.

(1) Observation (Gathering of Data)
Inductive Reasoning deals with observation and accumulating data to develop rules. This is the necessary approach for unbiased observation as the first step in the hermeneutical process. Robert Traina characterizes the inductive approach as foundational in this regard, due to the positioning of the interpreter as necessarily separate from that which he interprets:

> Now the Scriptures are distinct from the interpreter and are not an integral part of him. If the truths of the Bible already resided in man, there would be no need for the Bible....But the fact is that the Bible is an objective body of

literature which exists because man needs to know certain truths which he himself cannot know and which must come to him from without. Consequently, if he is to discover the truths which reside in this objective body of literature, he must utilize an approach which corresponds in nature with it, that is, an objective approach.[348]

While inductive and objective study is the ideal, there are obvious limitations when dealing with the human mind. Elliott Johnson extols certain advantages of inductive study but cautions that ultimately it

> Provides an inadequate model for a complete and sufficient study of Scripture...because there is no such thing as "pure" inductive study. We all necessarily bring premises or presuppositions to the study of the text. Those premises affect the way we comprehend the meaning, the way we understand – that is they have epistemological influence.[349]

Despite these limitations, inductive principles remain vital. Because of both the necessity and limitation of

---

348 Robert Traina, *Methodical Bible Study A New Approach to Hermeneutics* (Grand Rapids, MI: Francis Asbury Press, 1985), 7.

349 Elliott Johnson, *Expository Hermeneutics: An Introduction* (Grand Rapids, MI: Academie, 1990), 19.

the inductive approach, special care must be utilized in the undertaking of the interpretive task.

The observer must deal with a suitable sample size of observable material, understanding the primacy of context rather than simply text (the individual words themselves). The process of observation should consider *representativeness* – including in its scope like, or similar, subjects, making appropriate use of correlative data.

Deductive reasoning begins with a rule and applies it to observation. This type of reasoning is not ideal for basic observation as the first step of the hermeneutical approach, as it lends itself to eisegesis. Regarding inductive Biblical study, Chafer references as his second essential requirement the recognition that the laws of methodology are as essential to theology as to any science, denoting the importance in particular of the inductive approach.[350]

In practice, observe the use of key words and thoughts: repetition, emphasis, audience, setting, transitional words (therefore, thus, then, but, for this reason, etc.), imperatives, etc. Find the key thought of the sentence, then of the paragraph then of the chapter, then of the book.

Observe terms – normative terms, unique terms, frequently used terms, infrequently used terms, etc.

---

350 Chafer, *Systematic Theology*, 1:8.

Observe relationships – syntactical (subject to verb, pronoun to antecedent, etc.), comparison, contrast, repetition, continuity, continuation, climax, cruciality (e.g., Mt. 12 as a pivot point in Matthews Gospel), interchange, particularization, generalization, causation, substantiation, instrumentation, explanation, analysis, summarization, interrogation, harmony, etc.

Observe structural and contextual elements – biographical, historical, chronological, geographical, ideological, logical, etc. [351]

Ask the major questions: who, what, where, when, why, and how:

Who? Who is speaking to Hagar? Gen. 16:11-13 With whom is the New Covenant made? Jer. 31 Are all of Job's friends rebuked by God? Job 42:7-9 Who is the stated audience of Luke and Acts? Who is being discussed in Heb. 6 and 10?

What? What are the three obstacles of Eph. 2:2-3? What is the gift of Eph. 2:8-10? What is the occasion for Moses' song in Ex. 15? What are the divisions of the book of Habakkuk?

---

351 Adapted from Robert Traina, *Methodical Bible Study A New Approach to Hermeneutics*, 40-56.

Where? Gen. 22:2,14 and 2 Chr. 3:1 Eph. 1:3 Where is Timothy in 1 Tim. 1:3?

When? In Mt. 16:28 when would those standing there see His kingdom? When is eternal life given? Jn. 3:16? 2 Thes. 2:2, etc.

Why? Why did "the many" die, and who were they? Rom. 5:12-18 Why did Christ use parables, and to whom were they directed? Mt. 13:10-17.

How? How was Israel delivered from the hand of Egypt? Ex. 3:8, etc.

(2) Interpretation (The Hypothesis Based on Data)
    There are three particular dangers[352] of which to be wary: (a) misinterpretation – missing the message of the passage; (b) subinterpretation – failing to interpret the full message of the passage; and (c) suprainterpretation – reading too much into the meaning of the passage.

(3) Correlation (The Verification of Data)
    Cross reference, using immediate context first, then other contexts to understand similar ideas. How did the Thessalonians refer to the Gospel (1 Thes. 1)? On what is this based? Do we have this history (see

---

352 Robert Traina, *Methodical Bible Study A New Approach to Hermeneutics*, 181.

Acts 17)? How is the prophecy of Revelation 20:1-10 corroborated?

Corroborate (a) internally – within the book, (b) contextually – within other books of the Bible, and (c) externally – using other resources, commentaries, etc. (for case studies, examine Rom. 2:13, 3:20, 10:9-10; Jam. 1:22; 2:21-24)

(4) Application (The Correct Use of Data)

Just as the previous three steps required great care and discipline, the use of the data requires at least equal thoughtfulness. There is a prescribed order here that must not be confused.

Primary Application

As this first step, the interpreter is concerned with the meaning of the text *then* for the initial audience.

> In any interpretation it is most important to decide to whom the Scripture is addressed, as this involves the application of the statement.[353]

The audience will have already been identified in the interpretive process. Any exclusive truths must then be identified – those which apply specifically to that age or condition (e.g., Acts 15:23-29 – to the Gentile believers of Antioch, Syria, and Cilicia regarding how to relate to Jewish believers). General truths should also be

---

353 John Walvoord, *The Prophecy Knowledge Handbook*, 13.

recognized (again, regarding Acts 15:23-29– providing for this same audience a general principle of consideration toward sensitive cultural issues); these are pertinent to specific audiences for any age or condition.

Secondary Application

Kaiser aptly defines the significance of this step in the interpretive process:

> If the key hermeneutical question is..."What was the Biblical author's meaning when he wrote a particular text?" then we must address ourselves to another question, which has also become troublesome...: "What are the implications of that single meaning for those who live and read that text in a different time and culture?"[354]

It is here that the general principle makes connection with the general audience. The principle can be identified as generally doctrinal, as providing a case study or an example, or a historical narrative for the overall understanding of the unfolding of events. All Scripture is God-breathed and useful for the growth of the believer (2 Tim. 3:16), and therefore all Scripture is applicable to every believer – but only after it has been first rightly understood in context.

---

354 Walter Kaiser, "Legitimate Hermeneutics," 138.

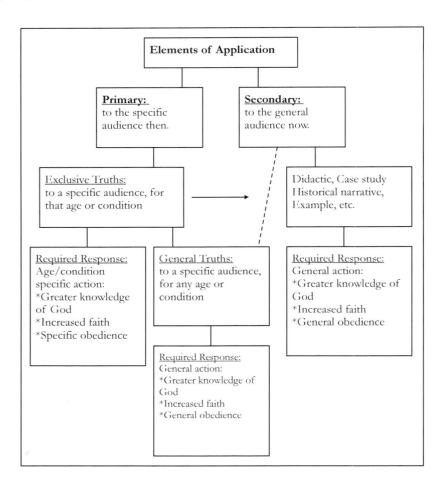

The interpreter must exercise extreme caution here, as a hurried application can often result in a misappropriated one. Also of importance is the effective carrying out of each step in the interpretive process to ensure continuous accuracy resulting in the proper usage and application of the text.

Approaching Individual Book Studies
(1) First reading   - for gleaning overall message, observation of standout words, themes, etc.

(2) Second reading - for major thought, thematic, and dialogic divisions.

(3) Third reading – further attention given to context and difficult passages.

(4) Outline the book based on identified internal divisions.

(5) Develop introductory material and setting by correlation using Biblical chronology (e.g., the relation of the ministries of Haggai and Zechariah to Ezra 5-6, and the Thessalonian letters to Acts 17-18).

(6) Verify outline based on context gleaned in correlation.

(7) Begin exegetical process for verse analysis.

Processes

in Biblical Theology

Three processes, in sequential order of importance, form the backbone of Biblical theology: (1) exegetical; (2) synthetic; and (3) systematic. To varying degree these three are interdependent – a healthy synthetic approach aids in formulating a proper systematic approach, and vice versa; likewise, healthy synthetic and systematic approaches help provide correlative evidence that sound exegesis has been achieved (Scripture interprets Scripture) – yet it is a vital reality that exegesis forms the foundation and must therefore be the first process in developing a Biblical theology.

In terms of the forest /trees analogy the exegetical approach is the examination of the individual trees – noting the minutest details; the synthetic approach looks at the forest as a whole; the systematic catalogs the types of trees in the forest into like kinds, subsets, etc. In other words, to gain an excellent understanding of the entire forest, all three approaches are helpful.

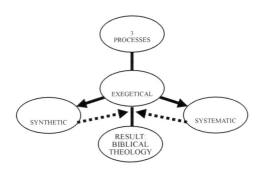

THE EXEGETICAL PROCESS
THE BUILDING BLOCKS OF BIBLICAL THEOLOGY

The first procedure of the theologian is exegetical.[355]

The term *exegesis* is derived from a compound Greek term meaning "to lead out," and refers to the application of hermeneutic principles. Whereas hermeneutics refers to the principles themselves, exegesis carries them out. Hermeneutics is the theory. Exegesis is the practice. Gordon Fee uses the term in reference to

The historical investigation into the meaning of the Biblical text. Exegesis, therefore, answers the question, What did the Biblical author mean? It has to do both with what he said (the content itself) and why he said it at any given point (the literary context). Furthermore, exegesis is primarily

---

355 W.G.T. Shedd, *Dogmatic Theology*, 1: 11.

concerned with intentionality: What did the author intend his original readers to understand?[356]

It should here be noted that study in the original languages is necessary for accuracy of understanding. The exegetical process can only be fully conducted in the original languages, and thus exegetical study in the English Bible is limited in effectiveness. It is notable that eras of significant growth in church history have been accompanied by renewed emphasis to Biblical study in the original languages, and that eras of stagnancy generally had no such emphasis.

It is this writer's intent to encourage the reader to pursue such studies, as this pursuit will afford the Bible student a much greater depth in Biblical study. Milton Terry is likewise emphatic that without such pursuit the grammatical-historical understanding is unattainable. He says,

> The grammatico-historical exegete...will investigate the language and import of each book with fearless independence. He will master the language of the writer, the particular dialect which he used, and his particular style and manner of expression. He will inquire into the circumstances under which he wrote, the manners and customs of his age, and the purpose or object which he had in view.[357]

---

356   Gordon Fee, *New Testament Exegesis, A Handbook For Students and Pastors* (Philadelphis, PA: Westminster, 1983), 21.

357 Milton Terry, *Biblical Hermeneutics*, 173.

The exegetical process involves conducting a detailed and thorough analysis of the text in order to arrive at a correct interpretation and proper utilization of the passage. The process can be laborious, and sometimes even tedious (it is not without reason that Paul demands diligence from Timothy in 2 Tim. 2:15), yet handling accurately the word of truth is a very rewarding process.

Exegesis is not a task simply for the scholar, but is a necessary task for developing a deeper relationship with the Lord, and resulting in a proper worldview – a Biblical worldview. The process is a challenging one, and certainly a joyful one. The exegete should be constantly aware, while studying the pages of Scripture, of direct encounter with God. God has spoken, and hearing and studying His word should have profound effect on the student of Scripture. As Schreiner says,

> If one's heart never sings when doing exegesis, then the process has not reached its culmination. And if one has never trembled when doing exegesis (Isa. 66:2), then one is not listening for the voice of God.[358]

The process begins, then, with excitement, sobriety, diligence, and constant prayerful consideration

---

358 Thomas Schreiner, *Interpreting the Pauline Epistles* (Grand Rapids, MI: Baker Books, 1990), 18.

throughout, as nine fundamental steps are undertaken: (1) verify text and translation; (2) understand background and context; (3) identify structure; (4) identify grammatical and syntactical keys; (5) identify lexical keys; (6) identify Biblical context; (7) identify theological context; (8) secondary verification; and (9) development of exposition.

(1) Verify Text and Translation

(a) Verify limits of the text. Try to deal with the passage as a propositional unit or a complete thought. Avoiding unnatural and clumsy divisions involves recognizing and identifying natural and elegant ones. Note the unnatural chapter division of Habbakkuk 2:1. The initial verse is a continuation of the previous dialogical unit beginning in 1:12. Also, compare the context of Mark 9:1-2 with the division between Matthew 16 and 17. As is the case in every step of the exegetical process, access to the text in the original languages is crucial.

(b) Verify the best reading/text based on the following evidences for a manuscript reading:

> External evidences:
> (1) That which is supported by earliest external sources is generally authentic.

(2) Age, location, and character, rather than number, of manuscript is more determinate of authenticity.

(3) When there is broadly evidenced conflict, special attention should be placed on agreement between manuscripts originally separated by the greatest distances.

(4) Great care and attention to detail must be used in following these evidences.

Internal evidences:
(1) The reading which is congruent with a writer's style, nature, and context is to be preferred over that which lacks these evidences.

(2) Shorter reading preferred over the longer.

(3) The difficult reading preferred over the simpler.

(4) The reading from which other readings most likely developed is to be preferred. (e.g., 1 Thes. 2:7 *nepioi* vs. *epioi*).[359]

---

359   Adapted from Terry's evidences, Milton Terry, *Biblical Hermeneutics*, 132-133.

Also note the *Majority Text/Textus Receptus* readings of John 7:53-8:11; 1 Timothy 3:16; and John 3:13. Note the phrase 'good will toward men' Luke 2:14. Was His body broken or not (see 1 Cor 11:24)? Compare Mark 3:20 with Matthew 8:20. Does Mark 3:20 indicate Jesus had a home? Or is *home* a less than desirable translation of *oikon*?

For study in the English Bible, study the passage in several different translations and identify any key differences or issues in the translations. Note key differences in the following passages:

Hosea 6:7 – KJV vs. NASB: Adam or no Adam? Does this imply an Adamic covenant?

Amos 4:4 – compare KJV, NIV, NKJV, NASB, three years vs. three days.

Luke 9:44 – compare KJV, NASB, and NIV – note the NIV's use of dynamic equivalency.

John 3:10 in the NASB Christ references Nicodemus as *the teacher of Israel*, while in the KJV Christ identifies him as *a master of Israel*. Note the differences in the article (definite versus indefinite). In English there is significant distinction between a master and a teacher. What about in Jesus' day? Which is the more accurate rendering?

John 3:36 – *believeth not* (KJV) vs. does not obey (NASB). This is an example of a translational dispute, which only arises in the translation from Greek to English.

John 6:47 – *on me* (KJV) vs. other translations which omit the phrase. This is an example of a textual dispute. In this case there is variation in the manuscripts of this passage.

Acts 12:4 – Easter (KJV) or Passover (NASB)?

Philippians 2:5 in the NASB records the command *have this attitude in yourselves*, while the KJV tells the reader to *let this mind be in you*. Is there a significant difference between attitude and mind? Which is the better rendering?

1 John 5:7 – compare the significant differences between the NASB and KJV renderings.

(c) Write your passage overview identifying the following elements:

(1) Identify variants and/or translation differences in the text.

(2) Briefly summarize the passage.

(3) Summarize your current understanding of the theological impact of the passage.

(4) Identify doctrinal presuppositions you have in approaching the passage.

(2) Understand Background and Context

(a) Identify, defend, and explain the significance of literary form/genre.

This writer suggests that there are essentially five basic literary forms in Scripture, and that the classification of Biblical material is as follows:

Primary Historical Narrative – historical narrative which carries forth in deliberate fashion the chronology of Biblical history: includes Genesis, Exodus, Numbers, Joshua, Judges, 1 and 2 Samuel, 1 and 2 Kings, Ezra, Nehemiah, The Gospels, and Acts.

Complementary Historical Narrative - Books of historical narrative which complement (inasmuch as they are contemporaries of) the primary historical narrative. This category includes Job, Leviticus, Deuteronomy, Ruth, 1 and 2 Chronicles, and Esther.

Poetry and Praise – includes Psalms, Proverbs, Ecclesiastes, Song of Solomon, and Lamentations.

Prophecy – interspersed with historical narrative and poetry, this form presents, usually, God's revelation of judgment and restoration. Isaiah, Jeremiah, Ezekiel, Daniel (although not included in the Nebi'im section of the Hebrew Old Testament, its form is prophetic and complementary historical), the twelve minor prophets, and the New Testament book of Revelation.

Epistles – letters including Pauline and General (Hebrews, James, 1 and 2 Peter, 1, 2, and 3 John, and Jude).

(b) Research key questions regarding the background of the book (authorship, composition, purpose, etc.). Answer key introductory questions:

(1) Who wrote this book? (2) To whom did he write? (3) Where did he write it? (4) When did he write it? (5) What was the occasion of his writing? (6) What was the purpose for which he wrote? (7) What were the circumstances of the author when he wrote? (8) What were the circumstances of those to whom he wrote? (9) What glimpses does the book give into the life and character of the author? (10) What are the leading ideas of the book? (11) What is the central truth of the book? (12) What are the characteristics of the book?[360]

(c) Summarize background and context highlighting the following elements: historical, social, geographical, authorship, date, literary form.

(d) Identify how these findings are significant to interpretation of the passage. For example, as Luke is a physician (Col. 4:14), does his perspective influence on

---

360   R.A. Torrey, *You and Your Bible* (Westwood, N.J: Revell, 1958), 97.

his Gospel or Acts (i.e., medical terms, etc.)? Why is the dating of Daniel crucial to the message of the book? What is the object of Paul's criticism in 1 Timothy, and how is that related to higher criticism of 1 Timothy? How should we understand the timing and chronology of Paul's imprisonment, cited in 2 Timothy? What internal clues are there regarding the authorship of the book of Hebrews?

(3) Identify Structure

(a) Identify structural keys/developments (development of narrative, development of argument, chiasm, etc.).

Note the narrative- by- character divisions, as well as the *toledoth* divisions of Genesis; compare 2 Kings 18-20 with Isaiah 36-39. The context of each passage provides further background information for the other.

Note the narrative and geographical divisions of Acts 1:8 providing an outline of the book. Also present is division based on prominent characters (i.e., Peter and Paul).

John 20:30-31 provides the identification of structural keys in John's gospel as signs pointing to the identity of Jesus. The book can therefore be outlined based on the manifestation of these signs. John's own characterization of the book impacts the understanding of chronological issues within the book; Luke 1:1-4 provides similar information on Luke's gospel; Revelation 1:19 provides a chronological key to the divisions of the prophetic book; observe chiasms in

John 1:1-2, Ecclesiastes 11:3-12:2, and Genesis 1-12, etc.

(b) Outline the book, identifying major and minor divisions.

(c) Identify the importance of the structure in the interpretation of the passage. Consider, for example the structure of Habakkuk's prophecy. The structure reveals a dialogue between God and Habakkuk.

Habakkuk: The Sovereignty of God	1st Petition: Why Is Wickedness Not Judged? 1:1-4
	God's Answer: Judgment Coming via the Chaldeans 1:5-11
	2nd Petition: Why Use the Wicked To Judge Israel? 1:12-2:1
	God's Answer: The 5 Woes 2:2-20
	Prayer of Habakkuk: God is Sovereign 3

(4) Identify Grammatical and Syntactical Keys

(a) Identify historical/cultural references, figurative language, rhetorical devices, quotations, key sentence structure, clauses, etc.

Revelation 12 is a narrative describing some important signs. What is sometimes understood to be figurative language in this context is actually not figurative at all, but rather is a literal description of a figure, i.e., a sign.

Notice the consistent *grace and peace* greetings of Paul appearing at the beginning of each of his letters. The only exceptions are found in his letters to Timothy and Titus. The greetings are culturally significant, grace appealing to the gentile mind and peace appealing to the Jewish mind. What then is the significance of Paul's alteration of the greeting?

Note rhetorical devices employed in the text. Dialogical method is used by Paul in Romans 9:14, 19, 22, 30, and 32. Question and answer adds to the clarity of the passage and demonstrates the use of logical reasoning in Paul's argument, but also indicates the limitations of human logic (9:19-20). Parenesis (encouragement) is found in Romans 12:1-15:13; 1 Thessalonians, etc. Other devices include judicial, deliberative, epideictic (demonstrative, persuasive), etc. Jesus uses figurative language (metaphor) in John 11:11 in describing Lazarus' death. The metaphor is also applied in Psalm 17:15 and 1 Thessalonians 4:14.

Acts 2:38 includes an important imperative regarding repentance and baptism that seems, in the English translation, to indicate that repentance and baptism are both necessary for forgiveness. However, the imperative *repent* is second person plural while the *be baptized* is third person singular (let him or her – each one – be baptized), and the pronoun (your sins) is also second person. This grammatical key, not seen clearly in the English, is critical to understanding the verse.

In the creation account of Genesis 1 each day is described as consisting of evening and morning. The order (evening first) is significant. How does this relate to Jewish culture? How impactful is this syntactical repetition in defining the scope of an individual day (i.e., 24 hours)? Does this phrasing lend credence to a literal six-day creation? How can there be evening and morning before the sun is created?

Notice the phrasing of Psalm 1:1. There is a progression from action to inaction (walk, stand, sit). How is this significant in describing the blessed man?

Identify the *mouth* and *heart* clauses of Romans 10:1-10. Notice the significance of these clauses and their relation to Deuteronomy 30:14 (quoted in Rom. 10:8) in revealing the clarity of the often misunderstood assertions of 9-10.

What is the *rock* in Mt. 16:18? What is the grammatical significance of the distinction between the two word endings: *petros* is a piece of rock or a stone, *petra* is a large rock or boulder. Note correlation of 1 Peter. 2:8, Romans 9:33, and 1 Corinthians 10:4.

(b) Diagram sentences in original language to ensure grammatical and syntactical understanding.

(c) Summarize the importance of these grammatical keys to the interpretation of the passage.

(5) Identify Lexical Keys

Ask this key question: What words appear most often in the whole section?[361]

(a) Identify key words by emphasis.

(b) Do word studies on key words in the passage using three basic steps:

(1) identify, define (grammar and etymology), and parse (morphology) the word with aid of a lexicon.
(2) examine usage of the word in other contexts (a concordance is particularly helpful here).

(3) summarize key concepts arising from key words.

Identify a significant connection between Exodus 3:14 and John 8:24, 28, 58; What is the key difference between Exodus 7:13, 22; 8:19; 9:7, 35 and 8:15, 32; 9:34? How many times is the phrase *under the sun* used in the book of Ecclesiastes, and why is it significant to the theme of the book? Note *yom* in the Old Testament, quantified by context, sometimes as 24-hour period (i.e., Gen. 1), sometimes including a longer period (such as the day of the Lord (Joel, etc.). What is meant by the term *weeks* as translated (NASB) in Dan.

---

361   Gordon Fee, *New Testament Exegesis: A Handbook For Students and Pastors*, 33.

9:24-27? What words for love are used in the dialogue recorded in John 21:15-17? Why are they significant?

What are some important words in John 1:1-18, Romans 5:1-11, Galatians 3:16-22, and Ephesians 1:1-14? How are they used? What is their significance? Note the NIV rendering of 1 Corinthians 5:5, *sinful nature* as a translation of the Greek *sarx*, what would be a better rendering? How is the meaning of *Savior* pivotal in 1 Timothy 4:10? What unique word is repeated six times in Revelation 19:1-7? What does it mean? How is the word connected to Psalm 111:1; 112:1; and 113:1, etc.?

(6) Identify Biblical Context

(a) Identify the overall theme of the book. By completing the first steps in the exegetical process, the theme of the chosen book should by now be apparent.

(b) Summarize the immediate context surrounding the passage.

Note how important it is to recognize the immediate context in relation to the following passages:

Genesis 49:10 (for context definition, see 49:1) — the immediate context demonstrates the significance of the statement regarding Judah. What *kind* of statement was it?

Exodus 20 – The Ten Commandments. Should this passage apply to the church today? Why or why not? How does the immediate context clarify the issue?

2 Chronicles 7:14-15 – This passage has often been applied by the church to the church. Is this appropriate? What does the immediate context say about the intended audience? What kinds of consequences are promised? What is the significance?

Job 34:37 – Does Elihu personally indict Job for sinning?

Psalm 58:6 – How is this an appropriate prayer?

Isaiah 6:8 – This sounds like a very bold response by Isaiah. How do the preceding events alter that perception of this passage?

Ezekiel 40-48 – What time period does the context suggest?

Matthew 13 – Why is Christ speaking in parables. What is the significance?

Mathew 16:27-28 – Contextually, to what event is Christ referring to? (Note the chapter division of Mk. 9, how it fits the context better than the chapter division between Mt. 16-17).

Acts 2:4 – How does the immediate context define *to speak with other tongues*? See 2:11.

Galatians 3:28-29 – How does the immediate context define and limit the elimination of all distinctions?

Ephesians 3:3 – How is *the mystery* defined contextually?

Hebrews 6:4-6 – Who is being described, believer or unbeliever?

(c) Compare the overall theme with the individual passage and the immediate context surrounding the passage. Identify how the individual passage, defined by the immediate context, contributes to the overall theme of the book.

(7) Identify Theological Context

(a) Identify theological principles in the passage.

Recognize that generally larger contexts must be observed in order to identify theological principles, although sometimes, key individual words can provide significant theological framework (i.e., justification, redemption, propitiation, predestination, etc.).

What theological principles of the church (ekklesia) are presented in Matthew 16:13-20? Who is building the church? What is the scope of the church? Note the importance of a sufficient lexical and grammatical study here, as "upon this rock" has been understood in several different ways: (1) the rock is Peter – a foundational understanding for the development of apostolic succession, (2) the rock is the earth – and argument for the earthly scope of the church and a cog in the defense of replacement theology, (3) the rock is the confession that Peter made – detaching this phrase from key prophetic significance, and (4) the rock is Christ (the view that properly considers each of the necessary exegetical elements).

Note Peter's explanation in 1 Peter 2:4-10 appealing to Isaiah 8:14, etc. If the previous steps (grammatical, syntactical, lexical, contextual, etc.) are not given sufficient attention, the theological principles in a passage can be significantly misunderstood, leading to wide ranging and inaccurate conclusions.

In John 14:1-3, how is the rapture theologically present, yet grammatically and syntactically absent? Christ here does not detail the rapture, yet through future revelation and theology developed later (i.e., 1 Thes. 4; 1 Cor. 15, etc.), the rapture is in view here. In Romans 3:21-31, what is the theological significance of righteousness? In Ephesians 1:1-14, what is meant by predestination? How does the principle of predestination impact the passage? In James 2:14-26, what is the theological relationship between faith and works?

(b) Connect the principles to the overall context of the book.

What significant theological principle arises from Romans 5:12, 17-19? How does it support the argument of the epistle? In Galatians 3:15-29, what was the purpose for the Law? How does this relate to the theological theme of the epistle?

(c) Compare with far reaching contexts to verify theological principles.

In James 3:1-12, regarding the theology of the tongue, compare Ephesians 4:15, 29-30; 5:4, Colossians 3:5-10; 4:5-6, and also Proverbs 6:17, 10:20 and 31, 12:18-19, 15:2 and 4, 17:4; 18:21, 21:6 and 23; 25:15 and 23, 26:28, and 28:23. What theological principle is clarified by a comparison of John 14:1-3, 1 Corinthians 15:50-58, and 1 Thessalonians 4:13-18 with the outline of the book of Revelation? What key theological principle is outlined in Ephesians 2-3, and how does a comparison of Jeremiah 31, Romans 9-11, 2 Corinthians 3, Galatians 3 and 6:16, 1 John 2:25, and Rev. 19:11-14, 20:1-6 clarify the issue?

(d) Summarize theological themes and principles based on context.

(8) Secondary Verification
Primary verification (as worked out in previous steps) comes from the contextual examination of Scripture – first the immediate context in an exegetical verification, and then more far reaching contexts in a systematic verification. By this point primary verification should be effectively completed. Secondary

verification offers a further opportunity to challenge one's exegetical work by comparing it to the exegetical work of other godly and learned exegetes.

Valuable external resources at this stage include introductions (generally to Old or New Testament studies), surveys (generally offering overviews of Old and New Testaments or individual books), handbooks and dictionaries (providing general outlines and definitions), and exegetical commentaries (providing verse analysis and other key exegetical information).

(a) Utilize a number of resources covering the selected passage.

Avoid locking into one commentator, but rather utilize a plurality. Comparing an exegesis with only one commentator generally does not offer enough of a broad view to soundly test the exegetical process. The purpose of this process is not to simply find agreement with an esteemed commentator, but rather to provide a critical look at the exegetical work already done.

(b) Identify hermeneutic method of the commentators.

This is a vital step, not only in assessing a commentary's validity and usefulness, but also in developing a critical approach to Biblical research literature. Developing an awareness of the commentator's presuppositions, theological bents, and methodologies is key in both areas.

(c) Summarize agreements and differences in the interpretations of the commentators.

Exegetically and critically examine each commentator's agreements and differences. Have they covered key elements, or have they glossed over difficult or controversial issues? Particularly in light of the hermeneutic method utilized, certain conclusions can be expected. An allegorical approach will generally lead to replacement theology conclusions. Spiritualization will often de-emphasize primary applications. Theological hermeneutics can often lead to wild and unverifiable conclusions. Do those commentators using similar methodologies arrive at similar conclusions?

(d) Defend your interpretation or alter it in light of your findings.

If secondary verification uncovers holes in one's exegetical process, the entire process should be reviewed in order to determine the cause. What is desired here is not only a refinement of the conclusions regarding the particular passage, but also a refinement in the overall process – ensuring that the next exegetical exercise is sounder than the previous.

(9) Development of Exposition

(a) Provide verse analysis - running commentary on the passage.

Generally this can be as simple as basic summary of each passage in relation to the overall context, or it can be as complex as including every discovered element of exegetical insight. In either case, and all those in between, the content should be the direct result of the exegetical study.

(b) Summarize principle, primary application, and secondary application.

If a universal principle is evident in the passage, it should be noted as crucial to both primary and secondary application. Primary application relates directly to the original intended audience, while secondary application relates to later audiences, including the exegete. Principles and applications should be stated with clarity and conciseness to ensure that keys have been grasped.

(c) Identify the impact of the passage on your own life and begin to act upon it.

Just as throughout the entire study process, the passage should have personal impact. James exhorts believers to be doers of the word and not merely hearers (Jam. 1:22-27), and later cautions against being too "ready" to teach. Before the edification of others must come the application to one's self. Ezra's attitude and actions were exemplary:

For Ezra had set his heart to study the law of the Lord, and to practice it and to teach His statutes and ordinances in Israel (Ezra 7:10).

Ezra's priorities show a focus on (1) diligence necessary for study and learning, (2) being an effectual doer and practitioner of all that God had said, and (3) only then being a faithful teacher of Scripture.

At this point it can be easy to focus on how the passage will be delivered to a target audience or congregation, but the godly examples of the Bible demonstrate how important personal devotion and godliness first is before God. Practice comes before teaching. The adage says, "Them that can't do, teach," but in reality the truer adage should be "Them that would teach (and them that wouldn't) must *do*."

(d) Develop a presentation of the passage for the edification of others.

Here is an effective basic pattern for the structure and delivery of an exposition: (1) reading of the entire passage to be covered, (2) prayer for guidance in study, (3) basic summary of background and context, (4) reading of individual section (sentence, verse, or paragraph), (5) relating of section to the overall context, (6) summary of each section's verse analysis and exegetical key points, (7) highlight principles and applications at appropriate points, (8) offer brief summary of overall exegetical context, highlights, and principles and applications, and finally, (9) prayer for wisdom and strength in order to be an effectual doer of the word, to the glory of God.

Examine the exposition recorded in Nehemiah 8:1-12. Note in particular the emphases regarding both the content and the response. The content – the textbook - was the word of God (8:1). It was prayerfully considered (8:6). It was opened and read from (8:3, 5). It was explained, to ensure that the hearers understood

(8:8), and it provided calls to action and encouragement (8:10). In response, the people gathered to hear it (8:1). It was heard attentively (8:3) and respectfully (8:5). It was received as true (8:6). It was received patiently (8:7). It elicited personal response (8:9). It resulted in worship of God (8:6). It was understood and acted upon (8:12).

SYNTHETIC PROCESS
OVERVIEW OF BIBLICAL THEOLOGY

> A view of the whole of Scripture and the relationship of the various parts which compose the whole is essential for fully appreciating the Biblical revelation. In brief fashion you are introduced to this approach, especially in the historical books of the Old and New Testaments. The emphasis is upon the total message or theme of each book or books and the relation of each part to that theme.[362]

The synthetic approach, from the Greek *sunthetos,* meaning *combined or brought together,* emphasizes a thematic thread within divine revelation. While there are a number of such threads that can be highlighted, the primary motif is the glorification of God, the means

---

362 C.I. Scofield, *Scofield Bible Correspondence Course Volume I Introduction to the Scriptures* (Chicago: Moody Bible Institute, 1959), 12.

to that end being the proclaiming and fulfilling of various promises and covenants.

A synthetic examination will handle not just the individual book, but will also seek to relate it to the whole of Scripture. For example the prophecies of Daniel can be well understood without the aid of the broader context of other Biblical books; however, the prophecies of Daniel fit like pieces of a jigsaw puzzle within this broader context, both contributing to the panorama of the ages, and having a great light shed upon their details by such related books as Ezekiel and Revelation. The synthetic process, then, becomes a very necessary element of Bible study.

Two key emphases (among perhaps many) of a synthetic approach are (1) the Biblical Covenants, and (2) the Dispensations.

Highlights of the Biblical Covenants

A covenant is an agreement or compact between two parties. The Hebrew word *berith*, from a root meaning *to cut* is translated covenant. A covenant is a "cutting," referring to the cutting of animals into two parts, and the passing between them by the contracting individuals (Gen. 15; Jer. 34:18, 19). This definition requires two parties to ratify in some form.

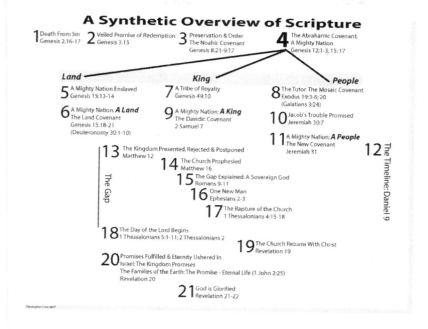

A Synthetic Overview of Scripture

1 Death From Sin
Genesis 2:16-17

2 Veiled Promise of Redemption
Genesis 3:15

3 Preservation & Order
The Noahic Covenant
Genesis 8:21-9:17

4 The Abrahamic Covenant:
A Mighty Nation
Genesis 12:1-3; 15:17

Land ——

King

People

5 A Mighty Nation Enslaved
Genesis 15:13-14

7 A Tribe of Royalty
Genesis 49:10

8 The Tutor: The Mosaic Covenant
Exodus 19:3-6; 20
(Galatians 3:24)

6 A Mighty Nation: *A Land*
The Land Covenant
Genesis 15:18-21
(Deuteronomy 30:1-10)

9 A Mighty Nation: *A King*
The Davidic Covenant
2 Samuel 7

10 Jacob's Trouble Promised
Jeremiah 30:7

11 A Mighty Nation: *A People*
The New Covenant
Jeremiah 31

12 The Timeline: Daniel 9

13 The Kingdom Presented, Rejected & Postponed
Matthew 12

14 The Church Prophesied
Matthew 16

15 The Gap Explained: A Sovereign God
Romans 9-11

16 One New Man
Ephesians 2-3

17 The Rapture of the Church
1 Thessalonians 4:15-18

The Gap

18 The Day of the Lord Begins
1 Thessalonians 5:1-11; 2 Thessalonians 2

19 The Church Returns With Christ
Revelation 19

20 Promises Fulfilled & Eternity Ushered In
Israel: The Kingdom Promises
The Families of the Earth: The Promise - Eternal Life (1 John 2:25)
Revelation 20

21 God is Glorified
Revelation 21-22

Christopher Cone 2007

Certain promises of God, traditionally identified as covenants, will not be considered as covenants here, due to a literal hermeneutic: they are never referred to as covenants, and they involve promises by God, and have no ratification as covenants, but rather serve as promises to be kept. These promises include: (1) the "Edenic" (Gen. 1:26-31; 2:16-17), (2) the "Adamic" (Gen. 3:16-19), (3) and the "Solomonic" (1 Kgs. 9:1-9). (Note: the Land Covenant of Deut. 30 is not referred to by the word *covenant*, however, as it is a recounting of the land element of the Abrahamic Covenant, it will be so identified as covenant rather than simply promise.)

These promises are absolutely foundational to a proper understanding of Scripture, and they must not be under-emphasized. But technically, it is better that they not be identified as covenants.

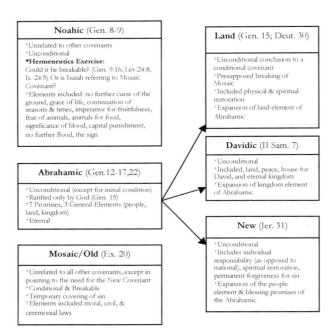

Noahic (Gen. 8-9)

⁺ Unrelated to other covenants
⁺ Unconditional
*Hermeneutics Exercise:
Could it be breakable? (Gen. 9:16; Lev.24:8; Is. 24:5) Or is Isaiah referring to Mosaic Covenant?
⁺ Elements included: no further curse of the ground, grace of life, continuation of seasons & times, imperative for fruitfulness, fear of animals, animals for food, significance of blood, capital punishment, no further flood, the sign.

Abrahamic (Gen.12-17,22)

⁺ Unconditional (except for initial condition)
⁺ Ratified only by God (Gen. 15)
⁺ 7 Promises, 3 General Elements (people, land, kingdom)
⁺ Eternal

Mosaic/Old (Ex. 20)

⁺ Unrelated to all other covenants, except in pointing to the need for the New Covenant
⁺ Conditional & Breakable
⁺ Temporary covering of sin
⁺ Elements included moral, civil, & ceremonial laws

Land (Gen. 15; Deut. 30)

⁺ Unconditional conclusion to a conditional covenant
⁺ Presupposed breaking of Mosaic
⁺ Included physical & spiritual restoration
⁺ Expansion of land element of Abrahamic

Davidic (II Sam. 7)

⁺ Unconditional
⁺ Included, land, peace, house for David, and eternal kingdom
⁺ Expansion of kingdom element of Abrahamic

New (Jer. 31)

⁺ Unconditional
⁺ Includes individual responsibility (as opposed to national), spiritual restoration, permanent forgiveness for sin
⁺ Expansion of the people element & blessing promises of the Abrahamic

Israel: The Eternal Promises

Genesis 12:1-3 - Abrahamic Covenant
Deuteronomy 30:1-10 - Land Covenant
II Samuel 7:8-17 - Davidic Covenant
Jeremiah 31:27-40 - New Covenant

EARTHLY

Daniel 9 - The 70 Weeks of Israel Prophecied
Matthew 12 - Israel rejects her Messiah

Romans 9-11

Veiled Allusion

The Church: The Eternal Promise

Genesis 12:3c - Blessing to the nations
Jeremiah 31:34b - Forgiveness of sin
Joel 2:28 - Holy Spirit predicted
John 16 - Holy Spirit promised

HEAVENLY

Direct Revelation

Matthew 16:13-20 - First prophecy of the church
Acts 2 - Birth of the church
Ephesians 1-3,5 - The mystery of the church
Galatians 3-4 - The economy of the church
I John 2:25 - The promise defined
Revelation 1-3 - The conclusion of the church
I Thessalonians 4:13-18 - the rapture of the church

Revelation 4-18 - Jacob's Trouble:
The Tribulation (Daniel's 70th
week)

(church in heaven)

Revelation 19 - The King Comes

Revelation 19 -Christ returns
with His bride

Revelation 20 - The Kingdom
Revelation 21-22 - Eternity

Revelation 20 - The Kingdom
Revelation 21-22 - Eternity

363

363 Chart from Christopher Cone, *The Promises of God: A Bible
Survey* (Arlington, TX: Exegetica Publishing, 2005), 181.

Chronological Factors of Division: The Dispensations
    One writer underscores an inadequacy in our understanding of dispensations, as he observes,

> ...an adequate definition of dispensationalism probably remains to be written. As soon as the suffixes are added to the word the subject is transferred immediately from Biblical to theological grounds. The recent literature on the subject has made it necessary to revise the theological definition....The current conception of the term in the popular mind is entirely inadequate.[364]

Despite their ring, these are not contemporary words. They are not banter akin to the present debate between classical and progressive dispensationalists. In 1945 Arnold Ehlert penned these words in a Dallas Theological Seminary doctoral dissertation (approved by John Walvoord), and they reveal dissatisfaction with traditional and contemporary definitions. This present discussion seeks to address certain inadequacies in definition and division.

    Dispensation, derived from the Latin *dispensatio (economy, management, or administration*[365]*)*, is the KJV translation of the Greek word *oikonomia* (e.g., 1

---

364 Arnold Ehlert, "A Bibliography of Dispensationalism," Th.D Dissertation, Dallas Theological Seminary, November 1945, 33.

365   D.P. Simpson, *Cassell's Latin Dictionary* (New York: MacMillan Publishing Co., 1959), 195.

Cor. 9:17; Eph. 1:10; 3:2; Col 1:25) from which the English word *economy* gets its derivation. The Greek term is a compound which literally means *house-law*, and refers to stewardship, administration, or appropriation and management of resources. It is understood to be an arrangement, order, or plan.[366]

It is quite evident that there are such administrations in Scripture, and that the chronology of Scripture is marked with changes (sometimes slight) from one administration to another. Even those who oppose the theological system of dispensationalism recognize differing administrations within God's sovereign plan.[367]

The Biblical writers clearly recognized that such distinctions exist. Note, for example, the various outlines/timelines within the Book of Daniel, Paul's use of terminology in the *oikonomia* passages, and also John's outline of Revelation (Rev. 1:19), which highlights a minimum of three such distinctions in his immediate context, etc.; and the second-generation church and beyond (including Justin Martyr, 110-165 AD; Irenaeus, 130-200 AD; Clement of Alexandria,

---

366 William F. Arndt and F. Wilbur Gingrich, *A Greek Lexicon of the New Testament and Other Early Christian Literature*, 4th Ed. (Chicago: The University of Chicago Press, 1957), 559.

367 Even the covenant system, holding to at least two basic divisions (law and grace) admits (at least) two distinct functional divisions in God's plan.

150-220 AD; Augustine, 354-430 AD, and others[368]), while certainly not recognizing the specific divisions we would speak of today, also observed chronological divisions in God's revealed plan. There has been much quality work revealing the historical recognition of these divisions, so the point is not belabored here, but John Calvin's acknowledgment of God's "dispensing"[369] activity is worthy to be noted, as Calvin points out how elementary and how reasonable the concept of a dispensation really is, saying (among other things, in a discussion of dispensation and distinction between various Biblical economies),

> God ought not to be considered changeable merely because he accommodated diverse forms to different ages, as he knew would be expedient for each....Why then do we brand God with the mark of inconsistency, because he has with apt and fitting marks distinguished a diversity of times?[370]

---

368   For a more comprehensive list see Arnold Ehlert, "A Bibliography of Dispensationalism," Th.D Dissertation, Dallas Theological Seminary, November 1945, 10-29.

369   John Calvin, *Institutes of the Christian Religion*, Edited by John T. McNeill, Translated by Ford Lewis Battles (Philadelphia, PA: Westminster Press, 1940), 1:61.

370 Ibid., 462.

Without perhaps too much ado it can be assumed that there is little question as to the existence/reality of dispensations[371], but rather the inquiry comes at the points of definition and division.

In recent years, definitions have been given more attention, and one definition has emerged to be, at present, perhaps most well known and commonly referenced: that of C.I. Scofield, who believed that a dispensation was

> ...a period of time during which God deals in a particular way with man in respect to sin and to man's responsibility.[372]

With further demarcation he says,

> These periods are marked off in Scripture by some change in God's method of dealing with mankind, or a portion of mankind, in respect of the two questions: of sin, and of man's responsibility. Each of the dispensations may be regarded as a new test of the natural man, and

---

371 Ehlert has done a noble job of citing the historical evidence for such a statement; also Ryrie summarizes well some highlights in "Update on Dispensationalism," Wesley R. Willis, John R. Master, and Charles C. Ryrie, *Issues in Dispensationalism*, 15-27 and provides an excellent historical summary in Charles C. Ryrie, *Dispensationalism*, 61-77.

372 C.I. Scofield, *Scofield Bible Correspondence Course*, (Chicago: Moody Press, 1959), 1:46.

each ends in judgment, marking his utter failure in every dispensation.[373]

This specific characterization gives rise to Scofield's classic delineation of seven dispensations:

(1) Innocence - Gen. 1:3-3:6
(2) Conscience – Gen. 3:7-8:14
(3) Government – Gen. 8:15-11:9
(4) Promise – Gen. 11:10-Ex. 18:27
(5) Law – Ex. 19:1-Jn. 14:30
(6) Grace[374] – Acts 2:1 – Rev. 19:21
(7) Millennium – Rev. 20:1-5

In his definition, dispensations are limited in scope to periods of *time*, thus necessitating that they fit within the *chronological* framework of Genesis-Revelation (meaning from day one of creation week to the instituting of the new heavens and earth[375]). Therefore, those events taking place before and after the advent of time are not incorporated into his dispensational panorama. In addition – and perhaps more significantly, this definition has greater soteriological emphasis than doxological. There is notable

---

373 C.I. Scofield, *Rightly Dividing the Word of Truth*, 12.

374 Although Scofield originally communicated his dispensational soteriology with some ambiguity (see *Scofield Reference Bible,* 1917, p. 1115), dispensationalists agree that salvation has always been by faith, with the content varying by dispensation.

375 Ibid., 58.

contemporary dependence on Scofield's definition, as illustrated by the definition provided by Paul Enns:

> Dispensationalism is a system of interpretation that seeks to establish a unity in the Scriptures *through its central focus on the grace of God* [emphasis mine]. Although dispensationalists recognize differing stewardships or dispensations *whereby man was put under a trust by the Lord* [emphasis mine], they teach that response to God's revelation in each dispensation is by faith (salvation is *always* by grace through faith). Dispensationalists arrive at their system of interpretation through two primary principles: (1) maintaining a consistently literal method of interpretation, and (2) maintaining a distinction between Israel and the church.[376]

Note the emphasis on the redemptive plan and the focus on man. It is this writer's view that these particular emphases are inappropriate, and that they result in a less than ideal framework.

Because of these nuances, Scofield's definition (although we are tremendously indebted to and grateful for it) seems to be less than ideal, particularly in light of three notable Scriptural emphases:

---

376 Enns, *Moody Handbook of Theology*, 547.

(1) There are major events which take place before the commencing of time: including God's own existence, Self-relating (Jn. 17:24; Rom. 1:20; 16:26; 1 Tim. 1:17; 1 Pet. 1:20), goings forth (Mic. 5:2), and His choosing and predestinating work (Eph. 1:4-5; 3:11; 2 Tim. 1:9), etc.

(2) There is continuation of reality after the cessation of recorded time: including the future glorification of God and His continual sovereign rule (1 Tim. 6:16; 2 Pet. 1:11; 3:18), ongoing salvation and life of believers (Is. 45:17; Mt. 19:28; Jn. 3:15-16, 36; 5:24, 39; 6:40, 54; 17:3; 2 Cor. 4:17; Heb. 9:12; 1 Jn 2:25), and ongoing judgment and punishment of unbelievers (Mt. 18:8; 25:41, 46; Mk. 3:29; 2 Thes. 1:9; Heb. 6:2).

(3) There is a weighty accent on the centrality of God's doxological plan, with the redemptive plan (to which Scofield here alludes, emphasizing man's sin and responsibility) subordinate to and fitting into the framework of the doxological (Ps. 86:9, 12; Ezek. 39:13; Jn. 17:3-5; Rom. 11:36; 12:1-2; 1 Cor. 6:20; 10:31; Eph. 2:8-10; 1 Pet. 4:11; Is. 6:3 and Rev. 4:11).

The centrality of God's doxological purpose is emphasized by Ryrie and included as the third element of his *sine qua non*, despite occasional suggestion by some that the doxological purpose is not germane to the dispensational viewpoint. In reality this element is *the most definitive result of a literal hermeneutic, and this writer would suggest therefore that it is the most necessary of the three elements.*[377] Scofield's definition of dispensations seems to fall short of recognizing this emphasis.

It is notable, in seeking a proper emphasis on this doctrine, that the major works of God revealed in Scripture *all* serve the doxological purpose (Ps. 86:9-10; Rev. 15:4); as a matter of fact, Scripture identifies no greater purpose for each of the following: God's predestining and calling works (Eph. 1:5-12; 2 Pet. 1:3); the ministry of Christ (Jn. 13:31-2; 17:1-5; 21:19; 2 Cor. 1:20; Heb. 13:21); creation (Ps. 19; Is. 40; Rev. 4:11); The Keeping of His Word (Rom. 3:1-7); salvation (Ps. 79:9; Rom. 15:7;16:25-27; Eph. 1:14; 1 Tim. 1:15-17; 2 Tim. 4:18; Jude 24-25); the church (1 Cor. 10:31; 2 Cor. 4:15; Eph. 1:12; Phil. 1:11; 2 Thes. 1:11-12; 1 Pet. 4:11,16); fruitfulness of believers (Jn. 15:8; 1 Cor. 10:31; the kingdom – Phil. 2:11; 1 Thes. 2:12; Rev. 1:6); sickness, death, and resurrection (1 Sam. 6:5; Lk. 17:11-18; Jn. 9:1-3; 11:4); judgment (Rom. 3:7; Rev. 14:7); deliverance of Israel (Is. 60:21; 61:3); the fulfilling of covenants and summing up of all things (Is. 25:1-3; 43:20; Lk. 2:14; Rom. 4:20; 15:8-9; 2 Cor. 1:20; 2 Pet. 1:3-4; Rev. 19:7).

---

377 Of course, the doxological purpose is derived through a literal reading of Scripture, and so it is also a resultant understanding from the consistent use of a literal hermeneutic; however, the centrality of the doxological purpose is clear nonetheless, and thus is placed as God's over-arching purpose in all things. Because of this emphasis it must be seen logically as the most essential element – or at the very least the most definitive result of a literal interpretation of Scripture.

While Chafer reckons the same number of dispensations as does Scofield, perhaps a greater emphasis on the doxological purpose led Chafer to offer a more spacious perspective on the scope of the word. Chafer defines a dispensation as

> ...a period which is identified by its relation to some particular purpose of God – a purpose to be accomplished within that period.[378]

In Chafer's estimation, the focus of the dispensational construct is namely the particular purpose of God. This definition seems a more precise one in that it allows for a dispensational epicenter not so much relating to man and his redemption as much as to God and His doxological purpose, avoiding the error of the soteriological center and the mistake which Walvoord calls *the reductive error* – "the use of one aspect of the whole as the determining element."[379]   Ryrie's elaboration on the third element of his *sine qua non* begs for an even more refined definition of this strange unit of measure that is a dispensation. He says,

> To the dispensationalist the soteriological or saving program of God is not the only program but one of the means God is using in the total program of glorifying Himself. Scripture is not

---

378 Chafer, *Systematic Theology*, 1:40.

379 Walvoord notes, in particular, that this is a mistake of covenant theology, in Walvoord, *The Millennial Kingdom*, 92.

mancentered as though salvation were the main
theme, but it is God-centered because His glory
is the center. The Bible itself clearly teaches
that salvation, important and wonderful as it is,
is not an end in itself but is rather a means to
the end of glorifying God.[380]

Therefore perhaps a more refined definition,
accounting for the doxological priority which Ryrie,
Walvoord, and others have recognized would be as
follows:

*A dispensation is a particularly distinctive economy or
administration in and by which God demonstrates or
expresses His own glory.*

Dispensational Divisions

If then the definition which directly leads to the
divisions is to be reconsidered, then perhaps the
divisions themselves could be better expressed to
accommodate the newly defined term. Historical
dispensational delineations emphasizing either a

---

380 Ryrie, *Dispensationalism Today*, 46.

primarily redemptive program[381] or a kingdom program[382] have come in all shapes and sizes, generally delineating anywhere from three (Gaebelein[383]), four

---

381   Including William Gouge (1575-1653); Pierre Poiret (1646-1719); John Edwards (1639-1716); Isaac Watts (1674-1748); Jonathan Edwards (1703-1758); John Fletcher (1729-1785); JN Darby (1800-1882); Robert Jamieson (1802-1880), A.R. Fausset (1821-1910), and David Brown (1803-1897) in their 6-volume commentary, reference the term dispensation/dispensations well over 100 times, seeming to take a redemptive approach based on comments on Gen. 2:17, etc.; Charles Hodge (1797-1878); R.L. Dabney (1820-1898); J.R. Graves (1820-1893); George Pember (1837-1910); James Gray (1851-1935); C.I. Scofield (1843-1921); I.M. Haldeman (1845-1933); W. Graham Scroggie (1877-1958); L.S. Chafer (1871-1952); H.A. Ironside (1876-1951); etc.

382   Adam Clarke's (1760/62-1832) and Richard Watson's (1781-1833) approaches have something of a kingdom overtone; John Cumming (1810-1881) places some focus on kingdom elements; Samuel Andrews (1817-1906) while based on a redemptive premise emphasizes gradual submission of mankind to the authority of God; G.B.M. Clouser highlights both redemptive and government elements; Clarence Larkin (1850-1924) has a kingdom emphasis; A.C. Gaebelein (1861-1942) and Alva J. McClain (1888-1968) both had a strong kingdom emphasis.

383 See Michael C. Stallard, "The Theological Method of Arno C. Gaebelein," Ph.D Dissertation, Dallas Theological Seminary, 1992.

(progressive dispensationalism[384]) five, seven (Scofield), sometimes up to eight dispensational divisions.[385]

However, a synthetic overview accounting for God's doxological purpose seems to unveil no less than 12 dispensational divisions in Scripture. And while the number of dispensations may not be of tremendous significance (perhaps 3, 5, 7, or 8 *are* most appropriate numbers, after all), in this writer's estimation it does seem that the following 12 divisions most suitably represent the Biblical narrative in three specific ways: (1) the synthetic overview of Scripture based directly on the covenants and promises of God fit very well within this framework; (2) each dispensation pre-announces (or at least logically necessitates) the coming of the next; and (3) this 12 division approach unites the kingdom and soteriological emphases cohesively *under* the doxological purpose as consistent with Ryrie's *sine qua non* and as a natural result of literal grammatical-historical interpretive approach.

---

384   Patriarchal (to Sinai), Mosaic (to Messiah's ascension), Ecclesial (to Messiah's return), Zionic (1.Millennial, 2. Eternal), from Craig A. Blaising and Darrell L. Bock, *Progressive Dispensationalism*, 123.

385   Blaising and Bock present an excellent chart of historical dispensational delineations in Craig A. Blaising and Darrell L. Bock, *Progressive Dispensationalism*, 118-119.

THE TWELVE DISPENSATIONS: THE UNFOLDING DRAMA OF PRAISE

(1) Planning: Eternity Past (Jn. 17:24; Acts 4:28; Eph. 1:4; 1 Pet. 1:20)

Before the foundation of the world, in eternity past, God is. He related to Himself (Jn. 17:24), existing in aseity, lacking in no way, and being in essence and in character holy, holy, holy (Is. 6:3; Rev. 4:8). He had no intrinsic need for fellowship with any other being (yet uncreated) nor had He the need to create anything at all. Yet, before the foundation of the world, God made determination about specifically how and with whom He would glorify Himself, presenting His character later to His creation as a divine Self-expression.

His predestining work provided the foundation of wisdom later to be revealed to His creation (1 Cor. 2:7), and set the stage for all that was to come (Acts 4:28), as all things would be in submission to the sovereign counsel of His will (Eph. 1:11). Included in His predestined plan some among His created beings would have unique relationship to Him (e.g., Eph. 1:5) by grace through faith (Hab. 2:4; Eph. 2:8-9). The revealed planning in eternity past demonstrated God to be sovereign, free to act, all-powerful, and worthy of worship by His creation.

Despite having at this point (in eternity past) no specific recorded announcement of the coming dispensation(s), logically the outworking of this planning stage is necessary.

(2) Prelude: Innocence of Man (Gen. 1:1-3:6)

In accordance with His own plan He created the heavens and the earth and all they contain (Gen. 1-2). The apex of His creative work was man, created in His own image. He placed him in the Garden as a beneficiary of the doxological plan, and gave him but one imperative. The consequence for violating this one command was spiritual death (Gen. 2:17). Adam, for an undisclosed period of time, walked innocently and in fellowship with God. This era demonstrated (1) the perfection of God's creative working; (2) God's allowance of His creation to have fellowship with Him under specific and delineated terms, i.e., obedience – although it is clear even at this stage that He would demonstrate man's inability to maintain obedience; and (3) by communicating and creating an alternative to willing human obedience (disobedience, Gen. 2:15);

God demonstrated that His plan of the ages was far more complex than even the creative work revealed, that ultimately fellowship with Him could only be achieved by righteousness only He could provide – by grace through faith (which can be clearly seen as the dispensations unfold), and that His plan's culmination would be dependent wholly upon Himself, and not upon His finite creatures. The imperative of Gen. 2:17 provides the backdrop for the following dispensation: either to be characterized by continued obedience or by dramatic disobedience. The command was given, and man would be tested. How he responded would define the mood of the next dispensation.

(3) Plight: Failure of Man (Gen. 3:6-6:7)

Man's willing disobedience, calculated by God in His pre-creation planning, within a very short period of time transforms man - the apex of creation, made in the image of God - immediately into a depraved being, falling short of the glory of God and ultimately into nothing short of a fully evil and violently rebellious entity (Gen. 6:5) deserving of the fullness of God's wrath. This period demonstrates that no being would be able or allowed to approach the glory of God independent of the working of God, as man would have no ability to work his way into right standing with God, and evidences a gap between the holiness of the Sovereign Creator and the ungodliness and unworthiness of man unbridgeable by any other than God Himself. Veiled elements of the bridging of this gap are in view particularly with the veiled promise of redemption (3:15), the slaying of an animal to cover the first sinners (Gen. 3:21), and again with God's show of regard for Abel's animal sacrifice and disregard for Cain's offering of vegetation (4:4-5).

Genesis 6:3 pre-announces the next dispensation. Just as God would blot out man because of his wickedness (6:7), He would preserve the seed of man, allowing a lifespan of 120 years. Additionally, if one considered 6:8 as the conclusion to this dispensation, there would be further pre-announcement in the form of Noah's identification as finding favor in the eyes of the Lord.

(4) Preservation and Provision: Common Grace and Human Government (Gen. 6:8-11:9)

In view of man's total and complete depravity, God would be rightly justified in the aggregate destruction of all mankind – specifically due to the conditional consequence of Genesis 2:17. But God limited Himself by His own word, as He had previously offered a veiled redemptive promise (3:15) that necessitated the survival and proliferation of man and woman. God therefore provided two elements for the protection of His promise, to His own glory: (1) the preservation of the seed of man through Noah and his family, by way of deliverance from the otherwise worldwide destruction of the flood; and (2) the provision of human government – the sovereignty of man over nature (Gen. 9:1-3) and over each other (9:5) - as a means whereby various controls would be in place to protect the life of mankind from both external threats (beasts of the field) and internal threats (the murderous sinfulness of man).

This era additionally offered a tremendous contrast between the holiness of God and the depravity of man, as after the preservation and provision were accomplished, man still revolts against God, asserting his own method and will to achieve independence from God (Gen. 11:1-4). Such rebellious efforts, even still, are subject to God's sovereign control, Who thwarts man's attempts at independence (11:5-9), demonstrating once again that man's best efforts are worthless in achieving godliness.

(5) Promises Pronounced (Gen. 11:10-Ex. 18:27)

Beginning with Abraham, God's soteriological and kingdom schematic is further unveiled. From this one man would arise a great nation (Gen. 12:2), possessing the definitive elements of a people, a land, and a kingdom — each element to be expanded and unveiled in future promises. This period traces the generations from Abraham, Isaac, Jacob and his twelve sons, to the birth of the Israelite nation as God extracts them, at just the right moment, from previously promised servitude in Egypt (Gen. 15:13-14). With this nation rapidly developing from Abraham's progeny God commences a grand work — both soteriological and kingdom oriented, yet focusing primarily on His character as the Covenant Keeping God — the One who rules and orchestrates to His own pleasure.

(6) Prerequisite Portrayed: The Broken Covenant, The Tutor (Ex. 19:1-Mal. 4:6 [Gal. 3:24-25])

Lest the people of God's choosing think that they have an inheritance of blessing apart from God's workings and unconditional promises, God initiates with Israel the conditional covenant through Moses — a covenant of obedience which if kept would result in the physical blessing of Israel in the land, and which if forsaken would result in a curse including the removal of Israel from the promised land (Deut. 28). Israel would be unable and even disallowed to fulfill this covenant (Deut. 31:16-21), characterizing this era as a graphic portrayal of man's incapacity to walk in accordance with God's holy demands, and effectively pointing to man's need for redemption which only Christ would be qualified to provide. The prerequisite to living under God's blessing and in His fellowship is a righteousness which only He can provide. During this era the holiness and righteousness of God is magnified, as the contrast between His character and that of man is accentuated.

Also of significance during this era is the expansion of the unconditionally promised elements of God's covenant with Abraham: (1) the land element from Genesis 15:18-21 is further delineated in Deuteronomy 30; (2) the kingdom element, providing necessary leadership for a great nation, is clarified in 2 Samuel 7; and (3) the people element, without which the great nation would be devoid of any citizens, is unveiled in Jeremiah 31, providing a springboard to the fulfillment of the universal blessing element (Gen. 12:3) for all peoples.

(7) Promises Proffered: The Kingdom Offered (Mt. 1:1-12:45)

The kingdom of God[386] refers to His universal and eternal rulership applied   physically on earth in direct fulfillment of the covenant promises, particularly to Abraham (Gen. 12-17) and David (2 Sam. 7). Matthew (exclusively, as none of the other Gospel writers do) refers to the kingdom of heaven frequently,

---

386 For an excellent discussion on the nature of the kingdom see Stanley Toussaint, *Behold the King* (Portland, OR: Multnomah Press, 1980), 19-20, 65-68, 171-173.

appealing to the Jewish mind via well understood terminology[387] and indicating that God's heavenly kingdom was poised to find an earthly home, fulfilling the promise to David. (Toussaint notably suggests these terms [kingdom of heaven and kingdom of God] as being used interchangeably[388] - this is a significant point in understanding the identification and nature of the kingdom.) Peters recognizes the significance of this kingdom offer and its earthly scope:

> This kingdom is one pertaining to the earth. Before the creation of the world, it only existed in the determination or purpose of God but at creation the very foundation of the world was laid in preparation for it... 'From the foundation of the world' is indicative that God purposed this very earth, when founded, for this kingdom.[389]

It was a kingdom designed for the earth, and so promised to Abraham and David. The disciples rightly understood the kingdom offer as referencing the restoration of the Davidic kingdom and thus the hastening of the covenant fulfillments.

---

387 George Peters, *The Theocratic Kingdom* (Grand Rapids, MI: Kregel, 1972), 1:195.

388 Stanley Toussaint, *Behold the King* (Portland, OR: Multnomah Press, 1980), 65-68.

389 Ibid., 35.

It can be safely asserted...that it is a well-grounded belief that the Kingdom was something that they [the disciples] were acquainted with, and concerning which, as to its nature or meaning, they *needed not*, owing to its plain portrayal in the Old Testament, any special instruction....

...nothing is alleged that they *misapprehended* the Kingdom of the prophets in its fundamental aspects....

...such supposed ignorance would *reflect severely* upon the covenants, prophecies, and preaching of the first preachers of "the Gospel of the Kingdom."[390]

Clearly then, Jesus' first public proclamation (Mt. 4:17) entailing the preliminary offer of this expected kingdom, was understood for what it truly was. This period of consideration was a unique time in Israel's history – an emphatically pivotal era (brief though it was), which if responded to positively would have certainly precipitated the fulfilling of the eschatological plan. Of course, in God's own predetermination and sovereignty, Israel's negative response to this offer had already been predicted (Is. 6:9-10). This temporary rejection would prove to be the opportunity God had designed to provide further fulfillment of the Genesis 12:3 universal blessing – in this case the specific element of blessing being God's

---

390 Ibid., 182-184.

righteousness being accessible through Christ by the gentiles as well as the Jews.

God's glory is demonstrated in this brief era through the outworking of His plan (1) to further refine and prepare the nation of Israel for promised future blessing, and (2) to pave the way for the unveiling of the mystery (later revealed in Rom. 11:25-36 and Eph. 2:11-3:12) – that God has provided a means whereby all mankind, both Jew and gentile, would have opportunity for salvation, by grace and through faith.

(8) Postponement and Propitiation: The Kingdom Postponed and the New Covenant Ratified (Mt. 12:46-Acts 1:26)

Immediately after Israel's prophesied (Is. 6:9-10, etc.) corporate rejection of Jesus as Messiah (and consequent rejection of the kingdom offer) begins an era of postponement which serves God's predetermined plan in a very significant way. Israel's covenant realizations are placed on hold while God provides the means for their ultimate fulfillment – namely the blood of Christ. Without the propitiatory work of Christ, as ratification of the New Covenant, there could be no fulfillment of the New Covenant, and thus all other covenant blessings would be rendered void as there could be no people to enjoy them into eternity since all men would otherwise stand eternally condemned. Therefore, this very brief period is pivotal in the execution of God's plan, as it provides the enablement to keep (literally and fully) the unconditional covenants of the Old Testament while also providing (in keeping with the universal blessing aspect of the Abrahamic Covenant, Gen. 12:3) an expansion of God's revealed focus to include the gentiles in the plan of eternal life.

This period is unique and set apart from the previous era, clearly delineated by Jesus' advancement of His mission and alteration of His teaching methods (beginning to teach the multitudes exclusively in parables, see Mt. 13). The most straightforward reading of Scripture demands an understanding that the Kingdom was postponed, and without this understanding the clarity of even Jesus' earthly ministry is compromised. Peters characterized this understanding as of significant import, saying

> The rejection of the postponement of the Kingdom, is a rejection of *the only key* that can unlock the singular and otherwise mysterious sayings of Jesus.[391]

This aspect of Jesus' earthly ministry seems at least to characterize this as a fully unique dispensation in the plan of God. Additionally, this era is distinct from the next particularly being defined by the ascension of Christ and the role of the Holy Spirit.

Ultimately God's glory is profoundly manifest in this short span as so many elements come together at this stage to bring continuity and cohesiveness to God's unfolding plan.

---

391 Peters, *The Theocratic Kingdom*, 1:622-623.

This era offers a unique characteristic in that all subsequent dispensations are pre-announced by Christ during this time: in Matthew 16:18 the Era of Participation (The Church Age), coupled with John 14-16, describing the coming role of the Holy Spirit during that time; in Matthew 24:1-28 the Era of Purification (The Tribulation Period); in Matthew 24:29-31 the Era of Promises Performed (The Kingdom Initiated); and in Luke 18:29-30 and John 6:40, 54 (in conjunction with His aggregate teaching on eternal life and eternal condemnation) the Postscript (Eternity Future) is certainly in view. Particularly in light of Christ's prophetic ministry during this time, these divisions seem quite natural.

(9) Participation: The Church Age (Acts 2:1- Rev. 3:22)

Perhaps this era serves as the most surprising of the dispensations as its leading lady (the church) is nowhere to be found in Old Testament prophecy (despite allusions to an additional focus on the gentiles, as found in such passages as Gen. 12:3b; Deut. 32:20-21, 43; 2 Sam. 22:50; Ps. 18:49; 117:1; Is. 11:10; and later in Lk. 21:24, etc.). The church first appears by name in Matthew 16:18, is noticeably absent from earthly perspective in Revelation 4:1-19:10, and reappears (by strong implication and in correlation with Rev. 19:7-8) in Rev. 19:14. The scope of the church's blessing and focus is, during this age, in the heavenlies in Christ (Eph. 1:3).

Mystery aspects of the church include (1) the translation (rapture) of saints at the end of the church era (1 Cor. 15:51); (2) God's partial hardening of Israel (i.e., fostering the rejection of the kingdom offer, see Mt. 13:10-17, etc.) in order that the fullness of the gentiles might be fulfilled (Rom. 11:25); (3) God's subsequent self-revelation to all nations (Rom. 16:25-26); (4) the unity of Jew and gentile together in the body of Christ (i.e., the church, Eph. 2:11-3:12); (5) the relationship of Christ as husband to the church (Eph. 5:32); and (6) the indwelling of Christ via the Holy Spirit in the believer (Col. 1:27).

The inheritance of the church lies in the promise (singular, see Eph. 3:6; 2 Tim. 1:1; 1 Jn. 2:25, etc.), underscoring a significant area of distinction from Israel, whose inheritance is found in the covenants and promises (plural, see Rom. 15:8; Gal. 3:16; Eph. 2:12; Heb. 6:12; 7:6; 8:6; 11:17). There are at least several key elements to be considered in this context which contribute significantly to the understanding of this dispensation, and those dealt with here are: (1) the new covenant and its relation or non-relation to the church, (2) the parenthesis problem, and (3) the illustration of the olive tree.

The New Covenant and the Church

Scripture contains by name eight direct (and other less direct but equally definite) references to the New Covenant:

(1) Jeremiah 31:31 – here the New Covenant is identified as including at least the following specific elements: it is made directly with the houses of Israel

320 Prolegomena on Biblical Hermeneutics and Method

and Judah (31:31); it is distinct from and unlike the Mosaic covenant (31:32); it is prophesied as still yet future (31:31); it is characterized by God at a future time writing His law on the hearts of the recipients (31:33); it signified a possession relationship between God and Israel/Judah (31:33); it resulted in universal knowledge of God within Israel/Judah (31:34); it entailed forgiveness of sin (31:34); and it included both physical and eternal restoration of Israel/Judah (31:27-28, 37-40).

(2) Luke 22:20 (Mt. 26:28; Mk. 14:24) – in this initiation of the New Covenant, the blood of Christ is pre-announced as the ratification of the New Covenant, which would be inaugurated with the coming of the kingdom (Lk. 22:18).

(3) 1 Corinthians 11:25 – Paul here recounts to the Corinthian church the initiation (Lord's Supper) of the New Covenant pointing to Christ's ratification (death and resurrection).

(4) 2 Corinthians 3:6 (Rom. 11:25-32) – this passage delineates "us" (the specific antecedent is identified in 1:19 as Paul, Silvanus, and Timothy) as servants (*diakonous*) of a *new covenant*. It is notable that while these servants of the New Covenant are *of* the church, there is no assertion or contextual indication that the New Covenant is made *with* the church. Rather it is most appropriate to understand that as ministers of the gospel, the apostles served to facilitate the New

Covenant, just as the church serves as an instrument to move Israel to jealousy – thus hastening the inauguration of the Covenant.

(5 and 6) Hebrews 8:6-13 (7:22) – in describing the superiority of Christ's ministry, here the contrast is drawn between the Law (8:4) and the better covenant (8:6). The focus here is on Jesus and His superiority as exemplified by His role as Mediator of the New Covenant – the context of the Covenant here then is in relation to Him and not the church. He is the (immensely qualified) High Priest for the believer (8:1). Herein is the connection between the New Covenant and the church: the same Mediator of the New Covenant is the High Priest for the believer, and resultantly the believer is a beneficiary of certain elements of the New Covenant (e.g., forgiveness of sins and eternal life, Is. 55:5; Jer. 31:34; 1 Jn. 2:25); however, the bestowing of such benefits to the church is not connected to the New Covenant (since it was made only with Israel/Judah, Is. 55:1-11; 59:21; 61:8-9; Jer. 31:31; 32:37-42; 50:4-5; Ezek. 16:59-63; 34:22-31; 37:21-28) but rather to the Mediator who grants forgiveness, righteousness, and life based upon the choosing of God, to His glory.

(7) Hebrews 9:15 – due to the death of the Mediator, the promise of the eternal inheritance can be received, for without eternal life, none of the eternal promises could be enjoyed. This promise magnifies the significance of the New Covenant, as it provided for the

people element of the Abrahamic covenant. Without this element literally fulfilled, the Abrahamic covenant rings empty.

(8) Hebrews 12:24 (10:15-18, 29; 13:20) — this passage speaks to the efficacy of the blood of Christ, again emphasizing His identity as the Mediator of this better covenant. The significance of the New Covenant in each of the Hebrews passages lies in its relation to Christ, not to the church.

The Parenthesis Problem

O.T. Allis, recognizes that the basis of distinction between Israel and the church is indeed the literal interpretation of Old Testament prophecy, saying,

> The parenthesis view of the Church is the inevitable result of the doctrine that Old Testament prophecy must be fulfilled literally to Israel.... [392]

Allis' mention of the parenthesis view references the understanding on the part of a number of dispensational theologians that the church is *parenthetical* — that it is an interruption of God's program with Israel. This understanding, while properly recognizing a distinction between Israel and the church, seems not to be an entirely accurate perspective.

---

392 Allis, *Prophecy and the Church*, 54.

There is indeed clear distinction between Israel and the church, but the church represents not a *parenthesis* but rather simply *one stage or aspect* of God's redemptive program, serving as a cog in His doxological program. The application of the term *parenthesis* to the church implies a discontinuity in God's eternal plan, which in the view of this writer does not exist, and which seems to do injustice entirely to the doxological plan.

The Olive Tree

In Romans 11:16-24 Paul presents the example of the olive tree, identifying (or at least alluding to) several key characters: The wild olive (the gentiles who are grafted in, 11:17); the branches (the Jews, 11:16); the root (the Messiah,[393] 11:16-18; 15:12; Rev. 5:5 – *riza* as in the LXX Is. 11:10; 53:2). In this picture Paul

---

393 Many see the root here as referencing Abraham or the covenants, but this seems quite unnatural, as (1) there is precedent for Christ as the root in prophecy – both contextually and grammatically, (2) there is not precedent for Abraham or the covenants as the root in prophecy, and (3) although this is simply an illustration here, Christ as the root seems to more forcefully illustrate the point of the gentiles having access to Christ due to the Jews' initial rejection of Him, (4) the gentiles were already promised blessing directly through the Abrahamic covenant, so the metaphor of grafting would seem unnecessary – the gentiles as blessed would be a natural result of the covenant, not a manufactured reality; whereas, to have a unity with Christ would seem to require grafting, (5) a grafting implies access to the full benefit of the root, whereas the Gentiles do not enjoy all the blessing of the Abrahamic covenant, but certainly do enjoy the fullness of access to Christ.

demonstrates that the gentiles have access to the Messiah (and consequently His salvation blessings) directly due to Israel's initial rejection of the Messiah. The gentiles, in this figure, are grafted not into Israel, nor to *all* the covenant promises, but to Christ Himself, reaping the profound benefit of His salvific work. It is here we see God's magnificent fulfillment of the seventh element of the Abrahamic Covenant (Gen 12:3b) – all the families of the earth blessed in Abraham - through Christ.

Thus the mystery of the partial hardening is unveiled (11:25) as a predetermined element of God's grand plan: This remarkable and unexpected (although somewhat pre-announced) twist in His redemptive plan serves His doxological purpose, demonstrating His superlative wisdom – leaving Paul in wonderment at the thought (11:33-36).

This era of participation fills a limited timeframe, constituting the gap between Daniel's 69th and 70th week (Dan. 9:26-27), and the initial times of the gentiles (Lk. 21:24) leading to the fullness of the gentiles (Rom. 11:25) - elements which are consummated in the next dispensation.

(10) Purification: The Tribulation, Jacob's Trouble (Rev. 4:1-19:10 [Jer. 30:7])

Returning the focus on the nation of Israel and providing a continuation of the Daniel 9 timetable, this seven-year era will be inaugurated as a covenant is made with the many by the (Roman[394]) prince who is to come (Dan. 9:27). This covenant is broken at the midpoint (three and a half years), at which time the *great* tribulation (a period of more severe testing, see Mt. 24:15-22[395]) begins, culminating with the shaking of the heavens and the 2nd coming of the Messiah King (Mt. 24:29-30). This is the time of Jacob's distress (Jer. 30:7), preceding the restoration of the nation.

God's glory is demonstrated during this period in at least three major ways: (1) His holiness is expressed as He faithfully judges (without any turning back) the nation for her failures (Jer. 30:24); (2) His protection of the nation, even as He watches over them "to pluck up, to break down, to overthrow, to destroy, and to bring disaster" (Jer. 31:28), provides a testament to His faithfulness and covenant keeping; (3) as a secondary purpose for this tribulation period, the wrath of the

---

394 cf. Dan. 9:26 and 27.

395 Walvoord agrees that the great tribulation takes place during the last 42 months of the tribulation, as he says, "The great tribulation, accordingly, is a specific period of time beginning with the abomination of desolation and closing with the second coming of Christ, in the light of Daniel's prophecies and confirmed by reference to forty-two months." (John Walvoord, *Matthew: Thy Kingdom Come* [Chicago, IL: Moody Press, 1974], 188). It should be noted that neither Walvoord nor this writer seek to divide this seven year period into two disassociated parts as Pentecost cautioned against (J. Dwight Pentecost, *Things to Come* [Grand Rapids, MI: Zondervan, 1958], 184). Rather there is an exegetical distinction made between the two halves, yet both sections are a part of the tribulation period as evidenced by a comparison between Mt. 24:9 and 24:21.

Lamb befalls the nations (Rev. 6:16-17), illustrating His worthiness as Judge and ultimately as King.

The period immediately following is preannounced in several key contexts, primarily (1) Jeremiah 31:27-34 – the time of judgment and refinement will be followed by a spiritual and physical restoration of the nation; and (2) Revelation 19-20 - The King will return triumphant with His redeemed, initiating the fulfillment of the Davidic promise of an eternal throne (2 Sam. 7).

(11) Promises Performed: The Kingdom Initiated (Rev. 19:11- 20:6)

Major events unfolding during this period include: (1) the return of the King (Zech. 14:4), (2) the binding of Satan, (3) the inauguration of the promised Davidic Kingdom, (4) the release of Satan and corresponding final revolt – a revolt which sets the stage for God's final demonstration of His glory within the framework of revealed time: namely, the execution of His judgment.

(12) Postscript: Eternity Future (Rev. 20:7 – 22:21)

Eternity future is inaugurated by the (1) great white throne judgment, and the (2) destruction of the old heaven and earth (Rev. 21:1). Although Chafer lists the destruction as taking place before the White Throne Judgment, note the like English phrases of the earth passing away (cf. Rev. 20:11 and Rev. 21:1), but this passing away is indicated by two different Greek terms (*ephugen* in 20:11 and *apelthan* in 21:1, the latter of which is anticipated in Mt. 5:18 with *parelthe* and Mt. 24:35 with *pareleusontai* – each from the same root, *erchomai*), implying two different actions or events, and (3) creation of the new heaven and earth, with the new Jerusalem described vividly, and God seen in all His glory, which shall be so magnificent as to eliminate the need for any external light:

> And there will no longer be any night; and they will not have need of the light of a lamp nor the light of the sun, because the Lord God will illumine them; and they will reign forever and ever (Rev. 22:5).

While differing conclusions regarding the actual number of dispensations seem rather significant and certainly worthy of examination, it should be understood that as long as basic core elements (e.g., Ryrie's *sine qua non*, due to its accurate representation of Biblical emphases) are acknowledged, such acute divisions are not integral to the overall conclusions of dispensational theology. Such matters need be handled with cautious levels of dogmatism, as these divisions are not expressly revealed in the text of Scripture, but are rather derived deductively.

Where there is minimal amount of revelation we must be exceedingly careful not to insert the maximum amount of commentary, Ryrie's observations in this regard are worthy of noting:

> ...the difference of opinion as to number [of dispensations] is not due to a defect in the dispensational scheme but rather is due to lack of detailed revelation concerning the earliest periods of biblical history. We do not have preserved in the written record all that God may have said or revealed to man in those early periods.[396]

He identifies the calculation of dispensational divisions as a deductive[397] enterprise, underscoring the need for thoughtfulness and consideration, as the deductive process here can and does involve different premises.

The premise asserted here to have inestimable significance is God's doxological purpose. If indeed it bears as great a role as is revealed in Scripture - stemming in all actuality from God's worldview - then it necessarily must also be a *central tenet* in our thinking and in our walking. As a result of this focused attention, our systematic conclusions will reflect an increased estimation of Him, coupled with a decreased

---

396 Ryrie, *Dispensationalism*, 53.

397 Ibid.

estimation of ourselves – developments requisite to a sound theology and a Biblical walk.

It may be argued, then, that this particular arrangement of divisions is lacking for one reason or another. It may also be argued that since the Bible does not directly identify any particular number of divisions that any codified enumeration is unwarranted. However, what is certain is the priority God places on His own purpose and His own glorification. This particular attempt at definition and enumeration is designed solely to respect that priority. Such singularly motivated attempts, this writer would hope, should result in an overall understanding of the flow of Biblical history – past, present, and future – as contributing to this very course of direction.

> In Him we have redemption through His blood, the forgiveness of our trespasses, according to the riches of His grace which He lavished on us. In all wisdom and insight He made known to us the mystery of His will, according to His kind intention which He purposed in Him with a view to an administration suitable to the fullness of the times, *that is,* the summing up of all things in Christ, things in the heavens and things on the earth. In Him also we have obtained an inheritance, having been predestined according to His purpose who works all things after the counsel of His will, to the end that we who were the first to hope in Christ would be *to the praise of His glory.* (Eph. 1:7-12, emphasis is mine)

398

The Dispensations: Number and Purpose		
12 Dispensations: *Doxological*	**7 Dispensations:** *Soteriological*	**3 Dispensations:** *Kingdom*
1. Planning Eternity Past Jn. 17:24; Eph. 1:4; 1 Pet. 1:20		
2. Prelude Innocence of Man Gen. 1:1-3:5	**1. Innocence** Gen. 1:3-3:6	
3. Plight Failure of Man Gen. 3:6-6:7	**2. Conscience** Gen. 3:7-8:14	**1. Preparation** beginning in Gen. 3:15
4. Preservation and Provision Common Grace and Human Government Gen. 6:8-11:9	**3. Government** Gen. 8:15-11:9	
5. Promises Pronounced Gen. 11:10-Ex. 18:27	**4. Promise** Gen. 11:10-Ex. 18:27	
6. Prerequisite Portrayed The Broken Covenant: The Tutor Ex. 19:1-Mal. 4:6 Gal. 3:24-25	**5. Law** Ex. 19:1-Jn. 14:30	
7. Promises Proffered The Kingdom Offered Mt. 1:1-12:45		
8. Postponement and Propitiation The Kingdom Postponed and New Covenant Ratified Mt. 12:46-Acts 1:26		
9. Participation The Church Age Acts 2:1- Rev. 3:22	**6. Grace** Acts 2:1 – Rev. 19:21	**2. Participation** beginning in Acts 2
10. Purification The Tribulation, Jacob's Trouble Rev. 4:1-19:10		
11. Promises Performed The Kingdom Initiated Rev. 19:11- 20:6	**7. Millennium** Rev. 20:1-5	**3. Consummation** beginning in Rev. 19
12. Postscript Eternity Future Rev. 20:7 – 22:21		

398 Chart reprinted from Christopher Cone, *The Promises of God: A Bible Survey* (Arlington, TX: Exegetica Publishing, 2005), 181.

THE SYSTEMATIC PROCESS
OUTLINES OF BIBLICAL THEOLOGY

Exegesis takes the Scripture and analyzes each part of it in detail. Biblical Theology takes the fruits of the exegesis and organizes them into various units and traces the revelation of God in Scripture in its historical development. It brings out the theology of each part of God's Word as it has been brought to us in different stages, by means of various authors. Systematic theology then uses the fruits of the labors of exegetical and Biblical theology and brings them together into a concatenated system.[399]

A systematic approach to a Biblical Theology unveils *eleven basic topics* of discourse (the doctrine of God consists of three categories, with the other studies numbering eight):

(1) The Doctrine of God: Theology Proper
Emphasizing the holiness of God (Is. 6:3; Rev. 4:8), His triunity (as Father, Son, and Spirit), and His personal interaction with His creation, an inquiry into the doctrine of God will   discuss His attributes, and those generally in two categories, as follows:
(1) those independent of His creation, including:
    a.   aseity and
    b.   holiness

---

399 Van Til, *Introduction to Systematic Theology*, 2.

(2) those relative to His creation (divine nature, eternal power, and invisible attributes, see Rom. 1:20)
   a. divine nature – greatness, eternity, immensity, immutability, incomprehensibility, knowability, etc.
   b. eternal power – transcendence, immanence, omnipotence, sovereignty, omniscience, etc.
   c. invisible attributes – justice, wrath, patience, faithfulness, mercy, grace, lovingkindness, etc.

In addition to reflecting on His attributes, theology proper will inquire as to the works of God, including His doxological purpose as a framework, His creative, redemptive, and kingdom works.

As the Sovereign Creator, He has all sovereign rights to rule over creation. The kingdom has the following elements: authority (the right of God to rule), scope (the realm in which the authority is manifest), and the exercise of the authority. The sovereignty of God is without beginning (Ps. 10:16; 145:13; Jer. 10:10; Lam. 5:19), and the scope of His authority extends everywhere (1 Chr. 29:11-12; Ps. 103:19).

He manifests that authority in whatever manner He wishes, and He has communicated the exercise of His authority, in His eternal kingdom, in two distinct elements. First, the Heavenly Kingdom represents God's eternal sovereign rule, and specifically in relation to creation. The scope is heavenly (Eph. 1:3; Php. 3:20;

2 Tim. 4:18; Heb. 3:1; 9:24; 1 Pet. 1:4), with the eternal (future) focal point being New Jerusalem (Gal. 4:26; Heb. 12:22; Rev. 3:12). That city is said to be coming down out of heaven (*katabainousin ek tou ouranou*, Rev. 21:10). The phrase is used earlier (10:1-3) describing an angel who stood on the land and the sea, and again (13:13), describing fire coming from heaven to the earth. The phrase is also used by John in his Gospel, recording Christ's description to His incarnation (6:41-42, 50-51, 58). Note Ezekiel 37:28; 43:7.

Secondary beneficiaries are believers of all dispensations. Qualification for entrance is the righteousness of God. In fruitless opposition to the kingdom is the morning star (Is. 14:12-15), king of Tyre (Ezek. 28:12-19), the god of this age (2 Cor. 4:4), the prince of the power of the air (Eph. 2:2), spiritual forces of wickedness (Eph. 3:10; 6:12), the dragon (Rev. 12).

Second, the Earthly Covenant Kingdom is the fulfillment of the Davidic Covenant (2 Sam. 7), as offered by Christ in the Gospels. The phrase kingdom of heaven (emphasizing its origin, in contrast to its scope does not originate on earth) occurs only in Matthew (31 times), directed to the Jews, as the earthly manifestation of God's authority over all as delineated by the Davidic Covenant. Note the use of kingdom of God in Matthew 12:28 (and again in 19:24; 21:31,43) – the kingdom is not identified as such (by Matthew) until Israel rejected the offer. The kingdom will be initiated based on the authority of the Messiah, the worthy King, and as the Son of David, fulfilling the

Davidic Covenant. The scope is earthly, with eternal (future) focal point being Jerusalem (Ezek. 43:7) – the throne is of the house of David, and will be literally in physical Jerusalem. After the millennial kingdom New Jerusalem replaces the old, yet the promises still have literal physical fulfillment. (2 Sam. 7:13; Heb. 11:10-16; Rev. 21:22).

The primary beneficiaries are those identified as true Israelites (Rom. 9:6; 11:5-7). The qualification for entrance is God's righteousness – the Gospels present to the Jews the necessary righteousness – the fruits of a regenerated heart – to enter this kingdom. The Gospels therefore hold direct application to the Jews in this regard, but since this manifestation of God's authority holds the same requirement as His other (righteousness), the Gospels therefore present the application of righteousness characteristic of all dispensations. In fruitless opposition to this kingdom is the dragon (Rev. 12:13, 17).

(2) The Doctrine of God: Christology

Discussing the person of Christ, Christology deals with such issues as the person and work of Christ. Regarding His person, studies include His deity, preincarnate nature(appearances include those to: Hagar: Gen. 16:7,11,13; Abraham: Gen. 18:2, 22; 22:11-15; Moses: Ex. 3:2; Balaam: Num. 22:22-35; Joshua: Judg. 2:1-4; Gideon: Judg. 6:11,22), incarnate dual nature (as both God and man[400]), names, role as an eternal Member of the Trinity, and His qualification as Savior.

Regarding His work, considerations include His identity as Messiah functioning as Prophet (Deut. 18:15 and Jn. 5:46 and Acts 3:22-26), Priest (Ps. 110:4 and Heb. 5:6; Zech. 6:12-13; 1 Tim. 2:5; Heb. 2:14-18, 4:14-16; 5:1-10; 6:19-20; 7:11-28; 8:1-13; 10:1-31; Phil. 2:5-11; Heb.5:9), and King   (2 Sam. 7:12-16; Is. 9:6-7; Mic. 5:2; Lk. 1:32-33), who will ultimately rule over all.

(3) The Doctrine of God: Pneumatology

From the Greek *pneuma* (*spirit*), pneumatology is a discourse on the Holy Spirit (Jn. 14:16; 15:26-27; Rom. 8:9; Tit. 3:5; 1 Pet. 3:21; Eph. 1:13-14, etc.). In similar fashion to the previous studies of Theology Proper and Christology, the two elements of person and work are highlighted.

The study of the Person of the Holy Spirit handles such issues as His deity (and consequent claims to the attributes of God) and personality evidenced by the use of personal pronouns, e.g., Jn.

---

400 Biblical Evidence For His Fleshly Nature
Jn. 1:14; Rom. 1:3-4, 5:12-21; 1 Cor. 15:45-47; Heb. 2:14-18, 7:14, 10:4-10; 1 Jn. 4:2; 2 Jn. 1:7.
Biblical Evidence For His Divinity
Jn. 8:58-59, 10:30; Rom. 1:3-4; Col. 1:15; Tit. 2:13; Heb. 1:3; 2 Pet. 1:1; (Is. 44:6; 48:12, 16 and Rev. 1:17, 2:8, 22:13).
Biblical Evidence For His Dual Nature
Rom. 1:3-4; Col. 2:9; (Is. 44:6; 48:12, 16 and Rev. 1:17; 2:8; 22:13).

15:26, etc. and numerous other demonstrated elements of personality, names, role as an eternal Member of the Trinity, His procession (sent from the Father: Ps. 104:30; Is. 48:16; Jn. 15:26; from the Son: Jn. 15:26; Gal. 4:6, Rom. 8:9).

An examination of the work of the Holy Spirit will include such elements as His work in creation (Gen. 1:2; Job 26:13; 33:4; Ps. 33:6; 104:30), inspiration of Scripture (2 Tim. 3:15-16; 2 Pet. 1:20-21), striving, restraining, and convicting (Gen. 6:3; Jn. 16:7-11; 2 Thes. 2:6-8), providing regeneration and rebirth (Mt. 19:28; 1 Cor. 15:24-28; Tit. 3:5; Jn. 3:6; 10:10; 2 Cor. 5:17; 1 Pet. 1:23), sanctification (2 Thes. 2:13; 1 Pet. 1:2), justification (1 Cor. 6:11), indwelling (Jn. 7:37-39; Acts 11:17; Rom. 5:5; 8:9-11; 1 Cor. 2:12; 3:16; 6:19-20; 12:13; 2 Cor. 5:5; Gal. 3:2; 4:6; Eph. 2:22; 2 Tim. 1:14; Jam. 4:5; 1 Jn. 3:24; 4:13), sealing of the believer (2 Cor. 1:22; Eph.1:13; 4:30), baptism (Mt. 3:11; Mk. 1:8; Luke 3:16; Jn. 1:33; Acts 1:5; 2:2-3, 11:16; Rom. 6:1-4; 1 Cor. 12:13; Gal. 3:27; Eph. 4:5; Col. 2:12), gifting (Acts 2:38; 10:45, Rom. 12:6-8; 1 Cor. 12-14; Heb. 2:4), filling (Acts 2:4; 4:8, 4:31; 9:17; 13:9; 13:52; Eph. 5:18), illumination (Jn. 16:12-15; 1 Cor. 2:9-12), helping/ comforting (Jn.13:1-17:26), intercession (Rom. 8:26-27), begetting of the incarnate Son (Lk. 1:35), and His general function within the Trinity.

(4) Bibliology

Bibliology is the study of the Bible (Ps. 19; 2 Tim. 2:15; 3:16; Heb. 4:12; 2 Pet. 1:20-21), and ponders such elements as the nature of revelation, the distinctions and definitions of natural and special revelation, as well as the inspiration, inerrancy, canonicity, transmission, and sufficiency of the Bible. Elements of higher and lower criticism are generally examined under this category as well.

Yet another important consideration here is Biblical interpretation. Ryrie's *Basic Theology* is exemplary for including a thorough handling of hermeneutics in its chapter devoted to Bibliology.

(5) Angelology

The study of angels (Gen. 19:1; 28:12; Ps. 91:11; 148:2; Is. 14; Ezek. 28) includes an inquiry into the origin, nature, fall, classification, function, and future of angelic beings. Discussions of Satan and demons would also fall in this category.

(6) Anthropology

The word derived from the Greek *anthropos* (*man*), anthropology references the study of man (Gen. 1:26-27; Rom. 9:16-21), and includes such elements as origin (creation), nature (image of God, image of Adam), purpose, fall (including consequences both immediate and long term), and future (resurrections, heaven/hell, etc.). Also considered are such controversies as free will, the nature of the soul, and thanatology (from the Greek *thanatos*, meaning *death*), which probes the origin, scope, and nature of death.

(7) Hamartiology

From the Greek *hamartia* (*sin*), hamartiology is the study of sin (Gen. 2:16-17; Rom. 5:12-14, 19; Is. 64:6; Rom. 3:23; 6:23). Important issues in this discourse include definition, origin, imputation, and impact of sin on creation in general and humanity in particular, demonstrating man's inability to approach God without divine working to offset the consequences of sin.

(8) Soteriology

From the Greek *soterion* (*deliverance* or *salvation*), soteriology is the study of salvation (Gen. 3:15; Is 53:5-6; Gen. 12:3; Jer. 31:34; Jn. 3:16; Rom. 5:6; Eph. 2:8-10; 1 Pet. 1:3-5). Concepts pondered here include definition of salvation (the nature of justification), need, provision (grace through faith), and results of salvation (including regeneration, reconciliation, baptism, and sanctification), the activity of God in regard to accomplishing the work of salvation (including the choosing, electing and predestining work of the Father, the forgiving, redeeming, and atoning work of the Son, and the sealing and baptizing work of the Holy Spirit), the positional (such as eternal security and positional sanctification) and practical (such as progressive sanctification and the Christian walk) realities of salvation, and the present (every spiritual blessing and assurance, etc.) and eternal inheritance of the saved.

(9) Israelology

The study of Israel (Gen. 12:1-3; Ex. 20; Deut 30; 2 Sam. 7; Jer. 31; Dan. 9; Rom. 9-11; Rev. 20:1-6), Israelology deals with such issues as the definition, identity, origin, purpose, past, present, and future of Israel. Arnold Fruchtenbaum deserves much credit for reminding us of Israel's significance in the plan of God. Fruchtenbaum rightly accurately assesses the centrality of Israel in God's plan of the ages, and observes that few systematic efforts have included the proper emphasis on Israelology[401]. If there should be a category of study dedicated to the church, then there must surely be an equal amount of attention − if not greater − committed to the nation of Israel.

(10) Ecclesiology

From the Greek *ekklesia* (*church* or *assembly*), this term references the study of the church (Mt. 16:18; Acts 2; Dan. 9; Lk. 21:24; 1 Thes. 4:13-18; Rev. 1-3, 19). Ecclesiology deals with such issues as the definition and identity of the church, the distinctions between Israel and the church (note passages such as Eph. 2:12-21); the Olive Tree (Rom. 11; Heb. 3:5-6 and Num. 12:7; Heb. 12:22-23; Mt. 21:43; Luke 12:32; Jn. 10:16; Gal. 6:16; 1 Pet. 1:1; Jam. 1:1; 2:2, etc.), the origin of the church (in prophecy − as referenced in Mt. 16 - and in actuality, as discussed in Acts 2), the economy, purpose, and future of the church as a spiritual

---

401   Fruchtenbaum, *Israelology* (Tustin, California: Ariel Ministries, 1989), 1.

organism – the body of Christ, organizational characteristics of the church (noting leadership, polity, and service issues), and the function of the church (including major roles such as worship, instruction, fellowship, and edification). Also considered are aspects of personal participation in the church, including spiritual warfare (noting three elements: (1) The world – Eph. 2:1-3; 6:12; 1 Cor. 3:19; Jam. 4:4; 1 Jn. 2:15-17; (2) The devil – Eph. 2:1-3; Gen. 3:1-5; Eph. 4:26-27; 1 Tim. 3:6-7; 2 Tim. 2:26; 1 Pet. 5:8; and (3) The flesh – Eph. 2:1-3; Rom. 7:24-25; Gal. 5:17-19), provision (Eph. 6:13-20; 2 Cor. 6:7; 10:3-5; Ps. 119:9-11; 1 Cor. 10:12-13; Mt. 4:1-11; against the world – Rom. 12:2; against the devil – Jam. 4:7; against the flesh – Gal. 5:16; Rom. 6; 1 Cor. 6:18; 10:14; 2 Tim. 2:22), gifts, and growth.

(11) Eschatology

From the Greek *eschatos* (*final* or *last*) the subject matter here is the study of last things and Biblical prophecy (Gen. 12, 15, 17, 49; Deut 30; 2 Sam. 7; Jer. 30-31; Dan. 9; Mt. 24-25; 1 Cor. 3; 2 Thes. 4; Rev. 1-3, 4-18, 19, 20, 21-22). Eschatology has at its root the Biblical covenants, and includes a study of such future events as the rapture (comparing post-tribulation, mid-tribulation, partial rapture, pre-wrath, and pre-tribulation views), the tribulation (with emphasis on its identified purpose as Jacob's trouble and Daniel's seventieth week, and its duration of seven years which is significantly divisible into two parts: the first three and one half years, and the second three and one half years – referenced by Christ as the Great Tribulation), the battle of Armageddon, the second coming of Christ, the various resurrections, the Millennial Kingdom, the various judgments, the new heaven, new earth, and new Jerusalem, and finally the ushering in of eternity. Of major emphasis in this study is an analysis of prophetic promises made and their literal fulfillments throughout history and the still yet future.

LAST WORD

It is my hope that this text gives the Bible student much to consider. To summarize, the reader should focus on six exhortations:

(1) The Bible student should be deliberate in understanding necessary prerequisites of Biblical doctrine. Presuppositions should not be ignored, and attention must be given to such introductory matters to ensure that the Bible student is beginning with solid foundations.

(2) The Bible student should be aware of available methods of interacting with Biblical doctrine, and must maintain a consistent and proper approach in hermeneutics and exegesis.

(3) The Bible student should be attentive to the development of the personal habit of Biblical exegesis. Far from being simply an academic exercise, Biblical exegesis forms a vital spiritual discipline.

(4) The Bible student should be diligent to synthesize and systematize central Biblical themes, remembering the importance of context, context, context.

(5) The Bible student should be ever aware of the doxological purpose of God, recognizing the majesty of

God and responding to Him with the appropriate fear, humility, and love.

Finally, (6) the Bible student must remember that Biblical study should result in an impacted life. As Paul reminds the reader in 1 Timothy 1:5, the goal of Biblical instruction is love from a pure heart and a good conscience and a sincere faith.

Let the word of Christ richly dwell within you...

Colossians 3:16

BIBLIOGRAPHY

Abravanel, Isaac. *Principles of Faith, Rosh Amanah.* Menachem Kellner, translator. Oxford, UK: Littman Library of Jewish Civilication.

Acosta, Ana M. "Conjectures and Speculations: Jean Astruc, Obstetrics and Biblical Criticism in Eighteenth Century France." *Eighteenth Century Studies*, No. 35 (Winter, 2002).

Allis, O.T. *Prophecy and the Church.* Philipsburg, NJ: 1945.

Ames, William. *The Marrow of Theology*, ed. and trans. John D. Eusden. Boston: Pilgrim, 1968.

Anderson, Sir Robert. *The Coming Prince.* Grand Rapids, MI: Kregel, 1984.

Archer, Gleason. *A Survey of Old Testament Introduction.* Chicago: Moody Press, 1995.

Armstrong, Karen. *The Battle for God.* New York: Ballantine, 2000.

Arndt, William F. and Gingrich, F. Wilbur *A Greek Lexicon of the New Testament and Other Early Christian Literature.* 4th Ed. Chicago: The University of Chicago Press, 1957.

Augsburg Confession. St. Louis, MO.: Concordia Publishing House, 2006.

Augustine, *City of God*, translated by Marcus Dods, in *Nicene and Post-Nicene Fathers of the Christian Church*, Vol. 2, edited by Philip Schaff. 1886 reprint, Grand Rapids: Eerdmans,1988.

Bahnsen, Greg. *The Concept and Importance of Canonicity.* Antithesis, Vol 1, No.5.

Bateman, Herbert IV. *Three Central Issues in Contemporary Dispensationalism.* Grand Rapids: Kregel, 1999.

Beaty, Michael, ed. *Christian Theism and the Problems of Philosophy.* Notre Dame: IN: Notre Dame Press, 1990.

Benware, Paul N. *Understanding End Times Prophecy: A Comprehensive Approach.* Chicago: Moody, 1995.

Berkhof, Louis. *Systematic Theology.* Grand Rapids, Eerdmans, 1941.

Bierlein, J. F. *Parallel Myths.* New York: Ballantine, 1994.

Blaising, Craig and Bock, Darrell. *Progressive Dispensationalism.* Grand Rapids: Baker Books, 1993.

_____, editors. *Dispensationalism, Israel, and the Church.* Grand Rapids, MI: 1992.

Bratton, Fred G. "Precursors of Biblical Criticism." *Journal of Biblical Literature,* No. 50, 1931.

Bray, Gerald. *Biblical Interpretation Past and Present.* Downers Grove: Intervarsity Press, 1996.

_____ *Creeds, Councils and Christ: Did the Early Christians Misrepresent Jesus?* 1984, reprint. Fearn, Rossshire: Mentor, 1997.

Brettler, Marc. "Rendsburg's The Redaction of Genesis." *The Jewish Quarterly Review,* No. 78 (July-Oct. 1987).

Bruce, F.F. *The Canon of Scripture.* Downers Grove: IL, 1988.

Callicott, J. Baird. "Genesis Revisited: Murian Musings on the Lynn White, Jr. Debate." *Environmental History Review,* No. 14 (Spring-Summer 1990).

Calvin, John. *Commentaries on Jeremiah.* Grand Rapids: Baker, 1989, volume 4.

Calvin, John. *Institutes of the Christian Religion,* edited by John T. McNeill, translated by Lewis Battles Ford. Vol. 1. Philadelphia, PA: Westminster Press, 1940.

Cate, Robert. *How to Interpret the Bible.* Nashville: Broadman, 1983.

Chafer, Lewis Sperry. *Systematic Theology.* Grand Rapids, MI: Kregel, 1993.

Charles, R. H. "A New Translation of the Book of Jubilees. Part I." *The Jewish Quarterly Review,* No. 6 (Oct. 1893).

Charnock, Stephen. *Discourses Upon The Existence and Attributes of God.* Grand Rapids, MI: Baker Book House, 1993.

Clement of Alexandria, *Miscellanies* in *The Ante-Nicene Fathers,* Vol. 2, edited by Alexander Roberts and James Donaldson. 1885 reprint, Grand Rapids: Eerdmans, 1989.

Cone, Christopher. *The Promises of God: A Bible Survey.* Arlington, TX: Exegetica, 2005.

_____ "Presuppositional Dispensationalism." *The Conservative Theological Journal* 10/29 (May/June 2006).

_____ "Considering Higher Criticism: The Relationship of Authenticity to Authority." *Journal of Diespensational Theology*, Vol. 16, No. 47 (April 2012).

Couch, Mal, ed. *An Introduction to Classical Evangelical Hermeneutics*. Grand Rapids, MI: Kregel, 2000.

Darwin, Charles. *The Voyage of the Beagle*, Edited by Charles Eliot. New York: PF Collier and Sons, 1909.

_____ *The Descent of Man*. 1871 reprint, New Jersey: Princeton University Press, 1981.

_____ *The Origin of Species*. 1859 reprint, New York: Modern Library, 1993.

Darwin, Erasmus. *Zoonimia*, Vol. 2. New York: AMS Press, 1974.

Davidson, A.B. *Theology of the Old Testament*. Edinburgh, TandT Clark, 1904.

DeBeer, E.S. *The Correspondence of John Locke*, 8 Vols. Oxford, MA: Clarendon Press, 1979.

Diprose, Ronald. *Israel and the Church, The Origin and Effects of Replacement Theology*. Waynesboro, GA: Authentic Media, 2004.

Ehlert, Arnold. "A Bibliography of Dispensationalism", Th.D Diss., Dallas Theological Seminary, November 1945.

Enns, Paul. *Moody Handbook of Theology*. Chicago, IL: Moody Press, 1989.

Erickson, Millard. *Christian Theology*. Grand Rapids, MI: Baker Books, 2001.

Fee, Gordon. *New Testament Exegesis, A Handbook For Students and Pastors.* Philadelphis, PA: Westminster, 1983.

Feinberg, John S.   "Systems of Discontinuity," in *Continuity and Discontinuity: Perspectives on the Relationship Between the Old and New Testaments*, ed. John S. Feinberg. Wheaton, IL: Crossway, 1988.

Feldman, Louis, H. "Josephus' Portrait of Moses." *The Jewish Quarterly Review*, No. 82 (Jan.-Apr. 1992).

Frame, John. *Apologetics to the Glory of God.* Philipsburg,   NJ: Presbyterian and Reformed, 1994.

Freeman, Kathleen. *Ancilla to the Pre-Socratic Philosophers.* Cambridge: Harvard Univ Pr., 1983 reprint edition.

Freud, Sigmund. The Question of Weltanschauung, in *New Introductory Lectures on Psycho-Analysis.* New York: Norton, 1965.

_____ A Philosophy of Life, in *New Introductory Lectures on Psycho-Analysis.* New York: Norton, 1965.

Friere, Paulo. *Pedagogy of the Oppressed.* New York: Continuum, 2002.

Fruchtenbaum, Arnold. *Israelology.* Tustin, CA: Ariel Ministries Press, 1989.

_____ *Biblical Lovemaking.* Tustin, CA: Ariel Ministries Press, 1995.

_____ *Footsteps of the Messiah.* San Antonio: Ariel Press, 2004.

Gaebelein, A.C. "The Dispensations" *Our Hope* 37 (Dec. 1930).

_____ *The Annotated Bible Volume V Daniel to Malachi.* New York: Our Hope, n.d.

Geisler, Norman L. *Systematic Theology.* Bloomington, MN: Bethany House, 2002.

_____ *Inerrancy.* Grand Rapids, MI: 1980.

_____ and Nix, William, *A General Introduction to the Bible.* Chicago: Moody, 1986.

Gentry Jr., Kenneth. *Postmillennialism: Wishful Thinking Or Certain Hope?* http://www.cmfnow.com/articles/pt568.htm, access date unknown.

Gerstner, John. *Wrongly Dividing The Word Of Truth.* Morgan, PA: Sole Deo Gloria, 2000.

Gould, Steven Jay. *Rocks of Ages.* New York: Ballantine, 1999.

Grant, Robert and Tracy, David. *A Short History of the Interpretation of the Bible.* Philadelphia: Fortress, 1985.

Grudem, Wayne. *Systematic Theology.* Grand Rapids, Mi: Intervarsity Press, 1994.

Hamilton, Floyd . *The Basis of Christian Faith.* New York: Harper and Row, 1964.

Hayes, P. Zachary. *The General Doctrine of Creation in the Thirteenth Century.* Germany: Verlag Ferdinand Schoningh, 1964.

Henry, Matthew. *Commentary on the Whole Bible.* and Rapids: Zondervan, 1961.

Hobbes, Thomas. *Leviathan*. Richard Tuck, editor. Cambridge,MA: Cambridge University Press, 1996.

Hodge, Charles. *Systematic Theology*. Peabody, MA: Hendrickson, 2001.

Hodges, Zane and Farstad, Arthur. *The Greek New Testament According to the Majority Text*, 2nd Ed. Nashville, TN: Thomas Nelson, 1985.

Ironside, H.A. *Wrongly Dividing the Word of Truth*, 4th Ed. Neptune, NJ: Loizeaux Brothers, 1989.

_____ *Proverbs and The Song of Solomon*. Nepture, NJ: Loizeaux Brothers, 1989.

Jacob, Benno and Hirsch, Emil. "Genesis, The Book of." The Jewish Encyclopedia, 1912. http://www.jewishencyclopedia.com/articles/6580-genesis-the-book-of.

Jamieson, R., A. R. Fausset, and D. Brown. *Bible Commentary*. Peabody, MA: Hendrickson, 2002.

Johnson, Elliott. *Expository Hermeneutics: An Introduction*. Grand Rapids, MI: Academie, 1990.

Johnson, Marshall D. *Making Sense of the Bible*. Grand Rapids: Eerdmans, 2002.

Josephus, Flavius. The Works of Josephus. William Whiston, translator. Peabody, MA: Hendrickson, 1987.

Keil, C.F and F. Deilitzsch. *Commentary on the Old Testament: Ezekiel and Daniel*. Peabody, MA: Hendrickson, 2001.

_____ *Commentary on the Old Testament, Ecclesiastes and Song of Solomon*. Peabody,MA: Hendrickson, 1989.

Kik, J. Marcellus. *An Eschatology of Victory*. Nutley, NJ: Presbyterian and Reformed, 1975.

Knudsen, Robert. "Progressive and Regressive Tendencies in Christian Apologetics," in E.R. Geehan, ed., *Jerusalem and Athens: Critical Discussions on the Theology and Apologetics of Cornelius Van Til*. Philipsburg, NJ: Presbyterian and Reformed Publishing, 1980, 275-298.

Kuyper, Abraham. *Principles of Sacred Theology*. Grand Rapids: Baker Book, 1980.

_____ *The Work of the Holy Spirit*. Grand Rapids: Eerdmans, 1975.

Ladd, George E. "Historic Premillennialism" in *The Meaning of the Millennium: Four Views*, ed. Robert G. Clouse. Downers Grove, IL, Intervarsity Press, 1977, 17-40.

LaSor, Hubbard, and Bush, *Old Testament Survey*. Grand Rapids: Eerdmans, 1982.

Leupold, H. C. *Exposition of Genesis*. 1942 reprint, Grand Rapids: Baker Book House, 1987.

Lewontin, Richard. "Billions and Billions of Demons," *New York Review of Books*, January 9, 1997.

Lin, Timothy. *Genesis: A Biblical Theology, 4th Ed.* Carmel, IN: Biblical Studies Ministries International, 2002.

Little, C.H. *Explanation of the Book of Revelation*. St. Louis: Concordia, 1950.

Lockhart, Clinton. *Principles of Interpretation*. Delight: AR: Gospel Light, 1915.

Maimonedes, Moses. *Commentary on the Mishnah, Tractate Sanhedrin*. Fred Rosner, translator. New York, NY: Sepher-Hermon Press, 1981.

Marshall, John. *John Locke: Resistance, Religion and Responsibility*. Cambridge, MA: Cambridge University Press, 1994.

Martyr, Justin. *Dialogue with Trypho*, ch. XC, as viewed on http://www.ccel.org/ccel/schaff/anf01.viii.iv.xc.html, access date unknown.

Mazar, Benjamin. "The Historical Background of the Book of Genesis." *Journal of Near Eastern Studies*, No. 28 (April, 1969).

McDowell, Josh. *Evidence That Demands a Verdict*. San Bernadino, CA: Here's Life Publishers, 1979.

Minear, Paul S. "How Objective is Biblical Criticism." *Journal of Bible and Religion*, No. 9 (Nov. 1941).

Morris, Henry, M. *The Genesis Record: A Scientific and Devotional Commentary on the Book of Beginnings*. Grand Rapids, MI: Baker, 1976.

Myra, Harold. "Ken Taylor: God's Voice in the Vernacular," *Christianity Today*, October 5, 1979.

Noble, Paul. *The Canonical Approach: A Critical Reconstruction of the Hermeneutics of Brevard S. Childs*. New York: EJ Brill, 1995.

Ott, Craig and Netland, Harold. *Globalizing Theology*. Grand Rapids, MI: Zondervan, 2006.

Pascal, Blaise. *Thoughts*. New York: PF Collier and Son, Co., 1910.

Pentecost, J. Dwight. *Things to Come*. Grand Rapids, MI: Zondervan, 1958.

Peters, George. *The Theocratic Kingdom*. Vol. 1. Grand Rapids, MI: Kregel, 1972.

Philips, D.Z. *Faith After Foundationalism*. London: Routledge, 1988.

Philo. *The Works of Philo*, translated by C.D. Yonge. Peabody, MA: Hendrichson, 1993.

Pinnock, Clark. *Biblical Revelation*. Chicago, Moody Press, 1971.

The Qur'an

Ramm, Bernard. *Protestant Biblical Interpretation*. Grand Rapids: Baker Book House, 1995.

Rendsburg. *The Redaction of Genesis*. Winona Lake, IN: Eisenbraun, 1986.

Rushdoony, Rousas John. "The One and Many Problem – the Contribution of Van Til," in *Jerusalem and Athens*, edited by E.R. Geehan. Philipsburg, NJ: Presbyterian and Reformed, 1980, 339-348.

Ryrie, Charles. *Basic Theology*. Wheaton, IL: Victor Books, 1986.

_____ *Dispensationalism Today*. Chicago, IL: Moody Press, 1965.

_____ *Dispensationalism*. Revised and Expanded, Chicago, IL: Moody Press, 1995.

_____ *The Basis of the Premillennial Faith*. Neptune, N.J.: Loizeaux Brothers, 1953.

Sagan, Carl. *The Cosmos*. New York: Ballantine, 1980.

Saucy, Robert. *The Case for Progressive Dispensationalism*. Grand Rapids, Zondervan, 1993.

Schaeffer, Francis. *The Complete Works of Francis Schaeffer*. Wheaton, IL. Crossway Books, 1982.

Schreiner, Thomas. *Interpreting the Pauline Epistles.* Grand Rapids, MI: Baker Books, 1990.

Scofield, C.I. *The Biggest Failure of the Church Age,* from http://www.biblebelievers.com/scofield/ scofield_church-age.html, access date unknown.

_____ *Scofield Reference Bible,* 1917.

_____ *Rightly Dividing the Word of Truth.* New York: Loizeaux Brothers, Inc., 1896.

_____ *Scofield Bible Correspondence Course Vouime I Introduction to the Scriptures.* Chicago: Moody Bible Institute, 1959.

Shedd, W.G.T., *Dogmatic Theology.* Vol 1. Nashville, TN: Nelson, 1980.

Shockley, Paul. "The Postmodern Theory of Probability on Evangelical Hermeneutics" *The Conservative Theological Journal* , 4/11 (March 2000): 65-82.

Sire, James. *The Universe Next Door.* Downers Grove, IL: InterVarsity Press, 1988.

Simpson, D.P. *Cassell's Latin Dictionary.* New York: MacMillan Publishing Co., 1959.

Smith, George. *Atheism: The Case Against God.* NewYork: Promotheus Books, 1989.

Soulen, Richard. *Handbook of Biblical Criticism.* 2nd Edition Atlanta, GA: John Knox Press, 1981.

Stallard, Mike. "Literal Hermeneutics, Theological Method, and the Essence of Dispensationalism" (Paper presented at the 1998 PreTrib Study Group).

_____ "The Theological Method of Arno C. Gaebelein", Ph.D Dissertation, Dallas Theological Seminary, 1992

Stam, Cornelius. *Things That Differ.* Chicago, IL: Berean Bible Society, 1959.

Strong, A.H. *Systematic Theology.* Philadelphia, Judson Press, 1947.

Swindoll, Charles   and Zuck, Roy, editors. *Understanding Christian Theology.* Nashville: Nelson, 2003.

Tan, Paul Lee. *The Interpretation of Prophecy.* Dallas, Bible Communications, Inc., 1993.

Tate, J. "On the History of Allegorism," *Classical Quarterly* 28 (1934): 105-114.

Taylor, John. *Ezekiel.* Downers Grove, IL: Intervarsity Press, 1969.

Taylor, W. R. "Biblical Criticism and Modern Faith." *The Journal of Religion*, No. 23 (Oct., 1943).

Terry, Milton. *Biblical Hermeneutics.* Grand Rapids: Zondervan, 1976.

The Catechism of the Catholic Church

"The Great Debate: Does God Exist? Dr. Greg Bahnsen versus Dr. Gordon Stein" University of California, Irvine, 1985

Torrey, R.A. *You and Your Bible.* Westwood, N.J: Revell, 1958.

Touissaint, Stanley. *Behold the King.* Portland, OR: Multnomah Press, 1980.

Traina, Robert. *Methodical Bible Study A New Approach to Hermeneutics.* Grand Rapids, MI: Francis Asbury Press, 1985.

Trigg, Joseph W. *Origen.* London: SCM Press, 1983.

Usher, Robin and Edwards, Richard. *Postmodernism and Education.* New York: Rutledge, 1994.

Vanhoozer, Kevin J. "One Rule to Rule Them All." in *Globalizing Theology*, edited by Craig Ott and Harold A. Netland. Grand Rapids, MI: Baker Books, 2006, 85-126.

Van Til, Cornelius. *Christian Apologetics*. Philipsburg, NJ: Presbyterian and Reformed, 2003.

_____ *A Christian Theory of Knowledge*. Philipsburg, NJ: Presbyterian and Reformed, 1969.

_____ *Why I Believe in God*. Philadelphia: Presbyterian and Reformed, n.d.

_____ *The Defense of the Christian Faith*. Phillipsburg, NJ, Presbyterian and Reformed Publishing, 1967.

_____ *An Introduction to Systematic Theology*. Philipsburg, NJ: Presbyterian and Reformed, 1974.

Virkler, Henry. *Hermeneutics*. Grand Rapids: Baker Book, 1981.

Wallis, Louis. "The Paradox of Modern Biblical Criticism." *The Biblical World*, No. 52 (July 1918).

Waltke, Bruce. "A Canonical Process Approach to the Psalms" in *Tradition and Testament*, edited by John Feinberg and Paul Feinberg. Chicago, IL: Moody Press, 1981, 3-18.

Walvoord, John. *The Millennial Kingdom*. Grand Rapids, MI: Academie, 1959.

_____ *The Prophecy Knowledge Handbook*. Dallas: Dallas Seminary Press, 1990.

_____ *Matthew: Thy Kingdom Come*. Chicago: Moody Press, 1974.

Warfield, B.B. *The Works of Benjamin Warfield*. Vol. 1. Grand Rapids, Baker Book House, 2003.

Webb, William J. *Slaves, Women and Homosexuals*. Downers Grove: InterVarsity Press, 2001.

Westcot, B.F., and Hort, F.J.A. *Introduction to the New Testament in the Original Greek*. Peabody, MA: Hendrickson, 1988.

The Westminster Confession and Shorter Catechism

Wenham, John. from Norman Giesler, *Inerrancy*. Grand Rapids, MI: Zondervan, 1980.

Whitcomb, John C. "Contemporary Apologetics and Christian Faith, Part I." *Bibliotheca Sacra*, 134 (April-June 1977): 99-106.

_____ and Morris, Henry. *The Genesis Flood*. Grand Rapids, Baker Book House, 1961.

White, James Emery. *What Is Truth?*. Nashville: Broadman and Holman, 1994.

White, Lynn. "Historical Roots of Our Ecological Crisis," *Science* 155 (March 10, 1967), 1203-1207.

Willis, Wesley R., John R. Master,, and Charles C. Ryrie, editors. *Issues in Dispensationalism*. Chicago, Il: Moody Press, 1994.

Zacharias, Ravi. *Can Man Live Without God..* Word Publishing, 1994.

44864560R00203

Made in the USA
San Bernardino, CA
25 January 2017